THE WELL-FILLED Cupboard

A collection of seasonal recipes, gardening hints, country lore and domestic pleasures

MARY ALICE DOWNIE
and BARBARA ROBERTSON

Fitzhenry & Whiteside

The Well-Filled Cupboard

First published by Lester & Orpen Dennys in 1987

Fitzhenry and Whiteside Limited
195 Allstate Parkway
Markham, Ontario L3R 4T8

In the United States
121 Harvard Avenue, Suite 2
Allston, Massachusetts 02134

www.fitzhenry.ca godwit@fitzhenry.ca

Fitzhenry & Whiteside acknowledges with thanks the Canada Council for the Arts, the Government of Canada through its Book Publishing Industry Development Program, and the Ontario Arts Council for their support of our publishing program.

National Library of Canada Cataloguing in Publication

Downie, Mary Alice, 1934-
The well-filled cupboard / Mary Alice Downie and Barbara Robertson.

Includes index.
ISBN 1-55041-748-7

1. Cookery, Canadian. 2. Gardening – Canada. I. Robertson, Barbara, 1931- II. Title.

TX715.D69 2003 641.5971 C2003-902686-5

U.S. Publisher Cataloging-in-Publication Data

Downie, Mary Alice.
The well-filled cupboard / Mary Alice Downie and Barbara Robertson.
[288] p. : ill. ; cm.
Includes index.
Summary: A collection of seasonal recipes, gardening hints, country lore and domestic pleasures.
ISBN 1-55041-748-7 (pbk.)
1. Recipes. 2. Gardening. 3. Home. I. Robertson, Barbara. II. Title.
646.7 21 TX714.D69 2003

Cover photograph by Christopher Campbell
Backcover photograph by John Spray
Interior illustrations by Wes Lowe
Cover design by Wycliffe Smith Design
Printed and bound in Canada

To our families

The poem "End of Summer" and excerpts from "Getting the High Bush Cranberries" from My Granddaughters Are Combing Out Their Long Hair, written by Colleen Thibaudeau and published by The Coach House Press, are reprinted by permission of the author.

The poems "Apple Jelly" and "Nasturtium" from Two Headed Poems and "Late August" from You Are Happy by Margaret Atwood are reprinted by permission of Oxford University Press Canada.

The excerpt from Wolf Willow by Wallace Stegner is reprinted by permission of Macmillan of Canada, a division of Canada Publishing Corporation.

The poem "Dorcas" from A Suit of Nettles by James Reaney is reprinted by permission of the author.

"Simples" from The Collected Poems of Anne Wilkinson by Anne Wilkinson is reprinted by permission of Macmillan of Canada, a division of Canada Publishing Corporation.

"Christmas Eve Market Square" from The Glass Air, written by P.K. Page and published by Oxford University Press Canada, is reprinted by permission of the author.

"Detail" from Collected Poems by Al Purdy is used by permission of the Canadian Publishers, McClelland and Stewart, Toronto.

The excerpt from Confessions of an Immigrant's Daughter by Laura Goodman Salverson is reprinted by permission of The University of Toronto Press.

"My Garden" from Sarah Binks by Paul Hiebert is reprinted by permission of Oxford University Press Canada.

The receipe "Cranberry Cordial" from Blanche Pownall's A Taste of the Wild is reprinted by permission of James Lorimer & Company Ltd.

The recipe "Apple Tart" from Margo Oliver's Weekend Magazine Cookbook is reprinted by permission of Optimum Publishing International.

Contents

Acknowledgements

We are grateful to those who provided recipes and answered innumerable questions: Una Beer, Miriam Bone, Lia Braun, John and Mary Coutts, Susan Dick, Jocelyn Downie, Jillian Gilliland, Jessica and Philip Haden, Mary Hamilton, Margery Hsu, Elizabeth Lovink, Paul Maclean, Jean Newell, Alison Oxlade, Kenneth Peacock, Maria Riley, Anneke Rogers, Mary Smith, Patricia Steer, Mary-Alice Thompson, Elizabeth Walker.

Our thanks to Shelley Tanaka who edited the manuscript with skill and enthusiasm.

A note of special thanks to the staff at the Queen's Faculty Club, who built roaring fires, poured us bumper glasses of wine and cheerfully served us every Wednesday during our three-hour working lunches.

Finally, we are grateful to our husbands, John Downie and Duncan Robertson, who patiently, if not always joyfully, ate their way through both our triumphs and our disasters. "What are those green things?" "Those are the Juniper Potatoes." There were many such doleful conversations. And our thanks to our children, Christine, Jocelyn and Alexandra, Elizabeth, Sarah and Katie — even if most of them still refuse to eat liver and mutter about Garbage Soup.

Introduction

"Why are you doing this?" asked a forthright friend. "Who is your audience and what are their lives like?"

We looked at each other nervously. *The Well-Filled Cupboard* had been envisioned as being very much like its title – a cheerful miscellany. But would this be enough? We had decided to write a book for people like us: those who were busy with other things, but who still tried to snatch time for the ancient pleasures of messing about in the kitchen, preparing good food for family and friends and pottering about in the garden or window box with flowers and herbs.

"Do you see it as the definitive Canadian cookbook?" she asked.

Appalled silence. We weren't planning an authoritative cookbook or gardening manual. There are shelves of these. We have many of them ourselves. Neither of us has run a cooking school or even attended one. Although Mary Alice has written cooking articles, as a teenager she was famous in her family for her Fallen Instant Cake. Even when her cooking improved, her children begged for "store-bought" birthday cakes. Barbara spent her summers more profitably on a farm in Huntsville, canning and pickling, and watching her family learn to appreciate the flavours of wild apples, Muskoka lamb and fresh-caught bass.

Despite our similarities (growing up in Toronto, professorial husbands, three daughters each), we have very different approaches to domestic life. One of us grows her own vegetables. The other, due to laziness and three 60-foot maples, has a tangle rather than a garden. (Recently, she has acquired an old cottage in the woods where the wild flowers look after themselves.) One of us coexists uneasily in a kitchen filled with equipment that she appreciates but fears, and a sociable smoke alarm that quacks when she cooks anything. The other believes in keeping kitchen equipment to a minimum and prefers operating with little more than a good sharp knife.

But we had compiled *The Wind Has Wings* together, and in doing so had learned to delight in Canadian poetry. We share an interest in Canada's history and a fondness for the indomitable Catharine Parr Traill whose *Settler's Guide* cheered and aided many a lonely pioneer wife. Through quotations from earlier writers, we hope to show that a connection with the past continues still.

We know that we cannot return to this past, nor would we want to. We advocate the use of food processor, blender and freezer, although not microwave. But through the use of quotations from early writers and modern poems sensitive to local and domestic character, we hope to encourage Canadians to look about them and make the best of their environment, just as their ancestors did.

Americans too will find much that is familiar: Vermonters cherish their apples and maple syrup. The Eastern seaboard, like the Maritimes, excels in seafood, and the French cuisine of St. Louis and Louisiana reflects the tastes of their founders, who were from Quebec.

Our main emphasis lies on recipes using the local produce of our seasons. It is best both financially and gastronomically to "eat it fresh" whenever possible, but it is also wise to tuck away fruits and vegetables in the freezer. Strawberry shortcake can be very cheering in February.

We are not pretending that this is cooking on a budget, but the prudent cook will find that buying fruits and vegetables in season, making one's own relishes rather than buying them and growing big plants from small will save money. We have included some unusual recipes: what to do if you find a basket of ground cherries at the market, or juniper berries during a fall walk in the woods. But you will find no deep-fried St. Paulin here, no chicken breasts with blueberry sauce (a concoction one of us was unfortunate enough to sample recently). We believe in adventurous, not contorted, cooking. Kiwi and green pasta will come and go as food-of-the-month. Fresh asparagus with melted butter and a touch of lemon will be here forever.

We have also included suggestions on gardening, indicating what can be done, even by apartment dwellers, to produce homegrown pleasures. There are occasional hints, too: things your mother may have forgotten to tell you, or if she did, you weren't listening.

A book such as this cannot be comprehensive in any area, but rather supplies a number of starting points. This is neither a book for the specialist nor one for the beginner. Most people are something in between. We are assuming that there are many activities in your life, but that you still enjoy the grace notes of plants on window sills and the odd jar of jelly to take to a friend. We suggest that this can be done by judicious planning, even if you are a VP of finance. Since most of us are pressed for time, we have concentrated on quick and delicious recipes. We have tried to avoid instructions so specialized and complicated that anyone with limited time – which is to say, almost everyone – would feel defeated before beginning. We want to make local pleasures of the table seem attainable as well as delicious.

Gone are the spacious days described by the great Californian writer M.F.K. Fisher when "There were times for This, and other equally definite times for That...," when there was a week for the sewing woman, for spring cleaning, and for a series of "short but violently active cannings." But it is still possible to find five minutes to make your own bread crumbs, to root ivy; a few hours for achieving your own chutney. The occasional hour or two spent thus will eventually produce a cupboard filled with relishes, jams and pickles, and a house filled with scents and blossoms.

Mary Alice Downie and Barbara Robertson

At the breakfast table we had nothing to eat but the hind quarter of a wild cat. It was very tough and tasteless; and while we were trying to make our breakfast from it, Mrs. Young said, "My dear, unless you shoot something for dinner, I am afraid there will be none."

Egerton R. Young
By Canoe and Dog Train Among the Cree and Salteaux Indians, 1892

Autumn

We feel bound constantly to urge upon the attention of our readers the profit and importance of a good garden. Its influence is good in every way. It spreads the table with palatable and nutritious food and fills the dessert dishes with luxuries, and thus saves the cash which might otherwise be paid for beef, ham, veal, and lamb; besides promoting the health and spirits more than the meat would. Then a good garden is a civilizer. The garden and orchard beautify the home wonderfully and kindle emotions which never die out of the heart.

Catharine Parr Traill
The Canadian Settler's Guide, 1854
(quoted from *The Old Countryman*)

Introduction

End of Summer

Coming home
to the various silver webs
spun in the trees,
ancestors holding out arms —
but cellarwebs sometimes
they choke the life out of you.

Sometimes coming home
silver webs draw other directions:
cellarwebs fight you back when
flight puts steely tentacles into the mind
draws you draws you.

My neighbour shakes out
summer's dustcloths,
invisible motes
go falling into the goldenrod
a fine time autumn neither
sad nor glad

But all spinning out
faraway belltowers
birds beautifully flocking
darken the wires, definite the frost
and indefinite the sulphur mists
and all the feathery asters in my head.

Colleen Thibaudeau

The true beginning of the year, autumn is scarcely the most restful of seasons, what with taking things (herbs and tender plants) out of the garden and putting other things (bulbs and perennials) in. But it is exhilarating.

First there are the September visits to the market for baskets of peaches, plums and, if you are very lucky, ground cherries. Later on, when the market really hits its stride, there will be bittersweet, dried savory and thyme, pumpkins, perhaps not so enormous as those John Geikie saw in the mid-nineteenth century ("I have known them so large that one would fill a wheelbarrow"), but large enough.

We gather supplies, taking excursions to the country to pick apples or wade ankle-deep in the swamp water to gather cranberries for the freezer. It is time to call the farmer for the yearling — larger, often more flavourful, and cheaper than the diminutive spring lamb.

Walks in the woods yield juniper berries (to be dried in the oven); by the roadside you may find milkweed pods and teasel for your own dried flower bouquets.

Thanksgiving, cottage-closing time for many, and Hallowe'en, with its jack o' lanterns and excited children, are upon us. And finally comes that eerily quiet November weekend, when one runs around the garden like a demented squirrel with frost-bitten paws, flinging in the last of the bulbs. "Why," one asks oneself, come the spring, "were the crocuses planted in the sandbox?"

Then there is a deep peace. The outside bulbs are nestled under their leaf covering, the cranberry cordial is steeping quietly down in the fruit cellar on the shelf above the pots of hyacinth and daffodil bulbs growing roots (one hopes) in the cool darkness. The blueberry wine is bubbling in the dining-room. It is time to settle back, put one's feet up and admire the first snowflakes drifting past the window.

The Garden

House Plants

Potting

September is the great month for harvesting. In addition to picking whatever is ripe, things wanted inside should be brought in before the frost kills them. All potential house plants should be potted as soon as possible in September, but can be left outside on the porch or deck. Then if an early frost threatens, the plants can hurriedly be brought in.

The question of what to bring in is always a vexing one. You'll probably want to bring in old standbys like the jade plant, clivia and Norfolk pine, but what of the fuchsia blooming so appealingly? A usually reliable old gardening book advised us to discard our fuchsia, but the temptation to keep it was too strong, and there sits one blooming right now, in March, while another is more reserved, but surviving. It takes a good deal of trial and error to discover which outdoor plants will thrive in your particular environment. Some people like to spray their outdoor plants with an insecticide before bringing them in, but we have never found insect life a problem.

As a general rule, small is beautiful. Plants grow; space does not. Often it is preferable to take a slip rather than the whole plant. Geraniums, impatiens and particularly ivies are easy to start from cuttings.

Take a cutting about 4 to 6 inches long from the top of a vigorous growing branch of the plant. Remove the leaves from the bottom half of the cutting and put it in a jar of rain water or tap water that has been allowed to sit for forty-eight hours to ensure that the chlorine has dissipated. (Chlorine inhibits the growth of bacteria in our drinking water and is largely a good thing, but not for encouraging the growth of roots on plant slips. Even for watering house plants, many people prefer to let tap water sit a few hours until most of the chlorine has dissipated.)

Put the cuttings in a jar and store the jars out of direct sunlight but near a kitchen window so that you can keep an eye on them. When the cuttings develop rootlets, they are ready to be potted. (It is also possible to buy rooting compounds, which allow one to plant the cuttings directly in soil. They don't always work, but then neither does rooting them in water. Take two cuttings to allow for one failure.)

Clay pots are the best containers, because the clay is porous and allows for root aeration. Choose a pot that allows one-third the space for the roots below to two-thirds the space for the foliage above. To avoid the messy and time-consuming business of repotting plants indoors, choose a slightly larger pot than the cutting requires.

The easiest way to obtain potting soil is to buy it from a supermarket or garden centre. However, garden soil can also be used. Sterilize it by letting it sit in the oven for 30 minutes at 350°F (180°C). For house plants use a mixture of two parts soil, one part peat moss and one part well-composted manure or, best of all, composted leaf mould.

Having assembled the plants, pots (with drainage holes) and soil, you need only add a small supply of gravel, stones or clay shards. Place a thin layer of stones in the bottom of each pot to facilitate drainage. Add a small layer of potting soil; then place the roots of the plant in the pot, filling around the sides with the potting soil until the plant is firmly in place. Do not fill the pot to overflowing with soil, or you will have difficulty watering it. Next, set the pot on a glass, hard plastic or china saucer. (Earthenware will eventually let the moisture through and ruin wooden window ledges.) Finally, water the plant thoroughly, for the potting soil will be entirely dry.

Apple-picking

Few of us have orchards. The thing to do is to emulate Isaac Weld (*Travels Through North America*, 1799) who, finding orchards in which "the trees, loaded with large apples of various hues, appeared bent down into the very water", could not resist the temptation of stopping and "for a few pence we were allowed to lade our boat with as much fruit as we could well carry away."

We do not "lade our boat", but rather load our car with as many bushels and half bushels as we seem likely to consume for the next four to six months. This makes an agreeable family outing in September, for even young children can pick from the small trees that are becoming increasingly common in orchards. The labour is easy, for apples are large; and the task is quickly accomplished, leaving plenty of time for a picnic and further exploration of the countryside.

The question of what to pick is a trifle complicated, since new varieties are always being introduced, and it is always tempting to hunt down old favourites. The summer varieties, such as Yellow Transparent, Melba and Tydeman's Red, should not be picked in large quantities because they spoil quickly; it's more sensible to buy them in small quantities from a farmer's market. The most obvious candidate for the picking expedition is the McIntosh Red, the best of all-purpose apples, which can with reasonable care be kept at least until Christmas. At the same time it is useful to have a small supply of Delicious apples (good for eating, not cooking) that can be used after the Macs are finished, for they are excellent keepers. And Northern Spies, admirable for cooking, keep even better: they ripen about Thanksgiving and can last until March. Consult the ads in your local newspapers as to when and where the apples are ready to pick. Or if a picking expedition is not feasible, buy whatever you need from a farmer's market, where you will likely find excellent quality at reasonable prices.

Macs, Spies, Delicious and other fall and winter apples keep well if stored in a cool, damp place. If the air is too dry, the apples will dehydrate, shrivel and become far less appetizing. A garage is excellent through October and into November, for apples do not merely keep but improve their flavour when temperatures are just above the freezing point. However, they should not be frozen. Throw a blanket over the bushels on cold nights, but when the frosts become severe, move the apples to the fruit cellar. In lieu of a garage or fruit cellar, apples can be stored in the trunk of a car, at least until the frosts become heavy. Check them occasionally to see whether any apples are spoiling — the odd one does.

Mushrooms

While mushrooms may be harvested at various times of the year — the highly prized morel (*Morchella esculenta*) occurs in May or June — probably the greatest quantity and variety occur in September, particularly during rainy Septembers. While others are whining about the weather, you will be far better employed moving purposefully through brushy areas of parks and waste places, gathering wild mushrooms. The essential piece of equipment is J. Walton Groves' booklet, *Mushroom Collecting for Beginners* (Ottawa: Agriculture Canada, 1983). As he wisely says, "eat only species that you know to be edible and avoid all others." With Groves' help, mushroom collecting becomes a practical and rewarding pastime. You may be able to find an experienced mushroom collector to help you get started, though mushroom collectors, like fishermen, are often a little reserved about showing you their best spots.

If you are of a timorous disposition, perhaps it is best late in August and early in September to search for the unmistakable giant puffball. The British naturalist P.H. Gosse described puffballs in a rather mysterious way in 1840: "They do not look much like plants, either when the inside is a soft green mud, or when it is become ripe, and resembles a lump of fine sponge, dipped in a box of impalpable snuff. If these atoms of dust be the seeds of the plant, as is supposed, it is surprising to me that the land does not become completely covered with them, instead of being scattered, as they are, here and there, half a dozen on an acre."

A full-grown puffball is about 15 inches in diameter, or even larger. It is white when young, becoming dingier as it matures. Do not pick a small one, because it is wasteful. Allow it to reach at least 10 inches in diameter. The inside should be white, not yellow (a sign of an old and bitter puffball). So large is the puffball, that it is wise to share it with friends and neighbours. That way everyone will be left with the feeling that they are enjoying a delicacy, instead of too much of a good thing.

As you explore the mushroom world more fully, you will no doubt develop preferences. Indeed, you will discover that some mushrooms are readily available in your locality and others not. Our favourite is the parasol mushroom (*Lepiota procera*), a rich and sumptuous mushroom beside which the commercial varieties pale. The more delicately flavoured shaggy manes (*Coprinus comatus*) have the engaging habit of growing on lawns, and so are easy to find.

Bulbs

Hardy Bulbs for Indoor Forcing

In the general hurry and rush of September, the idea of providing for winter flowers may not seem important. In January, however, when winter prowls and howls, the pleasure of having fragrant spring flowers indoors is considerable.

In the fall, the only thing you need to do about forcing bulbs is to buy them, for they are available in September. Without a cool room or fruit cellar, it is necessary to stick to narcissus — the delightfully fragrant paperwhites or the less fragrant golden soleil d'or. These do not require a cool rooting period, that slight artificial winter which we provide for bulbs so that we can "force" them into blooming early.

If a cool room is available, then tulips, daffodils, hyacinths and crocus may be forced. It is important to get hold of the right varieties (King Alfred daffodils, Bismarck hyacinths and William Pitt Darwin tulips, for example). The better sources of supply do provide indications of what is suitable for forcing. Choose bulbs the same way you choose onions: they should be firm and plump and free from blemishes.

Even before they are planted, the bulbs must be stored in a cool dark space. A corner of the refrigerator or a box in an unheated garage will do nicely, but if you're lucky enough to have a fruit cellar, it's the ideal location. They should not be frozen.

In deciding when to plant the bulbs, allow at least six weeks for them to develop a sturdy root system; some will take longer. If you want the bulbs to flower for Christmas or early January (there is nothing nicer than a Boxing Day hyacinth), they should be planted from early to mid-November. Narcissus, and some say hyacinths also, can be grown in china or pottery bowls, supported by pebbles. They need to be watered once a week, but they can do without soil.

If you are forcing a variety of bulbs, it is perhaps easier to treat them, more or less, all the same way. Plant them just like any other house plants, in clay pots, with a layer of pebbles at the bottom for drainage, and surrounded with good potting soil, lightened if possible by equal quantities of sand and peat moss. (Vermiculite is another possibility for lightening the soil.) Bulbs like to be planted close to one another, almost touching; and about one-third of the bulb should be above the surface of the soil.

After the planting is completed, water the bulbs thoroughly, and then store them in their cool dark place — the fruit cellar or whatever substitute you have settled on. You need to water them regularly, but just enough to keep them moist. Test the soil for dampness with your finger, and remember the immortal saying that more plants die by drowning than any other way. When the bulbs are ready to bring out, the sprouts will be 1 to 3 inches tall, and the roots will be visible through the drainage hole at the bottom of the pot. Paperwhites, if you do decide to give them a cool rooting period, will be ready first (plant them at two-week intervals if you can). Hyacinths are next.

Gradually acclimatize the pots of bulbs by moving them to a cool bright room. After a couple of days the foliage will turn green and you can move them to where you want them to bloom — a sunny window or a bright corner of the room. They will flourish best and last longest in rooms that are not too hot — about 65°F (18°C) is perfect. Try arranging pots of daffodils, hyacinths and crocuses on a large plate for a miniature spring garden to defy the wintry blasts.

It is wise to stagger the planting of bulbs, or come February your house will be full of daffodils. An agreeable problem.

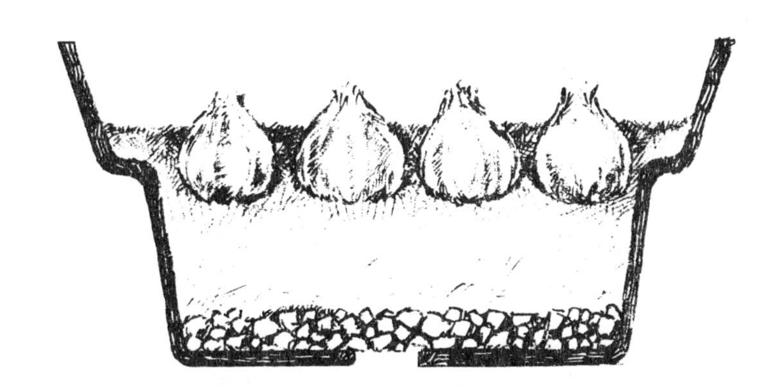

Tender Bulbs and Tubers

Tender bulbs, like amaryllis or gloxinia, need no forcing period, but they do need a great deal more warmth than hardy bulbs. Amaryllis bulbs are frequently on sale in November or December; sometimes they come equipped with their own pot and growing material, but the bulbs can be bought on their own and planted in good soil in a clay pot about 2 inches larger in diameter than the bulb itself. About one-third of the bulb should be above the top of the soil. The amaryllis will bloom in six to eight weeks from the time of planting. The flowers, ranging from red to white, are large and spectacular but not fragrant. Since the amaryllis likes warmth, it is particularly suitable for apartment dwellers or those confined to hospitals or schools.

After the flowers fade, cut them off; then fertilize the plant, allowing the green leaves to flourish. After all danger of frost is past in the spring, put it outside in its pot in a shady part of the garden. When the leaves die at the end of summer, bring the plant in for a few months' rest (without watering) in the fruit cellar or basement; then it can be started again in December, by bringing it out into a warm and sunny spot and recommencing watering.

Dried Flower Bouquets

If you want dried flowers in the fall, you must remember to plant the appropriate seeds in the spring, or to visit the local farmers' market. The most readily available of the everlasting annuals are helichrysum, double daisy-like flowers in a variety of bright colours, and statice, attractive sprays in colours ranging from pale yellow to dark blue.

It will take you two years to get a crop, but you may also want to try the biennial honesty, sometimes called silver dollars, or even (in these inflationary times appropriately) silver pennies. Its flowers are insignificant, but the seed pods — flat silvery discs — are very fetching. This is a plant that doesn't mind growing under trees. The Chinese lantern (*Phrysalis franchetti*) is a perennial rightly valued for winter decoration. Often for sale in farmers' markets, it can be readily grown from seed, although it needs sun to blossom and is a greedy plant whose roots spread mightily.

Honesty and Chinese lanterns combined together make a handsome bouquet and can be kept for as long as you care to look at it. They may get dusty, but it doesn't seem to show, and the Chinese lanterns retain their colour for at least a year. Indeed, a small bouquet of dried flowers in a little basket, bought seven years ago, still retains its charm, and the helichrysum most of its colour.

There are native everlasting plants, the most showy of which is the pearly everlasting (formerly called Mary, Mary, Last Forever, at least in some parts of Ontario), white clusters of bloom with yellow centres, to be found in dry pastures or by roadsides in midsummer. Where these are abundant, some may be gathered, though perhaps no more than ten per cent of the whole group, for one doesn't want to imperil the survival of the species. These days there are so many gatherers that it doesn't take much to convert a common weed into a rare wildflower. Pearly everlastings combine very prettily with blue statice, though Mary O'Brien in 1830 arranged her "white everlastings" rather differently: "We went to our cedar swamp and there I gathered some branches of cedar to form the background of a flower pot, the front of which is to be occupied by white everlastings. The whole will be stuffed into a little Indian basket and hung up against the wall."

To prepare dried flowers, gather them when they are just coming into bloom, for they will continue to open even after they have been picked. Tie them into small bunches and hang them upside down from any kind of hook, or perhaps a coathanger. The conventional advice is to let them dry in attics, but any airy place will do. They should be stiff and dry in less than a month, depending on the humidity of the season, and then they are ready to arrange. Remember to follow the same procedure with Chinese lanterns, commonly sold green in the markets; if arranged before drying, the weight of the lantern flowers is apt to break the stems.

There are many other possibilities. You can buy or plant ornamental grasses or gather wild grasses in the late fall. These, if chosen with discretion and arranged with care, are very ornamental indeed. Attractive for their shape are the dry milkweed pods, sprung open. Beware the temptation of bringing in the enchanting silken pods before they are empty, or your house will soon be filled with not-so-enchanting seeds. Some people paint the inside of the pods in a variety of colours, but this is gilding the lily.

Spray the heads of bulrushes with lacquer or hair spray so the fluff doesn't fly about the house.

Altogether, there are a variety of shapes and forms in nature — and November lays them all bare — from which to choose a winter bouquet. A drive along country roads, or better still a walk, should reveal a wealth of possibilities at the sides of the road, even teasel or bulrushes. Bare twigs, too, can have a bleak charm of their own.

Feeding the Birds

The question of feeding birds can be complicated. Is it moral for cat owners to do it at all? Do hand-outs destroy the moral fibre of birds, causing them to hang about the garden rather than migrating south? If one starts feeding birds, is it fair to take a winter holiday?

It is important to keep a sense of proportion: you are not establishing a bird sanctuary by providing modest amounts of food during the winter months. If you are away on holiday for a week, or down and out with the flu for several days, no doubt "your birds" will find their way to the feeders of a neighbour.

As to cats, few are keen about winter hunting. One grey tabby we know sometimes sits at the foot of a feeder, under the mistaken impression that he looks like a stone. No bird comes while he is there. And when you rap on the window to attract his attention, he looks up piteously and meows, then hurries to the door to be let in, for his feet are cold. Spring is a far different season, however. Cats are once again keen hunters and birds are distracted by the business of mating. Cat owners should stop attracting birds to their gardens at this point.

As to providing appropriate food for birds in the winter, it is unlikely to affect migratory patterns in the slightest, for we are feeding birds that are not in the habit of migrating, though they will wander to the degree necessary to find food.

The great practical problem of feeding winter birds is presented by squirrels. They like to eat bird food, and if you spread seeds and scraps of bread on a picnic table, they do tend to be first in and last out. Nor do they share. There can be no profound objection to feeding squirrels, but it is not the same as feeding birds. It is necessary, then, to devise squirrel-proof arrangements. We found a clothesline, wobbly and long, very useful for years. From it we hung simple plastic birdfeeders filled with sunflower seeds and net bags (such as the ones onions are sold in) filled with large pieces of fat. Eventually, however, the squirrels learned to walk the long, wobbly tightrope until they reached the seeds, which they ate, together with appreciable chunks of the plastic birdfeeders. More recently we tried birdfeeders on poles, which the squirrels shinnied up with incredible grace and speed. We have checked their progress by installing an inverted plastic dish, just slightly below the birdfeeder. For the moment we are ahead, but no doubt their keen minds are at work.

Start putting out feeders in November. The bags of fat will attract woodpeckers, chickadees and nuthatches. There are many varieties of seed — millet, cracked corn, mixed small seeds — but the most surefire, and therefore the best for the novice, is sunflower seed, which will bring chickadees, nuthatches, finches and grosbeaks. Birds that like to feed on the ground, if they are given a chance at the picnic table, will include juncos, sparrows and cardinals, though cardinals may come to a feeder if it is large enough. Who comes will depend to some extent on where you are.

It does take time for birds to discover new feeders, and a harsh winter will encourage them to search, whereas a mild one may leave them satisfied with natural sources of food. Certainly birds will be attracted more readily to a garden with lots of cover — shrubs and trees. Real bird enthusiasts may wish to plant with a view to attracting birds at all seasons of the year. High-bush cranberries, for example, are catnip to cedar waxwings in the spring, and hummingbirds adore delphinium in the summer. The fruit of the Virginia creeper (*Parthenocissus quinquefolia*) is said to attract as many as 39 species, including flickers, robins, purple finches and thrushes; and it is far exceeded by the shade-loving high-bush blueberry (*Vaccinium corymbosum*) which has drawn as many as 93 species, including kingbirds and pine grosbeaks. Trees like hemlocks and sugar maples, red and white oaks, and spruces are also attractive. And any gardener will tell you that birds like raspberries, strawberries, cherries and much else that we ourselves enjoy. If you are at all keen about gardening, you may feel that certain limits should be set to the business of attracting birds to the garden.

The Kitchen

Numerous apple and peach orchards ornament the sides of the road, and are, every season, loaded with a profusion of delightful fruit, which, however, appears to be very little valued by the owners, for in many places they allow their pigs to range among the trees, and pick up all that fall from ripeness, or are blown off by the wind. These animals, I am told, soon begin to be indifferent about delicacies of this kind, and often, at last, become so satiated, that they will eat those peaches only that have very recently dropt from the trees.

John Howison
Sketches of Upper Canada, 1821

Peaches

Peaches, yet another good thing from China, signify the end of summer and, at the same time, the pleasurable chores of preserving and pickling that loom ahead. But it is the first luscious bite, as the juice dribbles down the chin, that leads us to make pigs of ourselves. Mrs. Simcoe (*Diary*, 1792–96) confessed to eating thirty a day, and her share was trifling compared to the number the young men ate. ("They were very small but high flavoured. When tired of eating them raw Mr Talbot roasted them and they were very good.") Three standard peach trees behind the house kept the Simcoes supplied with tarts and desserts for six weeks.

Are the Redhavens really the best or is it just that they are first in late July and early August? Sources (as so often) differ over the merits of freestone and clingstone, but there is no doubt that the freestone is easier to work with.

Peach Chutney

It takes almost as much time to assemble the ingredients as to make this spicy chutney, but the results are worth the effort. The tamarind pulp (beware of lurking stones) can be found dried or canned in stores carrying Indian ingredients, or in places like Toronto's Kensington and Vancouver's Granville markets.

4 cups (1 L)	white vinegar
2 lb (1 kg)	granulated sugar
4 lb (2 kg)	peaches, peeled and chopped
6	cloves garlic, peeled and chopped
1	4-inch (10-cm) piece fresh ginger, peeled and chopped
1 tbsp (15 mL)	whole peppercorns, roughly ground
1 tbsp (15 mL)	ground coriander
1 tbsp (15 mL)	ground cumin
1 tbsp (15 mL)	ground turmeric (if possible grind cumin and turmeric together)
1 tbsp (15 mL)	paprika
2 tbsp (25 mL)	poppy seeds
2 tbsp (25 mL)	sesame seeds
1 tsp (5 mL)	ground mace
1 tsp (5 mL)	ground allspice
1	2-inch (5-cm) cinnamon stick
12	whole cloves
6	pods cardamom, or 1 tsp (5 mL) ground
1/2 cup (125 mL)	tamarind pulp
6 to 12	dried red chilies
3 tbsp (45 mL)	mustard seed
1	bay leaf, crumbled
3 cups (750 mL)	raisins

Bring the vinegar and sugar to a boil in large pot while assembling the other ingredients. Add everything but the raisins to the vinegar mixture and cook for 30 minutes, until the mixture begins to thicken and turns an evil dark brown. The peaches should almost disappear. Add the raisins and cook gently for another 10 minutes. Remove the cinnamon stick. Pack in sterilized jars and cover with wax. For the best flavour, let the chutney sit for at least one month before using. It is particularly good with chicken, lamb, pork and curries. Makes 12 to 16 cups (3 to 4 L).

The best way to peel peaches (and tomatoes) is to let them sit in boiling water for 1 or 2 minutes. Then plunge in cold water. The skin will come off easily with a sharp knife.

An old electric coffee mill is very handy for grinding spices.

If using dried tamarind pulp, soak it first in a little vinegar for a few minutes to soften.

Peach Pie

In John Geikie's day (*Adventures in Canada*, 1864), peaches "of the sunniest beauty and most delicate flavour" sold for a dollar a bushel on the Niagara River, and were "in some districts almost as plentiful as potatoes." No more. If they keep plunking factories into the orchards, peaches will soon become as expensive as saffron. So eat your peach pies while you may. Especially this one.

8	large ripe peaches
	Unbaked pastry for a double-crust 9-inch (23-cm) pie
1/3 cup (75 mL)	granulated sugar
2 tbsp (25 mL)	cake and pastry flour
1/4 tsp (1 mL)	salt
1/3 cup (75 mL)	maple syrup
1 tbsp (15 mL)	butter
1/4 tsp (1 mL)	grated nutmeg

Peel the peaches and slice them into the pie shell. Combine the sugar, flour and salt and distribute evenly over the peaches. Pour the maple syrup over the peaches and dot with butter and nutmeg. Cover with the top crust, prick with a fork and bake at 450°F (230°C) for 10 minutes. Reduce the heat to 325°F (160°C) and bake for 30 to 45 minutes longer, until the pastry is golden.

Freshly ground nutmeg, like freshly ground black pepper and coffee, cannot be equalled. In the seventeenth century, people carried their own silver nutmeg graters about with them. If you lack the king's ransom necessary to purchase one of these extravagant trifles, there are utilitarian stainless-steel graters available, with a space at the back for holding the nutmeg. Effective and attractive china graters can be found in kitchen specialty shops, and wooden nutmeg grinders (they look like pepper grinders with handles) are also appearing.

Broiled Peaches and Cream

The great pleasure of this elegant yet quick and simple dessert is that even though it is hot, the peaches still taste fresh.

4 oz (125 g)	cream cheese, softened
1/2 cup (125 mL)	unflavoured yogurt or sour cream
1/3 cup (75 mL)	brown sugar
1/4 tsp (1 mL)	ground ginger
6	fresh peaches

Beat the cream cheese in a small bowl. Add the yogurt slowly, then 2 tbsp (25 mL) brown sugar and the ginger, beating until thoroughly mixed. Peel the peaches and slice them into an 8-inch (2-L) square buttered ovenproof dish. Spread the cream cheese mixture evenly over the peaches. Sprinkle the remaining brown sugar on top.

Place the rack about 4 inches (10 cm) from the broiler element in the oven. Preheat the broiler for 10 minutes, then broil the peaches for 3 to 4 minutes, or until the sugar has caramelized. Serves 6.

To prevent peeled or sliced peaches from browning, dip them in lemon juice.

Peach Marmalade

You can get a head start on the season with this light and agreeable marmalade. Redhavens are particularly good in it. Spread it on toast or mix it with yogurt.

3	oranges
1 cup (250 mL)	water
12	large peaches
6 cups (1.5 L)	granulated sugar, approx.

Cut the oranges in half, then slice very thinly. Place the oranges in a large saucepan, then add the water and simmer for 15 minutes to soften the skins. Stone the peaches (do not peel them) and slice. Measure the quantity by packing the pieces tightly into cups. Add 1 cup (250 mL) sugar to each cup of peaches before stirring into the simmering oranges. Boil for about 40 minutes. Pour the marmalade into sterilized jars and cover with melted wax. Makes 12 to 16 cups (3 to 4 L).

For peach rum marmalade, stir in 2 tbsp (25 mL) rum at the end.

Tomatoes

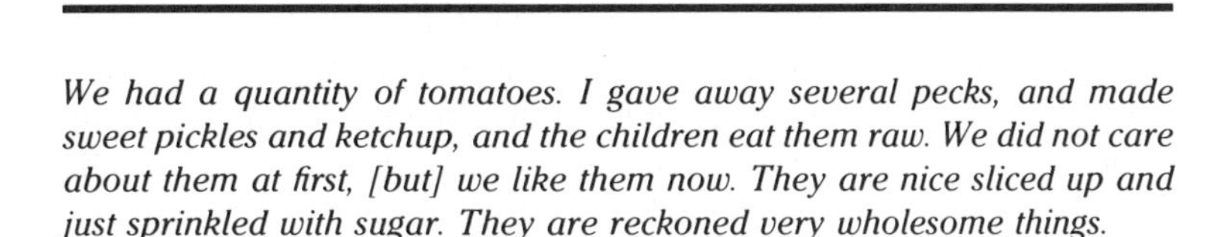

We had a quantity of tomatoes. I gave away several pecks, and made sweet pickles and ketchup, and the children eat them raw. We did not care about them at first, [but] we like them now. They are nice sliced up and just sprinkled with sugar. They are reckoned very wholesome things.

Anna Leveridge
Your loving Anna: Letters from the Ontario Frontier, 1883–91

The Spaniards brought back tomatoes with their gold from the New World (cherry-sized tomatoes grew wild in the lower Andes), and according to the herbalist Gerard, ate them "prepared and boiled with pepper, salt, and oyle." Until the middle of the nineteenth century most Englishmen, like Gerard, regarded "the golden apple" with contempt: "...they yeeld very little nourishment to the body, and the same naught and corrupt." The tomato quickly became a staple of Italian cooking, but was used in England chiefly as an ornamental garden plant, or was hung in houses as a decoration (one wonders for how long).

Today the tomato has come into its own. Home gardeners love the hearty beefsteak for its flavour, the cherry tomato is used for shishkabobs and garnishes, and the pointed Italian plum for tomato paste and pasta sauces.

The best thing to be done with a fresh tomato is to pick it sun-ripened from the vine. Slice it, salt it lightly, sprinkle with chopped

A simple vinaigrette is made by combining one part vinegar to two parts oil (olive oil is usually the best). Season with fresh herbs and spices.

fresh basil and eat it immediately with thin slices of brown bread and butter. Equally good are marinated tomatoes. Cut the tomatoes into thick slices, arrange in circles on a plate and sprinkle with a little sugar. Chop green onions (green and all) finely and toss over the tomatoes. Pour over vinaigrette dressing. Just before serving, add chopped fresh parsley or oregano.

Chili Sauce

There's no use pretending that brewing up a vat of chili sauce won't mess up most of the afternoon and the kitchen, too, and the children will wail that the house smells of vinegar again. This fresh and light chili sauce has a less pickley flavour than most.

30	tomatoes — about 6 quarts (6 L)
6	large onions, thinly sliced
4	red peppers, finely chopped
2 or 3	hot peppers, seeded and finely chopped
1 cup (250 mL)	cider vinegar
2 tbsp (25 mL)	coarse salt
2 cups (500 mL)	granulated sugar
1/2 cup (125 mL)	mixed pickling spice (wrapped in cheesecloth bag)

Don't bother canning tomatoes yourself. Save time by buying a case of canned tomatoes when they're on special in the fall.

Peel and chop the tomatoes and heat them in a large saucepan until they are thoroughly softened. Strain off about 4 cups (1 L) of the juice (keep it for drinking). Add the remaining ingredients to the tomatoes. Simmer gently for about 2 hours, or until the chili sauce is the desired thickness. Remove the pickling spice. Bottle in hot sterile jars and seal. Makes approximately 18 cups (4.5 L).

Cold Tomato Soup

For that all-too-brief season of the year when tomatoes are vine-ripened, abundant and full of flavour and the days are hot. Serve as a prelude to sandwiches and a salad.

1	very large tomato — about 12 oz (375 g)
1/2 cup (125 mL)	unflavoured yogurt
1	small onion, chopped
pinch	salt
dash	Worcestershire sauce
5	fresh sweet basil leaves

To seed a tomato, cut it in half crosswise and squeeze gently.

Wash and core the tomato. (Fastidious cooks may peel and seed it. We don't bother.) Cut it in pieces and spin in the blender with the remaining ingredients. Adjust the seasonings to taste and let the soup chill in the freezer for a few minutes. (Basil makes a lovely garnish for the soup as well.) Serves 2.

Green Tomato and Green Apple Chutney

The green tomatoes are an asset because of their texture. There's no need to peel or seed them because the skin is tender and the seeds are small.

3 cups (750 mL)	chopped green tomatoes
2 tbsp (25 mL)	coarse salt
4 cups (1 L)	white vinegar
2 tbsp (25 mL)	salt
3 1/2 to 4 cups (875 mL to 1 L)	brown sugar
6 cups (1.5 L)	chopped unripened, peeled green apples
1 cup (250 mL)	chopped onion
3 cups (750 mL)	seedless raisins
1/4 cup (50 mL)	peeled and chopped ginger root
2 tbsp (25 mL)	mustard seed
2 tbsp (25 mL)	all-purpose flour
1/4 cup (50 mL)	cold water

Sprinkle the tomatoes with the coarse salt, let stand for 12 hours and drain.

Combine the vinegar, salt and brown sugar in a large pot. Add the apples, onions, tomatoes, raisins, ginger and mustard seed and cook gently, stirring, until soft (30 to 60 minutes).

Combine the flour and cold water and add to the chutney. Cook for 5 minutes. Bottle in hot sterilized jars. Let the chutney stand for at least 6 weeks. Makes 8 cups (2 L).

When frost is expected, the remaining green tomatoes should be picked. If they are not required for chutney, ripen them slowly in a cool dark place, such as the fruit cellar. Traditionally they are wrapped individually in newspaper, but this is not necessary as long as the tomatoes do not touch one another. Keep a few on your window sill for everyday use.

If you have no green tomatoes in your garden, buy local ones from the market and ripen them at home. They do not have the flavour of sun-ripened tomatoes, but then, neither do the expensive imported ones.

To keep fresh ginger root indefinitely, peel the root and store it covered with dry sherry in a jar in the refrigerator.

Devilled Tomatoes

These are a good accompaniment for broiled lamb or pork chops, and have the merit of being cooked along with them.

1/4 cup (50 mL)	butter, softened
1 tsp (5 mL)	icing sugar
2 tbsp (25 mL)	finely minced onion
1/4 tsp (1 mL)	salt
1/2 tsp (2 mL)	dry mustard
pinch	cayenne
4	tomatoes

Cream the butter in a small bowl with the sugar, onion and spices. Cut the tomatoes in half and spread or dot with the butter mixture. Bake at 350°F (180°C) for 20 minutes. Better still, if you are broiling chops, broil the devilled tomatoes at the same time, removing after 6 to 8 minutes, or when they have browned. Serves 4.

Banyan Broil

A simple yet substantial lunch. Lightly toast 1 slice wholewheat bread (homemade if possible). Butter the toast and cover it with thinly sliced onion and tomato slices. Add alfalfa sprouts if you have them and top with slices of old Cheddar cheese. Broil for 1 or 2 minutes, or until the cheese melts. Serves 1. For carnivore's banyan, add a slice of ham between the onion and tomato layer.

Cucumbers

My husband had a large piece of land behind our house plowed up for a garden and had twelve hundred fruit trees planted there, which made a very pleasant and at the same time very useful garden,...every evening we went into it and plucked one hundred and fifty to two hundred cucumbers, which I made into pickles, which were not known there and of which I made presents to all the people, especially our good General Haldimand, who found them excellent.

Baroness von Riedesel
Journal, 1776 – 83

Cucumbers are at their best from the time the local ones start yielding in August, and they are at their most abundant in September. They flourish until the frost gets them, all too soon. Within this short space of time they must be enjoyed and preserved, for the ones grown by you or by commercial gardeners near you are incomparably better in flavour than those that have travelled great distances to reach you in the winter months (talk about jet lag!). Occasionally there is a problem with bitterness — the result, it seems, of the cucumber suffering from stressful situations like drought. This doesn't matter at all for pickling, but it isn't pleasant for eating fresh. Evidently the bitterness, if it exists, is concentrated under the skin and is especially strong at the stem end, so cutting off a chunk here, and removing the skin, should solve the problem.

The cucumber is an ancient vegetable; seeds found near the Burma-Thailand border date back to 7750 B.C. Apicius provided cucumber recipes for the ancient Romans, but it does not seem to have reached England and France until the fourteenth century. In an interesting reversal, the Spaniards took the cucumber with them to the New World and introduced it to the Indians.

Cucumbers are like tomatoes, in that one begins the season by enjoying them fresh and with very little adornment. And the season is so short that one need never travel far from simplicity. Adornment for cucumbers means pickling.

Cucumbers with Dill

Dr. Johnson remarked that "a cucumber should be well sliced, and dressed with pepper and vinegar, and then thrown out, as good for nothing." He hadn't tried this simple yet delectable salad.

2 tbsp (25 mL)	white vinegar
1 tbsp (15 mL)	water
1 tsp (5 mL)	granulated sugar
	Salt and pepper
2 tbsp (25 mL)	chopped fresh dill
1	medium cucumber

Combine all the ingredients except the cucumber in a small serving bowl. Peel the cucumber if the skin is tough, and slice. Add the cucumber slices to the dressing and combine thoroughly. Cover and let sit for about 1 hour. Serves 4.

They [the Canadians] cut cucumbers into slices and eat them with cream, which is a very good dish. Sometimes they put whole cucumbers on the table and everybody that likes them takes one, peels and slices it, and dips the slices into salt, eating them like radishes.

Peter Kalm,
Travels into North America, 1753–61

Cucumbers in Sour Cream

We like to think of Peter Kalm, the great Swedish naturalist, revelling in this wholesome treat.

3	medium cucumbers
1 tsp (5 mL)	salt
1	small onion, thinly sliced
3/4 cup (175 mL)	sour cream
1/4 cup (50 mL)	cider vinegar
1/2 cup (125 mL)	granulated sugar
	Pepper
2 tbsp (25 mL)	chopped chives

Peel the cucumbers and slice them thinly into a medium bowl. Sprinkle them with salt, cover with a weighted dish and drain after 2 hours. Add the onion.

Mix the sour cream, vinegar, sugar and pepper in a small bowl and pour over the cucumbers. Cover and chill for at least 1 hour. Sprinkle with chives. Serves 8 to 10.

Cucumber Yogurt Salad

If there is any leftover salad, it can be freshened up the next day with a bit more fresh dill and green onion, whipped in the blender and served for lunch as a cold soup (any lingering black olives should be removed before using the blender).

	Juice of 1/2 lemon or 1 lime
1/4 cup (50 mL)	olive oil
	Salt and pepper
3	large green onions, chopped
2 tbsp (25 mL)	chopped fresh dill
1	medium cucumber
1 cup (250 mL)	unflavoured yogurt
1/2 cup (125 mL)	whole black olives

In a salad bowl, combine the lemon or lime juice, olive oil, salt and pepper. Add the green onions and dill.

Peel and slice the cucumber, add it to the dressing and combine well until the slices are coated. Add the yogurt and mix again. Let the salad sit for about 1 hour in the refrigerator to allow the seasonings to blend. Serve garnished with black olives. Serves 4.

The great want of spring vegetables renders pickles a valuable addition to the table at the season when potatoes have become unfit and distasteful. If you have been fortunate in your maple-vinegar, a store of pickled cucumbers, beans, cabbages, etc., may be made during the latter part of the summer; but if the vinegar should not be fit at that time, there are two expedients: one is to make a good brine of boiled salt and water, into which throw your cucumbers etc.....Another plan, and I have heard it much commended, is putting the cucumbers into a mixture of whisky and water, which in time turns to a fine vinegar, and preserves the colour and crispness of the vegetable; while the vinegar is apt to make them soft, especially if poured on boiling hot, as is the usual practice.

Catharine Parr Traill
The Backwoods of Canada, 1836

Bread and Butter Pickles

Nowadays we are scarcely spurred on by the necessity that drove Mrs. Traill, but pickles still serve as brighteners to an otherwise bland meal or dull season. And the fact is that the home-pickler can out-perform all but the most gourmet of commercial producers any day of the week.

4 quarts (4 L)	small cucumbers — about 6 inches (15 cm) long — sliced
1 quart (1 L)	small cooking onions, sliced
5	sweet red peppers, cut in small strips
1/2 cup (125 mL)	coarse salt
6 cups (1.5 L)	white vinegar
6 cups (1.5 L)	brown sugar
2 tbsp (25 mL)	mustard seed
3 tbsp (45 mL)	celery seed

Combine the cucumbers, onions and red peppers in a large bowl or crock. Sprinkle most of the coarse salt on the vegetables, and mix briefly together so that the salt and vegetables are evenly distributed. Sprinkle the remaining salt on top, cover and let stand overnight. In the morning lift the vegetables from the brine, put in a sieve and squeeze slightly until thoroughly drained.

Combine the vinegar, brown sugar, mustard seed and celery seed together and bring to a boil in a large pot. Add the vegetables. Heat thoroughly, bringing the mixture nearly to a boil. (Do not allow it to boil or the pickles will be soft instead of crisp and crunchy.) Stir to help distribute the heat.

In bottling the pickles, if you run short of liquid and do not have enough to cover the last jar or two, boil up brown sugar and white vinegar, cup for cup, as needed. (More spices are unnecessary.) Bottle in hot sterilized jars and seal. Allow the seasonings to mellow for 6 weeks. Makes about 5 quarts (5 L).

Dill Pickles

These are the easiest pickles of all pickles. Make them in small quantities day by day from the garden, or buy the cucumbers in larger quantities from the market.

6 cups (1.5 L)	white vinegar
6 cups (1.5 L)	water
4 quarts (4 L)	small cucumbers — about 5 inches (12 cm) long
6 tbsp (90 mL)	granulated sugar
12 tsp (60 mL)	coarse salt
18	large cloves garlic
12	dill flowers

Put the vinegar and water in a large pot and bring it to a boil; keep it simmering. Place the thoroughly washed cucumbers in hot sterilized 1-quart (1-L) jars. To each jar add 1 tbsp (15 mL) sugar, 2 tsp (10 mL) coarse salt, 3 cloves garlic and 2 dill flowers. Fill the jars with the boiling water-vinegar mixture and seal at once. Do not use for at least 1 month. Makes 6 quarts (6 L).

Green Peppers

Originally grown by the Aztecs, peppers come in various shapes (bell-shaped, or thin and pointed), colours (green, red or yellow) and tastes (sweet or hot). Those used in the recipes below are the sweet bell peppers.

If you can grow tomatoes and cucumbers, you might like to try growing sweet peppers, which are even fussier about cold weather. They should be started indoors and shouldn't be planted out for at least two weeks after the threat of frost has passed. Exposure to cold weather in June can mean healthy plants but no fruit. (Perhaps these exacting requirements explain the absence of references to green peppers in pioneer gardens.) At any rate, they are abundant in September markets, when their flavour is delightful and their cost negligible.

Cheese and Green Pepper Sandwich Filling

For an appetizer, toast bread fingers on one side under the broiler. Spread this filling on the other side, then bake the fingers at 350°F (180°C) for 15 minutes.

1 cup (250 mL)	granulated sugar
1 tsp (5 mL)	salt
1 tbsp (15 mL)	dry mustard
2 cups (500 mL)	grated old Cheddar cheese
3	eggs, lightly beaten
1	large green pepper, chopped
1	large red pepper, chopped
3/4 cup (175 mL)	white vinegar
1/2 cup (125 mL)	light cream
1/2 cup (125 mL)	butter

Combine the sugar, salt and mustard in the top of a double boiler. Add the cheese and eggs. Mix together and cook over medium heat, stirring constantly, until the mixture is smooth.

Add the peppers, vinegar and cream. Stir and cook again for a few minutes. Add the butter. Continue cooking and stirring until the eggs have thickened the spread and the peppers are tender. Remove from the heat, let cool slightly and store in the refrigerator in a covered jar. Makes about 3 cups (750 mL).

Pepper Relish

A good relish for hot dogs and hamburgers.

4 quarts (4 L)	green or red peppers, or a combination
3	onions
4 tsp (20 mL)	coarse salt
1 cup (250 mL)	granulated sugar
1 cup (250 mL)	white vinegar
1 tsp (5 mL)	celery seed
1 tsp (5 mL)	mustard seed

Chop the peppers and onions finely in a food chopper or processor. Put them in a large saucepan, cover with boiling water and let stand for 10 minutes. Drain.

Cover with boiling water again, bring to a boil, remove from the heat and let stand for 10 minutes. Drain as dry as possible.

Return the vegetables to the pan and add the remaining ingredients. Bring to a boil and let simmer for 15 minutes. Pour the relish into hot sterilized jars and seal at once. Makes 6 cups (1.5 L).

Stuffed Green Peppers

This is an unusual dish, excellent for lunch or a light supper or even as a substantial appetizer at a dinner party.

4	large green peppers
4	eggs
1 cup (250 mL)	grated Cheddar cheese — about 4 oz (125 g)
1 cup (250 mL)	cottage cheese
	Salt and pepper

Cut the peppers in half lengthwise. Carefully remove the seeds and core. Beat the eggs and combine with the remaining ingredients. Fill the pepper shells and bake at 375°F (190°C) for about 45 minutes, or until lightly brown. Serves 4.

Veal Patties with Sweet Pepper Sauce

A striking change from the usual ground-beef patties, this simplified version of one of Craig Claiborne's recipes works extremely well in September, when the flavour of sweet peppers is at its best.

	Veal Patties:
1 lb (500 g)	ground veal
3 tbsp (45 mL)	unflavoured yogurt
1/2 cup (125 mL)	fresh breadcrumbs
1 1/2 tsp (7 mL)	paprika
1 tbsp (15 mL)	chopped onion
	Salt and pepper to taste
1 tbsp (15 mL)	chopped fresh dill
	Sweet Pepper Sauce:
1	sweet red or green pepper
1/4 cup (50 mL)	vegetable oil or butter, or a combination
1/4 cup (50 mL)	chopped onion
1/2 cup (125 mL)	white wine
1/2 tsp (2 mL)	paprika
1 cup (250 mL)	unflavoured yogurt

In a large bowl, combine all the ingredients for the veal patties. Mix well and shape into patties.

Core and seed the pepper and cut in strips. Heat half the oil in a medium frying pan. Add the peppers, cooking for about 4 minutes, then add the onion and cook until nearly transparent. Add the wine and paprika and cook gently for 30 minutes.

In a separate frying pan, cook the patties in the remaining oil for about 15 minutes until they are brown on one side, then turn and cook them gently until tender. As the patties near completion, add the yogurt to the sweet pepper mix. Heat, but do not boil, or the yogurt will curdle. When the patties are done, pour the sauce over them and serve with corn on the cob and a tossed green salad. Serves 4.

Mushrooms

If, accompanied by Groves' *Mushroom Collecting for Beginners* and a kind and experienced collector, you search for mushrooms in vain, there is still the possibility of finding them for sale in your local market. Following either route, sooner or later you will find your persistence rewarded.

Puffball: The simplest way to prepare a puffball is to slice it as you would a round loaf of bread. Remove the outside peel from the slice and discard; then cut the slice in strips. Dredge the strips in flour, shaking off any excess, then cook in butter until they are golden. Serve at once, seasoning them gently at the last minute with salt and pepper. Or you can dip the slices in beaten egg, then in breadcrumbs and cook in butter until golden.

Parasol Mushrooms: Parasol mushrooms may be substituted for cultivated mushrooms in most recipes. A few added to the sage and onion stuffing of the Thanksgiving turkey increase the savoury flavour. Dry them gently on cookie sheets in an oven put on its lowest setting, turning them occasionally. When they are thoroughly dry, remove them from the oven, let them cool and store them in clean jars in a dry place. They retain their flavour very well, though not their texture, so dried mushrooms are best used in soups or stews.

Shaggy Manes: Shaggy manes have a very delicate flavour, and if cooked in garlic butter should not be overwhelmed by the use of garlic. They are excellent for breakfast, sliced and fried with eggs in butter. Or try them with fried fish, adding them to the frying pan just a few minutes before the end of the cooking time.

Puffball Casserole

1 1/3 cups (325 mL)	fine breadcrumbs
3 tbsp (45 mL)	melted butter
3	slices puffball — about 1/2 inch (1.5 cm) thick
2	eggs
1 1/2 cups (375 mL)	milk
	Salt and pepper to taste
1/3 cup (75 mL)	grated Cheddar cheese

Combine the breadcrumbs and melted butter in a small bowl. Slice the puffball thickly and peel. Line the bottom of a buttered 1-quart (1-L) casserole with a layer of puffball. Top with one-quarter of the buttered breadcrumbs and repeat layering until you have three layers of puffball and three layers of breadcrumbs.

Beat the eggs with the milk and season with salt and pepper. Pour over the casserole (add a little more milk if necessary to cover, or combine another egg with 3/4 cup (175 mL) milk and add if you are seriously short of liquid). Top with the remaining breadcrumbs and the cheese. Bake at 350°F (180°C) for 30 minutes or until the mixture is firm and brown on top. Serves 6 as a side dish.

To make fine breadcrumbs, bake stale slices of bread to a golden brown, then grind finely in a food processor or mash with a rolling pin. Store in a covered container.

Pickled Mushrooms

If no fresh mushrooms are available, use two 6-oz (175-mL) cans of little whole mushrooms, drained.

1/3 cup (75 mL)	dry white wine
1/3 cup (75 mL)	white wine vinegar
1/3 cup (75 mL)	vegetable oil
1	small onion, thinly sliced
2 tbsp (25 mL)	chopped fresh parsley
1	clove garlic, chopped
1	bay leaf
1 tsp (5 mL)	salt
1/4 tsp (1 mL)	dried thyme
	Pepper
1 lb (500 g)	fresh mushrooms

Combine all the ingredients except the mushrooms in a medium saucepan and bring to a boil. Add the mushrooms and return to a boil. Simmer, uncovered, for 10 minutes. Chill in a covered container for at least 24 hours. This will keep for 2 weeks in the refrigerator. Serves 8 as a condiment.

Lamb

During the winter of the first Riel Rebellion, when all our supplies had been cut off, my good wife and I got tired of dining twenty-one times a week on fish diet, varied only by a pot of boiled musk rats, or a roast hind-quarter of a wild cat. To improve our bill of fare, the next summer, when I went into the Red River settlement, I bought a sheep, which I carefully took out with me in a little open boat. I succeeded in getting it safely home, and put it in a yard that had a heavy stockade fence twelve feet high around it. In some way the dogs got in and devoured my sheep.

Egerton R. Young
By Canoe and Dog Train Among the Cree and Salteaux Indians, 1892

One admirable meat to store in your freezer is Canadian lamb. No part need be wasted, even when the succulent legs have been consumed. The stewing lamb can be used in curries, and the kidneys are good for steak and kidney pies.

The highly efficient New Zealand lamb marketing board ships spring lamb all through the year, and very good it is, too, but one wonders just how old it is. A good butcher or farmer should be able to supply you with Canadian lamb in the late spring, summer or fall.

Two-year-old lamb becomes mutton, not much prized in North America, but some of us prefer it for its rich flavour.

Roast Lamb

1	large leg lamb — 5 to 6 lb (2.5 to 3 kg)
4	cloves garlic
	Fresh rosemary
2 tbsp (25 mL)	olive oil
3/4 cup (175 mL)	white wine

Place the lamb on a rack in a large roasting pan. Peel and sliver the garlic and stuff it into incisions in the lamb. Sprinkle generously with the rosemary sprigs (dry will do, though the children do complain about "twigs in the gravy") and spoon over the oil.

Bake at 350°F (180°C) for approximately 30 minutes per pound. To make the gravy, skim the fat from the juices in the roasting pan, add the wine, bring it to a boil and stir until thickened. Serve the roast with oven-baked potatoes or pommes canadiennes (see page 152) and green peas sprinkled with mint. Serves 8.

Beg, borrow or steal a small rosemary plant for your garden in summer and your window sill in winter. There is no comparison at all between the silvery-green needles of the fragrant bush and the prickly slivers of dried rosemary.

Most cookbooks sternly advise removing the fell, the papery white membrane that covers lamb. But it's always a struggle, and we no longer bother.

Shashlik

This Middle Eastern dish has many variations and names. The Greeks call it souvlakia and season it simply with lemon juice, olive oil, salt, pepper and oregano. Few of us can broil it the traditional way — skewered on a sword over a fire — but the more mundane oven still produces worthwhile results.

1/2 cup (125 mL)	lemon juice
1/2 cup (125 mL)	olive oil
2	cloves garlic
	Salt and pepper
3/4 tsp (4 mL)	dried oregano
3/4 tsp (4 mL)	paprika
2 lb (1 kg)	lamb loin or leg, boned and cut in 1 1/2-inch (4-cm) cubes

Combine all the ingredients except the lamb and pour over the lamb cubes. Let stand at room temperature for 4 hours or chill in the refrigerator overnight.

Thread the cubes on metal skewers and barbecue or broil, turning and basting frequently. Sprinkle with more oregano and serve with rice and marinated tomatoes (see page 30). For a variation, thread the lamb alternately with large mushroom caps, quartered green peppers and onion chunks brushed with oil. Serves 6.

Fried Lamb Liver

A recipe to help you deal with those ominous little packages that always accompany the lamb. Slice 1 1/2 pounds (750 g) lamb liver as thinly as you can. Soak for 15 minutes or longer in lemon juice, pat dry and then flour lightly. Cook sliced onions gently in butter until they are soft. Add the liver and cook quickly for a few minutes. Add a little dry vermouth to the pan juices, blend and pour over the lamb and onions. Sprinkle generously with paprika and cumin and serve as a light lunch for 6.

Julia Child suggests keeping a bottle of very dry white vermouth in your cupboard as a substitute for white wine in recipes. Use equal amounts.

Roast Lamb

Lay down to a clear good fire that will not want too much stirring or altering, baste with butter, dust on flour, and before you take it up add more butter, sprinkle on a little salt and parsley shred fine; send to table with an elegant sallad, green peas, fresh beans or asparagus.

The Cook Not Mad, 1831

Wild Rice

Wild rice (*Zizania aquatica*)is actually not a rice at all, but a member of the grass family. It is also called Indian rice, water oats, *riz sauvage* or *folle avoine* and was a source of much interest to early travellers, who described its appearance and harvesting fully. It ranges from New Brunswick to Saskatchewan and ripens from early summer to fall.

Jolliet and Marquette chronicled it on their Mississippi voyage in the seventeenth century. Robert Gourlay (*Statistical Account of Upper Canada*, 1822) describes how the "Wild fowls feed and fatten on this spontaneous grain. The Indians also gather it, by thrusting their canoes into the midst of it, and then beating it into the canoes with sticks. They eat it themselves, and sell it to the white inhabitants, who use it in puddings and other modes of cookery. It is rather larger than the Carolina rice, and its shell is of a dark brown colour."

And Catharine Parr Traill, as so often, provides a vivid picture in a letter to her sister (July 13, 1834): "Our rice-beds are far from being unworthy of admiration; seen from a distance they look like low green islands on the lakes: on passing through one of those rice-beds when the rice is in flower, it has a beautiful appearance with its broad grassy leaves and light waving spikes, garnished with pale yellow green blossoms, delicately shaded with reddish purple, from beneath which fall three elegant straw-coloured anthers, which move with every breath of air or slightest motion of the waters."

Nowadays we search for wild rice in gourmet stores and treasure our little half-pound bags jealously. In order to stretch this grainy gold, and for flavour, too, many people like to eke it out with ordinary rice. Some swear by a blend of white and wild; others prefer a mixture of brown and wild, which has the benefit of being cooked for the same length of time and in the same pot. Try it with shashlik (see page 42) and cucumbers in sour cream (see page 34).

Cooking Wild Rice

Soak 1/2 cup (125 mL) wild rice in 1 1/2 cups (375 mL) cold water for 2 hours in a large pot, covered. Drain well and rinse under cold running water. Add 1 1/2 cups (375 mL) cold water and 1/4 tsp (1 mL) salt. Bring to a boil and simmer, covered, for 30 minutes. Fluff and drain. Makes about 2 cups (500 mL).

Savoury Wild Rice

This was first served to us at a neighbourhood potluck dinner, as an accompaniment to Paprika Beaver. The beaver had been soaked overnight in water and vinegar, then boiled, dredged in flour, fried until brown and simmered with onions and red wine. The gravy was then flavoured with sour cream and paprika. The beaver was amazingly tender, though somewhat nondescript in flavour; the sauce rich and sustaining.

1/2 cup (125 mL)	wild rice, carefully washed
1/2 cup (125 mL)	long-grain rice
2 1/2 cups (625 mL)	water
1/2 tsp (2 mL)	salt
2 tbsp (25 mL)	butter
1	small onion, finely chopped
2	stalks celery, finely chopped
4	mushrooms, thinly sliced
2 tbsp (25 mL)	finely chopped fresh parsley

Combine the rices, water and salt in a saucepan and bring to a boil. Reduce the heat and simmer for about 45 minutes or until all the water is absorbed.

A few minutes before the rice is ready, melt the butter in a small frying pan. Add the onion and celery and cook for 3 minutes. Add the mushrooms, cook briefly and then cover the pan. Cook gently for about 4 minutes or until the mushrooms are soft. Add this mixture and the chopped parsley to the rice when it is ready and combine thoroughly. Serve at once. Serves 4 to 5.

Variation: Instead of using fresh mushrooms, add a sprinkling of dried ones, preferably parasol, to the top of the rice 5 minutes before it finishes cooking.

Wild Rice Pancakes

An equally dramatic potluck meal was a school lunch in Norway House (an old Hudson's Bay post in northern Manitoba). It featured moosemeat stew, wild plum jam, bannock and these pancakes served with wild blueberry sauce (see page 216).

1/4 cup (50 mL)	wild rice
1 cup (250 mL)	water
1/2 tsp (2 mL)	salt
1 1/2 cups (375 mL)	boiling water
2	eggs, well beaten
2 cups (500 mL)	buttermilk
2 cups (500 mL)	all-purpose flour
2 tbsp (25 mL)	granulated sugar
2 tsp (10 mL)	baking powder
1 tsp (5 mL)	baking soda
1 tsp (5 mL)	salt
2 tbsp (25 mL)	melted butter

Boil the rice in 1 cup (250 mL) water for 5 minutes. Cover, remove from the heat and let stand for 1 hour. Rinse well and drain.

Add 1/2 tsp (2 mL) salt to 1 1/2 cups (375 mL) boiling water. Add the prepared rice, and cook for 10 to 15 minutes, or until softened and partially puffed. Drain.

Combine the eggs and buttermilk in a large bowl. Sift together the flour, sugar, baking powder, baking soda and 1 tsp (5 mL) salt. Gradually add the dry ingredients to the liquid, beating well to make a smooth, thin batter. Stir in the melted butter and the rice. Drop the batter onto a hot buttered frying pan. Turn once. Serve with sausages and the Wild Blueberry Sauce. Makes 16 to 18 pancakes.

Apples

Apple Jelly

No sense in all this picking,
peeling & simmering
if sheer food is all
you want; you can buy it cheaper.

Why then do we burn our hours
& muscles in this stove,
cut our thumbs, to get these tiny
glass pots of clear jelly?

Hoarded in winter: the sun
on that noon, your awkward leap
down from the tree,
licked fingers, sweet pink juice,
what we keep
the taste of the act,
taste of this day.

Margaret Atwood

Some apples are better for eating fresh, others for cooking; some keep well, others must be used promptly. New varieties are constantly being developed and old favourites altered. Some seem to have disappeared altogether. Where is the *pomme caille* that Isaac Weld so enticingly described: "It is of an extraordinary large size, and deep red colour; not confined merely to the skin, but extending to the very core of the apple; if the skin be taken off delicately, the fruit appears nearly as red as when entire" (*Travels Through North America*, 1799)? Or the *bourassa* that Baroness von Riedesel in the late eighteenth century found "large, red and good-tasting" as well as excellent for storing? Her judgement was confirmed by Catharine

Parr Traill in 1855, but we have never seen one. Among the survivors is the Gravenstein, also commended by Mrs. Traill and still a favourite in Nova Scotia. Others are listed below. With the new varieties, it is well to keep in mind that commercial considerations are uppermost in the minds of developers: flavour comes last in their priorities. Essentially what they want is something that looks good, travels well and keeps a year. Still, it's worth sampling the new ones, for some are useful.

Apples vary with locality, so you need to learn what grows best near you. What follows is a very incomplete list of varieties and their uses.

Cortland: An old McIntosh spinoff, a good all-purpose apple that keeps well, still a favourite in Nova Scotia.

Delicious: Visually, the red Delicious is a treat: its flavour is mild and sweet and improves with age. Good for eating, though not for cooking.

Duchess: An old variety of summer apple, excellent for pies and sauce. Not a keeper.

Empire: Offspring of the McIntosh and Delicious, it has a mild flavour and is a good keeper. Useful for eating in the late winter and spring, when other varieties are in decline. It is said to be good for cooking, too.

Ida Red: Not to be used until after Christmas — and some say February. This excellent keeper is quite good for eating and reportedly for cooking in the late winter and early spring.

McIntosh: Certainly a survivor (the original seedlings were discovered by John McIntosh early in the nineteenth century when he was clearing land for his farm in eastern Ontario). A magnificent all-purpose apple, it dominates the scene from the beginning of October until Christmas. After that, it must accept competition from other varieties, for its flavour declines, even though kept otherwise intact by commercial cold-storage techniques.

Melba: A fresh-flavoured and early eating apple, good for cooking also, but not a keeper.

Northern Spy: Its quality was noted by Catharine Parr Traill, so it has been around for a long time and for good reason. A late apple, especially valued for cooking — the best for pies and baking. For eating, it is pleasant and it keeps very well.

Snow (La Fameuse): An old variety which is listed by Catharine Parr Traill as ripening in September, but which she used for "pies or puddings much earlier." She thought it "a fine, sweet, juicy apple", and so will you if you are able to find it.

Tydeman's Red: Related to the McIntosh, its chief merit is to fill the gap between Melbas, which don't last long, and McIntoshes, whose flavour does not really mature much before Thanksgiving. Tydeman's are for eating, not cooking, nor do they keep long.

Yellow Transparent: Originally from Russia, these used to be the first of the eating apples, yellow and juicy and easy to bruise; now they are green and hard, but very good for cooking. Not a keeper.

Applesauce

Though they vary in quality, wild apples often have a superior flavour to cultivated ones, and if you find a tree along some country road, and the fruit is reasonably free of worms, then you are in luck. They are worth picking for both pies and applesauce. The riper they are, the less sugar they will require for sweetening. A 6-quart basket is a reasonable quantity to deal with and will provide about seven pints of applesauce.

Wash the apples and core them. Simmer in enough water to prevent scorching. Stir and add more water as the apples cook, in small amounts as needed.

When the apples are thoroughly soft and the texture of the sauce is thick and smooth, put it through a coarse sieve to remove the skins and any surviving pieces of core. Add sugar to the sieved applesauce. The amount will vary with the apples, but for a 6-quart basket, it will be about 2 1/2 cups (625 mL). Add 1 tsp (5 mL) salt and 3 tbsp (45 mL) butter. Bring to a boil and pack in hot sterilized jars. Seal at once.

Unflavoured yogurt sweetened with a little honey makes a good topping for many desserts, like apple crumble or baked apples.

Variation: If no suitable wild apple tree meets your eye, you can make an excellent applesauce from Yellow Transparents or Duchess. You can avoid the messy business of sieving the applesauce by peeling as well as coring the apples, then cooking them in enough water to prevent scorching. When they are soft, beat with an electric handbeater until thoroughly smooth. Add sugar (not nearly as much as for wild green apples), salt and butter. Bring to a boil, then seal as previously described.

You can hardly go into any house in the bush, however poor, without having a large bowl of "apple sass" set before you — that is, of apple boiled in maple sugar.

John Geikie
Adventures in Canada, 1864

A slice of apple in your brown sugar will prevent it from hardening so much that you have to attack it with a hatchet.

Apple Jelly

The choice of apple is important: bland fruit will produce bland jelly. Crabapples will produce a jelly that is beautiful in colour as well as flavourful. Wild green apples will likely produce the best-tasting jelly of all.

Wash the apples — about a 4-quart (4-L) basket — and cut them in quarters, removing the stems and blossom ends. Do not peel or core them. Put the quarters in a large pot, cover with cold water and simmer gently until soft. Sieve through several layers of cheesecloth. Measure the resulting juice and for each cup add 1 cup (250 mL) sugar. Bring rapidly to a boil and cook hard, stirring constantly. Since crabapples and green apples have a high pectin content, begin testing to see whether the gel point has been reached after about five minutes of boiling. Use a wooden spoon to see whether the jelly "sheets" off, or put a teaspoonful on a saucer in the freezer until it cools to see whether it gels. When the jelly is ready, taste it. If the flavour seems a little boring, put a clove in each jar. Pour the jelly into hot sterilized jars and seal. Makes 3 1/2 cups (875 mL).

Apple Tart

An enlarged version of a tart developed by Margo Oliver, which never fails to please guests.

	Pastry:
1 1/2 cups (375 mL)	all-purpose flour, sifted
1/4 tsp (1 mL)	salt
3 tbsp (45 mL)	granulated sugar
3/4 cup (175 mL)	butter
4 tsp (20 mL)	white vinegar
1/2 tsp (2 mL)	grated nutmeg
	Filling:
1 1/2 cups (375 mL)	granulated sugar
3 tbsp (45 mL)	all-purpose flour
3/4 tsp (4 mL)	cinnamon
4 1/2 cups (1.125 L)	coarsely grated apples
	Icing sugar

For the pastry, combine the flour, salt and sugar lightly with a fork in a medium bowl. Cut in the butter with a pastry blender until crumbly. Stir in the vinegar and pat the dough into the bottom of a 9-inch (23-cm) springform pan. Sprinkle with grated nutmeg.

For the filling, combine the sugar, flour and cinnamon in a large bowl. Stir in the apples and spread the filling evenly over the pastry. Bake at 400°F (200°C) for 1 hour or until golden-brown. Remove the tart from the oven, cool it and remove from the pan. Just before serving, sift icing sugar over the top to produce an attractive snowy effect. Serve with whipped cream. Serves 10.

Apple Knobby Pudding

John Geikie describes how "the young folks of both sexes" entertained themselves with a lively evening of coring apples. "The object of all this paring is to get apples enough dried for tarts during the winter, the pieces when cut being threaded in long strings and hung up till they shrivel and get a leather-like look. When wanted for use, a little boiling makes them swell to their original size again, and brings back their softness." These strings of apples must have been used when this agreeable dessert was first made in Nova Scotia.

If you don't own a food processor, this dessert can be made easily by hand. Should there be any left for the following night, warm the pudding gently in the oven and serve with warmed maple syrup laced with a spoonful of rum.

1 cup (250 mL)	brown sugar
2 tbsp (25 mL)	shortening
1	egg
3 cups (750 mL)	finely chopped apples
1/2 cup (125 mL)	chopped nuts, optional
1 tsp (5 mL)	vanilla
1 cup (250 mL)	all-purpose flour
1/2 tsp (2 mL)	cinnamon
1/2 tsp (2 mL)	nutmeg
1 tsp (5 mL)	baking soda
	Freshly grated ginger to taste

Process the sugar, shortening and egg in the bowl of a food processor. Add the apples, nuts and vanilla and process briefly. Sift together the flour, spices and baking soda. Add to the apples with a little freshly grated ginger and process for a few seconds. Pour into an 8-inch (2-L) square pan and bake at 350°F (180°C) for 40 minutes or until brown. Serve with whipped or sour cream. Serves 6.

Apples in Pastry

Simple, delicious and elegant enough to serve to guests. The traditional jams for this recipe are plum or quince, but apple or red currant jelly will do.

The old-fashioned rolling pin cover can be a revelation. No more scraping off bits of dough, which then stick to fingers.

2 cups (500 mL)	all-purpose flour
pinch	salt
1 cup (250 mL)	butter
3 tbsp (45 mL)	granulated sugar
8 to 10 tbsp (120 to 150 mL)	ice water
8	baking apples
8 tbsp (120 mL)	quince or plum jam
2	eggs, beaten

Sift the flour and the salt into a large bowl and cut in the butter until the mixture is in crumbs. Add the sugar and enough water to make a smooth dough. Divide the dough into 8 pieces and roll each into a square large enough to cover an apple.

Peel and core the apples and set one in the centre of each square. Fill each centre with 1 tbsp (15 mL) jam. Brush the edges of the pastry with water and mould around the apples. Trim off the extra pastry and seal. Use the pastry scraps to decorate.

Set the apples on a baking tray, brush the pastry with beaten eggs and bake at 325°F (160°C) for 30 minutes, or until golden-brown. Pour cream or warmed maple syrup on top and eat with a fork or spoon. Serves 8.

Cranberries

Before we know it, Thanksgiving is upon us — that golden-leaved time when we tuck into the traditional turkey, cranberry sauce and pumpkin pie.

You can grow the high-bush cranberry (*Viburnum opulus*) or guelder rose, in your garden, but for the real cranberry (*Oxycoccus macrocarpus*) you must head for the swamps — or the supermarket.

Cranberry Relish

1 orange, unpeeled, seeded and quartered
2 cups (500 mL) cranberries
1 apple, unpeeled, cored and quartered
1/2 cup (125 mL) orange juice
1 cup (250 mL) granulated sugar

Combine the orange, cranberries and apple in a food processor and chop with the steel blade until coarsely chopped. Do this in batches if necessary. Stir in the orange juice and sugar. Store the relish in a covered container in the refrigerator. Makes about 3 cups (750 mL).

This recipe can be made easily in a blender, but then it *must* be done in batches.

Cranberry Salad

Old-fashioned jellied salads aren't nearly as popular as they used to be, but here's a recipe for those who miss them.

1 3-oz (90-g) package raspberry jelly powder
2 cups (500 mL) cranberries
1 orange, quartered
1 apple, cored but not peeled, chopped
1 stalk celery, finely chopped
1 cup (250 mL) granulated sugar

Make the jelly according to instructions on the package, in the bowl in which you intend to serve it (thus avoiding the nuisance of unmoulding).

Puree the cranberries and orange (including peel but with seeds removed) in a food chopper or processor. Add the apple, celery and sugar to the cranberry-orange mixture and stir. When the jelly begins to thicken, but before it sets, stir the cranberry mix into it. Refrigerate for at least 2 hours. Serves 6 to 8.

Cranapple Pie

A succulent use for leftover cranberries and a consoling dessert for those facing their umpteenth night of cold turkey.

2 cups (500 mL)	peeled and sliced apples
1 cup (250 mL)	cranberries
	Unbaked pastry for a double-crust 9-inch (23-cm) pie
1/2 cup (125 mL)	brown sugar
3/4 tsp (4 mL)	cinnamon
1/2 tsp (2 mL)	grated nutmeg
1/4 tsp (1 mL)	ground cloves
1/4 tsp (1 mL)	salt
2 tbsp (25 mL)	butter

Combine the apples and cranberries and place in a pie shell. Mix the sugar and spices in a small bowl and stir into the fruit. Dot the fruit with butter and cover with pastry. Prick the crust and bake at 350°F (180°C) for 1 hour, or until the pastry is golden. Serve with whipped or sour cream.

One of the wonderful things about these children of the Barrens is the great size of the fruit and flower compared with the plant. The cranberry, the crowberry, the cloudberry, etc., produce fruit any one of which might outweigh the herb itself.

Ernest Thompson Seton
The Arctic Prairies, 1911

Pumpkin

Pumpkins also are abundant in the farmers' gardens. They prepare them in several ways, but the most common is to cut them through the middle, and place each half on the hearth, open side towards the fire, till it is roasted. The pulp is then cut out of the peel and eaten. Better class people put sugar on it.

Peter Kalm
Travels into North America, 1753–61

Roasted Pumpkin Seeds: Pat the seeds dry and spread them on a cookie sheet. Sprinkle with salt and dot with butter. Bake at 325°F (160°C) for 1 hour, or until golden brown.

After many profligate years of throwing out the jack o' lantern, All Souls' Day is now spent peeling, cutting and cursing, but the resultant pumpkin puree resting in the freezer makes this hectic time worthwhile. As you peel the pumpkin, you may notice your cat sitting devotedly beside you hoping for scraps. This is not to be encouraged, because pumpkin seems to make cats sick.

To make the puree, peel the pumpkin and cut in cubes. Cover

with water and cook gently. When the pumpkin is cooked, drain it well, mash and pack in freezer containers.

Another method is to cut the pumpkin in half, remove the seeds and the slithery bits and bake in a 325°F (160°C) oven for about 1 hour or until very soft. The skin should then peel off easily.

Pumpkin au Gratin

Traditionally pumpkin goes into pies, but it is also excellent as a vegetable, as in this recipe.

Peel the pumpkin and cut it in pieces. Boil it briefly in salted water, drain well and dry. Arrange the pieces in a buttered casserole and sprinkle with 1 cup (250 mL) grated Cheddar cheese. Dribble 1/4 cup (50 mL) melted butter over the top and bake for about 30 minutes at 350°F (180°C).

An agreeable variant is to top the pumpkin pieces with slices of onion, which have been lightly cooked in butter, before sprinkling with the cheese. Or use alternate layers of cooked rice and pumpkin and proceed as above. Or omit the cheese and sprinkle generously with almond slivers.

Pumpkin Soup

This idea did not appeal — until we tasted it.

2 tbsp (25 mL)	butter
1	medium onion, minced
2	stalks celery, finely chopped
2 tbsp (25 mL)	all-purpose flour
2 cups (500 mL)	fresh pumpkin puree
4 cups (1 L)	chicken stock
	salt and pepper
2 tsp (10 mL)	dill seed
1 cup (250 mL)	light cream or evaporated milk

Melt the butter in a large saucepan. Add the onion and celery and cook until the onion is translucent. Remove from the heat and add the flour, mixing together carefully. Add the pumpkin and mix again, then return to the heat. Stir in the stock and seasonings and simmer for 30 minutes. Add the cream and, if necessary, correct the seasonings. Heat but do not boil. Serves 8.

Pumpkin Pie

Don't be afraid to be generous with the spices in this recipe, especially if you are using fresh pumpkin. Use heaping spoonfuls.

1 cup (250 mL)	granulated sugar
1 tbsp (15 mL)	all-purpose flour
1 tsp (5 mL)	ground ginger
1/2 tsp (2 mL)	allspice
1/2 tsp (2 mL)	mace
1 tsp (5 mL)	cinnamon
3/4 tsp (4 mL)	grated nutmeg
pinch	pepper
1/4 tsp (1 mL)	ground cloves
3	large eggs
2 cups (500 mL)	fresh pumpkin puree
1 cup (250 mL)	evaporated milk
1	unbaked 9-inch (23-cm) pie shell

Mix together the sugar, flour and spices in a large bowl. Blend the eggs, pumpkin and milk in a blender or food processor. Pour this mixture into the dried ingredients and mix well. Pour the filling into the pie shell. Bake for 15 minutes at 425°F (220°C), then at 350°F (180°C) for 50 minutes, or until firm. Test by sticking a fork in the centre. When the fork comes out clean, the pie is done. Let cool and serve with whipped cream flavoured with sugar to taste and 1 tsp (5 mL) Viennese vanilla (see page 85).

Pumpkin Bread

If you make this in the food processor, the bread is transformed into a light and delicate loaf, fit for the most particular of tea-tables.

Pumpkin Banana Bread: If you run short of pumpkin puree use 2/3 cup (150 mL) pumpkin and 1 mashed banana. Add 1 tsp (5 mL) grated fresh ginger and 1 tsp (5 mL) sherry in place of the vanilla.

The flavour of fresh pumpkin, more delicate than canned pumpkin (which is often strengthened with squash), requires additional spices.

1 3/4 cups (425 mL)	all-purpose flour
1/2 tsp (2 mL)	baking powder
1 tsp (5 mL)	baking soda
1 tsp (5 mL)	salt
3/4 tsp (4 mL)	cinnamon
1/2 tsp (2 mL)	ground cloves
1/2 tsp (2 mL)	grated nutmeg
1/4 tsp (1 mL)	mace
1 1/3 cups (325 mL)	granulated sugar
1/3 cup (75 mL)	shortening
2	large eggs
1 cup (250 mL)	fresh pumpkin puree
1/3 cup (75 mL)	milk
1 tsp (5 mL)	vanilla

Sift together the flour, baking powder, baking soda and spices. In a food processor, cream together the sugar and shortening, then add the eggs and process until fluffy. Add the pumpkin and the dry ingredients and process briefly, then add the milk and vanilla

Whipping cream (which should always be whipped cold) is usually flavoured with 1/2 tsp (2 mL) vanilla for 1 cup (250 mL) cream, but other flavourings are possible, too (such as kirsch, almond or rose water). An interesting discovery made one day, when alone in the kitchen with a bottle of Marsala and rather a lot of cream, was instant syllabub. Beat 1 cup (250 mL) whipping cream with 1/3 cup (75 mL) Marsala and 2 tbsp (25 mL) fruit sugar until stiff. Fold in a small can of mandarin oranges, drained, and 1 sliced banana. Serves 6.

and process for a few seconds. Pour the mixture into a greased 9 × 5-inch (2-L) loaf pan and bake at 350°F (180°C) for 1 hour or until a toothpick inserted into the centre of the loaf comes out clean.

Pumpkin Pudding

3/4 cup (175 mL)	granulated sugar
1 tbsp (15 mL)	all-purpose flour
3/4 tsp (4 mL)	salt
1/4 tsp (1 mL)	mace
1/4 tsp (1 mL)	allspice
1 tsp (5 mL)	ground ginger
1/2 tsp (2 mL)	grated nutmeg
4	large eggs
1 1/2 cups (375 mL)	fresh pumpkin puree
1 1/2 cups (375 mL)	milk
2 tbsp (25 mL)	light molasses
3 tbsp (45 mL)	melted butter

Place all the ingredients in a blender and mix well. Pour into a 1 1/2-quart (1.5-L) casserole. Bake at 350°F (180°C) for 1 1/2 hours or until firm. Serve warm or cold with whipped cream. Serves 8.

Grapes

Champlain observed wild grapes growing in southern Ontario early in the seventeenth century, though not uncritically: "Grapes ripen there, but they always leave a sharp, acid taste, which comes from not being cultivated" (*Voyages*, 1604–16). What he saw and tasted was the *vitis riparia*, the more common of the two wild grapes that grow in Canada, its range extending from New Brunswick to Manitoba. He was right about the flavour: they are too tart for eating fresh, but excellent for juice and jellies. They are found in moist places, along riverbanks and roadsides, along fences and in thickets where they can clamber; the ones used in the following recipes emerged in the wild part at the back of the garden. Their flavour is best after the first frost, around the end of September.

Evidently the wild grape can be confused with the poisonous Canadian moonseed (*Menispermum canadense*), but the distinction should be easy to make: the edges of wild grape leaves are sharply toothed, whereas those of the moonseed are smooth; the fruit of the wild grape contains many seeds; that of the moonbeam, only one.

If you are unable to find wild grapes, you can use Concord grapes. Their flavour is less intense, but otherwise similar, and they appear in stores and markets in late September.

Wild Grape Jelly

Because wild grapes have a strong flavour, we like to use a commercial pectin with them, which gives a larger quantity of jelly.

4 quarts (4 L)	wild grapes
2 1/2 cups (625 mL)	water, approx.
7 cups (1.75 L)	granulated sugar
1/2	170-mL bottle liquid commercial pectin

Wash and stem the grapes and measure them. You should have 7 to 8 cups (1.75 to 2 L).

Place the grapes in a large kettle and add barely enough water to cover—about 2 1/2 cups (625 mL). Mash the grapes, then bring to a boil and simmer gently until thoroughly soft (about 20 minutes if the grapes are ripe). Put the grapes through a sieve. This should give you about 4 cups (1 L) juice. Add the sugar, mix well and bring to a boil, stirring. Add the pectin and return to a full rolling boil. Boil hard for 1 minute and remove from the heat. Pour into sterilized jars and seal or cover with hot paraffin. Makes about 7 cups (1.75 L).

Concord Grape Pie

1 quart (1 L)	Concord grapes
3/4 cup (175 mL)	granulated sugar
3 tbsp (45 mL)	all-purpose flour
	Pastry for double-crust 9-inch (23-cm) pie
2 tbsp (25 mL)	butter

Slip the skins off the grapes. Put the skins in one bowl; collect the pulp in a saucepan. Cook the pulp gently for about 10 minutes, until the seeds are separated. Put the pulp through a sieve; then add it to the skins and mix with the sugar and flour. Add to a pastry-lined pie dish. Dot with butter and cover with pastry. Prick the top pastry and bake for 10 minutes at 450°F (230°C); reduce the heat to 350°F (180°C) and bake for 30 minutes longer.

Ground Cherries

Happiness is finding a cache of ground cherries at the market. This edible member of the nightshade family and cousin of the Chinese lantern is sometimes known as the strawberry or husk tomato. It is planted nowadays chiefly by squirrels, although it is increasingly listed in seed catalogues. Look for them by the wayside, or in fallow land — even in the back of your garden. Wallace Stegner remembers them on the prairies (*Wolf Willow*, 1955): "It may be that some of the ground cherries my mother brought as seed from Iowa and planted in the fireguard have grown and fruited and been spread by wind and birds. If so, field mice opening the papery husks and dining on the little yellow tomatoes inside may bless us too."

There's no denying that it's time-consuming to husk the papery shells, but the flavour of the tiny golden balls concealed within is subtle and unique, hinting perhaps at a cross between a cherry and a grape? A tomato and a melon? One begins to sound like a wine snob. Ground cherries freeze well but must be husked first. Green ones will ripen if left alone for a few days.

Ground Cherry Upside-down Cake

A surprising variation on an old theme. Demerara sugar adds a warm molasses flavour to the dish, but brown will do.

3/4 cup (175 mL)	melted butter
1 1/2 cups (375 mL)	Demerara sugar
2 1/2 cups (625 mL)	ground cherries, husked, washed and dried
1	banana, sliced, optional
2 tbsp (25 mL)	lemon juice
1/2 tsp (2 mL)	ground cardamom
1 1/2 cups (375 mL)	all-purpose flour
2 tsp (10 mL)	baking powder
1/2 tsp (2 mL)	salt
1/4 tsp (1 mL)	grated nutmeg
1	egg
1/2 cup (125 mL)	sour milk

In a 9-inch (2.5-L) square baking dish, combine 1/4 cup (50 mL) melted butter with 1 cup (250 mL) Demerara sugar. Cover with the ground cherries and sliced banana. Sprinkle the lemon juice and cardamom on top.

Sift together the dry ingredients in a medium bowl. Blend the egg, milk and remaining butter and sugar together in a small bowl and add gently to the flour mixture. Pour this over the fruit and bake at 400°F (200°C) for 30 minutes or until brown and crusty. Serve with sour cream or yogurt. Serves 6.

Ground Cherry Pie

4 cups (1 L)	ground cherries, husked, washed and dried
1/4 cup (50 mL)	all-purpose flour
2 tbsp (25 mL)	lemon juice
1/2 cup (125 mL)	granulated sugar
1/4 tsp (1 mL)	grated nutmeg
1/4 tsp (1 mL)	cinnamon
1 tbsp (15 mL)	melted butter
	Pastry for 9-inch (23-cm) pie plus lattice top

Mix the ground cherries gently in a large bowl with the other filling ingredients until they are evenly coated. Fill the pie crust with the fruit and top with a lattice. Bake for 1 hour at 350°F (180°C).

Juniper

If you rub the small, hard blue-black berries of this flat shrub that sprawls on rocky poor soil, they will exude a strong smell of gin (of which juniper oil is an important component). Juniper berries look rather like giant peppercorns. They were highly regarded by English cooks for spicing meats, and by herbalists as a remedy for plague, pestilence, poison and — less dramatically — chilblains and toothache. They grow plentifully in our woods, too. Since they are expensive to buy, when you manage to find them at all, it seems a pity not to harvest your own supply. Crushed, they make a good seasoning for veal or roast lamb.

Dry the berries by placing them in a slow oven — about 300°F (150°C) — until they have shrivelled slightly. Store them in small airtight jars in your spice cupboard (they seem to keep indefinitely). Add 3 or 4 crushed berries to pâtés, marinades or gravies.

Juniper Butter

This is an unusual flavoured butter for use with grilled fish or steak. Just spread it on before grilling.

1/4 cup (50 mL)	finely chopped onion
1/2 cup (125 mL)	melted butter
2 tsp (10 mL)	chopped garlic
8	crushed juniper berries
1 tbsp (15 mL)	chopped fresh parsley
1 tsp (5 mL)	lemon juice
	Salt and pepper

Cook the onion in the butter until soft. Add the garlic and remove from the heat. Add the remaining ingredients. Chill and store in a small covered jar in the refrigerator. Makes about 1/2 cup (125 mL).

Juniper Berry Stuffing

Use this spirited stuffing when you are preparing a large roast of pork. (For instructions on how to grow your own cress, see page 82.)

2	oranges
4 cups (1 L)	soft white breadcrumbs
1/2 cup (125 mL)	melted butter
1/4 tsp (1 mL)	grated nutmeg
3 tbsp (45 mL)	chopped cress
1 tbsp (15 mL)	chopped fresh parsley
4 tsp (20 mL)	dried sage
20	juniper berries, crushed
1/2 tsp (2 mL)	salt
2	eggs

Grate the rind of one orange. Squeeze the juice from both oranges and reserve.

In a large bowl, combine the orange rind and juice with the remaining ingredients and mix well. Bake with your roast or chicken.

Making Jellies, Jams, Pickles and Relishes

Because of the amount of sugar used in preparing jams and jellies, and the amount of sugar, salt and vinegar in pickles and relishes, there is no great danger of spoilage. So it is safe to use the old-fashioned open-kettle method of preparation, that is to say, boil the mixture in a large pot until it is ready and then pour it into hot sterilized jars. There is no need to process the jars further in a boiling water bath, as is the case when you are preserving most fruits and vegetables. This simplifies life a lot, particularly for novices.

Even so, there are a number of things to keep in mind.

1. Use fruit or vegetables of good quality and flavour. For jams and jellies it is best to use fruit that is slightly under-ripe. Over-ripe fruit will have less natural pectin and therefore will not gel so readily.

2. Prepare carefully. Remove all small worms and leaves and extraneous matter. Most fruit and vegetables should be washed, but it is best to avoid washing a soft fruit like raspberries if possible, for they tend to disintegrate.

3. In pickling, use coarse (pickling) salt; ordinary table salt will make the liquid cloudy. Use fresh spices for the best flavour — ground spices go stale quite readily. Where possible, take several thicknesses of a square of cheesecloth, put the whole spices in the centre, tie with string into a little bag and put the bag in the mixture to disseminate the spicy flavours while cooking. Remove the bag before bottling.

4. Use a large pot for making jams and jellies. Rapid boiling causes the mixture to expand enormously, if temporarily.

5. Use enamel (unchipped) or stainless-steel pots for making pickles or in dealing with an acidic fruit like rhubarb. Acid, whether in vinegar or in various fruits, will react chemically with aluminium, iron, copper and brass.

6. The merits of using commercial pectin are much debated. Using commercial pectin makes it necessary to use much more sugar, greatly reduces the cooking time and greatly increases the yield; it produces a light, fresh-flavoured jam or jelly. The arguments in favour of using commercial pectin seem persuasive in dealing with strawberries, which have practically no natural pectin and a very strong flavour. It takes ages to make a thick strawberry jam by boiling fruit and sugar together, and the yield is correspondingly small. The flavour is rich and satisfying, however. There seems no case at all for using commercial pectin where fruits such as currants, gooseberries and black currants are concerned, for these have much natural pectin and gel easily. Generally, the flavour is stronger when just fruit and sugar and no commercial pectin are used.

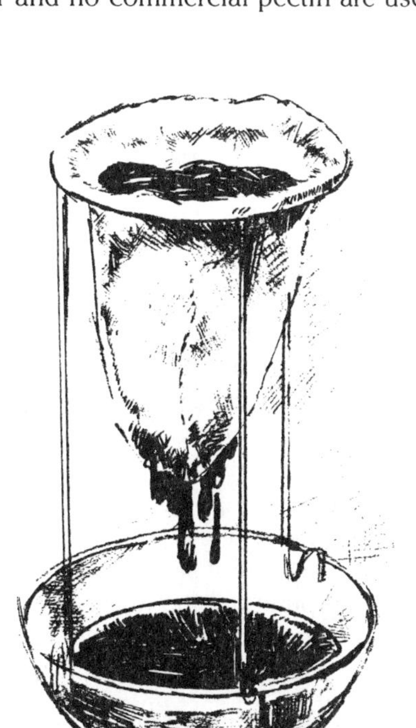

7. Jams are easier to make than jellies, which require an extra stage: juice must be extracted. This is done by simmering the fruit in a little water until it is thoroughly softened. Purists then move on to the jelly bag, letting it hang overnight and never squeezing it at all. They will be rewarded by a sparkling jelly. In this book, using a sieve is recommended. It is far faster, and meant principally to exclude seeds. It will also produce more, if less sparkling, jelly. In either case the flavour will be the same.

8. Testing is the chief worry in making jams and jellies. A candy or jelly thermometer will register 220°F (112°C) when the gel stage is reached, though fruits rich in pectin will gel at a slightly lower temperature. Other ways of testing can be equally satisfactory. There is the spoon test, which may be begun about 5 minutes after the sugar and fruit have begun to boil vigorously. Lift some of the mixture up in a wooden spoon; pause to let it cool for a moment or so, then slowly pour the mixture back into the pot. When the jam or jelly is nearly ready, the mixture will thicken together or "sheet". This test may be supplemented by pouring a little of the jam or jelly on a plate and putting it into the freezer to cool. When cool, it should have the desired consistency. If too runny, then try again in a minute or so.

Sterilizing Jars and Bottling

For jams, jellies, pickles and relishes, this is a relatively relaxed procedure. Some people keep their pickles in crocks, always making sure they are covered by the preserving liquid, but we have always used sterilized one-quart Mason jars for the large ones. Jams and jellies may be safely poured into commercial jars — preferably with wide mouths — and covered with melted paraffin. For gift-giving, buy proper jelly jars and small Mason jars. In some respects Mason jars are the easiest to deal with, although fresh lids must be used each year.

First wash and rinse the jars, then place them inverted in a large kettle — a large covered roasting pan works well — with about 2 inches of cold water at the bottom. While cooking the jam, jelly or relish, bring the water in the kettle to a boil and let the jars simmer gently in readiness, so that they will be hot and sterile when needed. (Strictly speaking, they will be sterile after 15 minutes of simmering.) Remove each jar as needed, shake off the excess water, then fill carefully with the prepared mixture. Jelly pours easily; jams and relishes are lumpier. A clean, heatproof, glass measuring cup is useful in transporting the mixture from pot to jar. In any case, wipe off any spills around the top and sides of the jar. Fill the jar to within 1/4 inch of the top and seal immediately.

If using Mason jars, put the lids briefly into the kettle with the simmering water — the manufacturers advise boiling for 5 minutes. Remove with a slotted spoon and shake to remove any excess water. Place the lid on the jar; screw tightly. It is probably easiest to complete one jar at a time. As the jars cool, each one will give an agreeable pop. That is the vacuum seal working, and you can now feel that the process of preservation is complete.

If there is no pop, and if the lid does not snap down to form a vacuum, then the jar is not sealed. You can either repeat the process, a rather painful prospect, or use the improperly sealed jar first. Jellies, jams and pickles do not spoil in a hurry.

If you are using paraffin, melt it carefully in a small pan from which you can pour it easily. Let the jelly cool slightly, perhaps for 15 minutes. Then add a thin layer of liquid paraffin; tilt the jar so that the paraffin covers the whole surface of the top. Add a second layer later if the paraffin covering is not perfect. Because paraffin can be difficult to pour and is certainly annoying to clean up, melt it little by little. It will be easier to manage. You may prefer to dedicate one little pan solely to melting paraffin, thus saving much time in cleaning.

Storage

When the jars are cool, wipe off with warm soapy water to remove any sticky bits that have spilled. Put lids, or plastic wrap held in place by an elastic band, on the paraffin-covered jams and jellies. This protects them from dust while they are being stored.

Label the jars, identifying the contents and date of making. Store in a cool dark place. A fruit cellar is ideal.

The Cellar

Now these new things of which you've never heard
Let me explain; first the cellar where they
Keep preserves and roots and cream and white curd,
Butter and cheese, pitchers of milk and whey.
Close to each other, but not too, they lay
Apples, red brown and yellow in their bins,
And all in shadows deep dark down from day
Rows of cider barrels huge as dead kings,
Beside a cistern where a trapped cloud lies
Beside the air where Scug the bat scallops and flies.

James Reaney

Plum Gin

Prick the damson plums all over with a needle and pack into 1-quart (1-L) Mason jars. For every jar filled, add 1/2 cup (125 mL) granulated sugar. Cover the plums with gin, but leave a space at the top of the jar so that the gin does not touch the metal. Keep in a warm place for about 3 months, shaking from time to time. About Christmas time, strain the liquid through a filter, then bottle and cork. Or, it can be poured into a decanter. Serve plum gin in small quantities, as you would a liqueur. The plums themselves are delicious.

I brandied some wild plums which I will never do again as you have to pierce each dratted little plum with a needle

Colleen Thibaudeau

Wild Grape Juice

This recipe will bring out the splendid rich flavour of wild grapes. Pick as many as is convenient, wash and separate from the stems. Put the grapes into a large kettle, add enough water to cover the fruit, but no more, and bring to a boil. Simmer gently for about 30 minutes. Press the fruit through a sieve and add sugar to taste. For 7 cups (1.75 L) juice about 1 1/2 cups (375 mL) sugar may be necessary. Simmer the juice for 5 minutes, bottle in sterilized jars and seal. To drink it, mix half and half with water, ginger ale or soda water.

One bottle of this grape juice, somehow, kept getting itself shoved to the back of the refrigerator. Two years later, when opened, it had become rich and mellow, having turned itself, if not into a liqueur, certainly halfway into a cordial. We were almost as fortunate as Mrs. Simcoe's friend (*Diary*, 1792–6), who put "some of the Juice in Barrels to make vinegar &...it turned out very tolerable Wine."

Cranberry Cordial

Recipes are like folktales; they turn up everywhere in different guises. Just when you think someone has invented one, it pops up somewhere else. But we have never encountered this delicate ruby-coloured liqueur except in Blanche Pownall Garrett's *A Taste of the Wild*.

3 cups (750 mL)	cranberries
1 cup (250 mL)	granulated sugar
1	6-oz (175-g) can frozen orange juice, thawed
3 cups (750 mL)	apricot brandy

In a blender, puree the berries, sugar and orange juice. Empty the contents into a large glass jar and pour the brandy over it. Cover tightly, give it a good shake and put it away in a cool dark place for at least one month. Give it a shake about once a week.

When you are ready to use the cordial, strain it several times, first through a colander and then through cloth. Pour the cordial into a clear decanter. Makes about 1 quart (1 L).

Rather than discarding the cranberry puree left over from your cranberry cordial, try making brandied cranberry butter. In a saucepan, combine the puree with 2 tbsp (25 mL) fresh orange juice, 2 tbsp (25 mL) finely grated orange peel, 1/4 cup (50 mL) cranberry or cranapple juice, 1/4 tsp (1 mL) salt, 1 tbsp (15 mL) butter and 2 cups (500 mL) granulated sugar. Boil until thick, approximately 15 to 20 minutes, stirring from time to time. Pour the butter into sterilized jars and seal with wax. This butter is particularly good with toast or hot English muffins.

Cider

Cider was mostly used for making apple-sauce, but a few barrels called by some rack cider, were kept for drinking purposes, for the different bees, and harvest time, and social gatherings. After temperance sentiments gained ascendancy the custom was abolished, for, after the cider had been kept a while, it became "hard." Hard cider, because it contained a percentage of alcohol, was very intoxicating. It was sometimes called "Apple Jack." Cider was also made into vinegar, and of the best quality; by being left exposed to the air, i.e., not corked up, it became vinegar in a few months' time.

A "Canuck"
Early Pioneer Life in Upper Canada, 1905

When the market is offering freshly pressed cider, buy a few gallons extra and stick them in the freezer. (Cider freezes beautifully in bags or plastic jugs, but don't freeze it in glass bottles as they may crack.)

Mulled Cider

1/2 cup (125 mL)	brown sugar
1 tsp (5 mL)	whole allspice
1 tsp (5 mL)	whole cloves
2 quarts (2 L)	cider
1/4 tsp (1 mL)	salt
pinch	grated nutmeg
	Orange slices and cinnamon sticks for garnish

Combine all the ingredients in a large saucepan and heat slowly to a boil. Cover and simmer for 20 minutes. Strain and serve in small punch cups with an orange slice on top. Use cinnamon sticks as stirrers.

Winter

The winters there [in Quebec] are very healthy, though severe, for since the weather is not changeable, one can take good precautions against the cold. Thus one takes cold there less than in our country. At the beginning of November people lay in their winter provisions. I was very surprised when people asked me how much fowl, and particularly how many fish, I wanted and where I should like to have the latter left, since I had no pond. In the attic, I was told, where they would keep better than in the cellars. Accordingly I took three to four hundred which kept very well through the winter. All that had to be done when a person wanted meat, fish, eggs, apples, and lemons for the midday meal was to put them in cold water the day before. Thus the frost is thoroughly removed, and such meat or fish is just as juicy, even more tender than what we have at home. In addition to this, poultry is packed in snow, which forms such a crust of ice that one must chop away with a hatchet.

Baroness von Riedesel
Journal, 1776 – 83

Introduction

With luck and a cupboard full of jams, jellies and pickles, the pre-Christmas culinary crunch can be a relatively relaxed affair of producing little luxurious treats like Stilton pâté (page 88) and smoked salmon yogurt dip (page 90).

And Christmas shopping, if you don't view it as a crusade or a wearisome obligation, can be an enjoyable excursion, although perhaps not as colourful a scene as that described by an observer in mid-nineteenth-century Toronto:

If the weather chanced to be cold, you would see huge files of frozen pigs standing on their four legs in front of the stalls, as if they had been killed when at a gallop; countless sheep hung over-head, with here and there one of their heads carefully gilded, to add splendour to the exhibition. Some deer were almost always noticed at some of the stalls, and it was not unusual to see the carcase of a bear contributing its part to the general show. As to the oxen, they were too fat for my taste, though the butcher seemed to be proud of them in proportion to their obesity. The market was not confined to a special building, though there was one for the purpose. Long ranges of farmers' wagons, ranged at each side of it, showed similar treasures of frozen pork and mutton, standing entire at the feet of their owners, who sat among them waiting for purchasers. Frozen geese, ducks, chickens, and turkeys abounded, and that household was very poor indeed which had not one or other to grace the festival.

John Geikie
Adventures in Canada, 1864

There is the gradual adornment of the house from Advent Sunday on — cards trickle in and then the tree itself enters the scene, to be decorated with popcorn and cranberry chains, tinsel and ornaments, with the oldest and most battered baubles the most treasured. Lights, wreaths, candy canes. Not only the children are enchanted.

And then, suddenly, it's Boxing Day. With luck, the first hyacinth refreshes the jaded household. In January we curl up with seed catalogues while visions of gardens dance in our tired heads. Gradually the bulbs begin to blossom, the daffodils bringing splashes of sunlight to grey days and cheering the sniffling invalids. (Someone is always sick in January, but there's a certain cosiness to convivially sipping a hot toddy together and sharing the commiserations and the Kleenex.)

Once recovered, we cheer ourselves up with various indoor domestic pursuits: growing little boxes of cress, making marmalade and quickbread. And we enjoy substantial peasant soups or red cabbage and sausage after a day in the frozen wastes.

The days grow visibly longer, the snow, once glistening, is piled in grimy heaps by the roadside. And then one afternoon, as we stagger through the mud with the groceries, while the cat waits reproachfully by the front door, through the tattered snow pokes the first snowdrop. Spring!

The Garden

Simples

To damp the fire that burns in Billy
Extract of the water lily.
Man who eats a cabbage quite
Can drink and not get drunk that night.
If falling sickness trouble you
Down a glass of Dutch sundew.
Your lungs are clogged? Kind Sir consent
To hyssop, horehound, calamint.
If head's at fault, then betony.
Or sage or rue or peony.
Should stomach prove the house of pain,
Wormwood, sorrel, and purslane.
For liver's yellow melancholy
Decoction make of agrimony.
Finger-fern and maiden-hair
And a dodder of thyme the spleen restore.
Kidneys clear for those who swallow
Parsley, saxifrage and mallow.
Mugwort will the womb renew,
And pennyroyal, and featherfew.
Hearts on roses fed grow calm
With borage, bugloss, basil, balm.

Anne Wilkinson

Herbal Gifts

As Christmas approaches, it's time to begin creating herbal gifts. An appropriate place to start is with pot-pourri, an art that stretches back at least as far as the ancient Egyptians, who combined dried rose petals with spices like myrrh. Pot-pourri is a French term that literally means "rotted pot"; no doubt this refers to the classic way of making a moist pot-pourri by combining half-dried rose petals (or other fragrant petals) with salt. This process is harder and more authentic than dry pot-pourri, which requires added fragrance.

You can grow all the flowers yourself, or seek blooms from friends. (They may want to hide their gardens when they see you coming.) These days it is hard to find nearly enough fragrant flowers in a garden. Not any old rose will do, but only certain kinds of old-fashioned ones like the rugosas — Belle Poitevine, Frau Dagmar Hastrup and Hansa. Most of the modern hybrid tea roses are not suitable. Sweet woodruff, dianthus, hardy lavender, lemon- and rose-scented geranium, and that delightful annual, mignonette, are among the other garden possibilities.

The leaves (if scented) and flowers (just coming into bloom) should be gathered in the late morning, after the dew has evaporated and before the heat of the day has arrived. Spread the petals and leaves on a screen and keep in a warm, dry place (an attic is ideal) for several days until they are thoroughly dry. Then store them in a plastic bag until you are ready to make your pot-pourri.

Perhaps it is best to start in a plain way, buying dried lavender and rose petals from a health-food store. Two other ingredients will be necessary: a fixative such as orris-root powder to absorb and retain the perfume; and essential oils, such as lavender or rose. Concentrated essences of these and other perfumes are usually needed these days to emphasize the natural fragrances. If they're not available in your health-food store, try a nursery that specializes in herbs.

Spices — cinnamon, cloves and nutmeg — may be added, or various combinations of herbs such as lemon verbena, thyme and rosemary. Of course, it is not advisable to try everything at once, but there are vistas of fragrant possibilities. You can be complicated and subtle, devising mixtures appropriate for each room in the house — roses for the living room, the refreshing lemon verbena for a bedroom, and lavender in drawers.

Though invention and variation are the order of the day in composing pot-pourri, it is useful to start from a basic sort of recipe like the following:

Lavender and Rose Pot-Pourri

3 cups (750 mL)	dried lavender flowers
3 cups (750 mL)	dried rose petals
1/2 cup (125 mL)	dried lemon verbena leaves
2 tbsp (25 mL)	dried rosemary
1/3 cup (75 mL)	orris-root powder
3 drops	oil of roses
3 drops	oil of lavender

Mix the flowers, petals and leaves carefully together in a bowl. Add the orris powder and mix again. Add the essential oils, mixing after each drop. Place the mixture in a glass jar or plastic bag and seal. Store in a warm dry place and shake it from time to time. Let cure for 6 weeks.

If you want the pot-pourri for Christmas gifts, then make it in early November at the latest. The mixture can be presented in small ornamental glass jars with tight lids. The jars should be uncovered in a warm place; the pleasing fragrance will soon fill the room.

Depending on the amount of use, the pot-pourri should last for years. When the scent declines, it can be revived by adding a drop or two of the essential oils originally used.

Some people like to arrange pot-pourri in ornamental saucers, in which case you may want to improve its appearance by adding some colourful dried flowers — a few sprigs of statice or calendula petals or rosebuds. (The scent of pot-pourri will not last more than a few weeks in an open bowl. It can either be freshened up with essential oils or simply enjoyed for its appearance.)

Sachets

Some of the pot-pourri may be used to make sachets. About 1/4 cup (50 mL) of the mixture will fit into a small bag about 3 by 5 inches (8 by 12 cm). Cotton prints such as those from Laura Ashley are marvellously appropriate, especially if remnants can be found. You can trim the bag with lace and tie it with a ribbon that suits the print of the fabric. These are gifts that children can readily make. For a more bracing scent, perhaps for a grandfather, try combining 2 tbsp (25 mL) pot-pourri with 2 tbsp (25 mL) dried rosemary or thyme. Throw in 6 whole cloves as a finishing touch. The scent will linger pleasantly in drawers for years.

Sleep Pillows

Make sleep pillows larger than sachets and fill them with either pot-pourri or a mixture of pot-pourri and herbs such as lavender and lemon verbena. Tuck the pillows under regular pillows for a pleasing and relaxing scent at bedtime.

Herbal Bath Bags

Make a small bag of cotton and fill it with a mixture of 2 tbsp (25 mL) fine oatmeal (traditionally believed to keep the skin soft and produced by putting regular oatmeal in the blender or food processor and whirring until fine) and 1 tbsp (15 mL) pot-pourri or mixed dried herbs (rosemary is invigorating; lavender and lemon verbena refreshing).

Let the bag soak in the warm bath water or let it hang on the tap so the warm water pours over it. You can use it twice.

Elizabethan Pomander

Of all herbal gifts, none is more distinctive than an Elizabethan pomander — a clove orange. As a Christmas gift it can be made by children; it should be prepared six weeks ahead of the event, in early November.

Take a small firm orange and wrap plain cotton seam binding tape around it so that the orange is divided into four quarters. Pin the tape in place. (Later it will be replaced by decorative ribbon.)

In each of the quarters, make holes with a nail and fill each one with a clove. Except where the tape is, the whole orange should be covered with cloves, about 1/4 inch (5 mm) apart. (As the orange dries, it will get smaller and the cloves will move closer together.)

When completed, put the clove-covered orange in a brown paper bag and sprinkle about two spoonfuls of orris-root powder on it, shaking the bag gently to make sure the powder is well distributed. Put the bag in a warm dry place for about six weeks.

When the orange is dry, shake off any excess powder and remove the cotton tape. Replace it with ribbon (red or green velvet is handsome and seasonal) tied in a bow at the top.

According to Eleanor Farjeon, in her poem *The Clove Orange*, the pomander once had a multiplicity of uses. Sniffed during dull sermons, it promoted wakefulness. Sniffed in pestilential rooms, it warded off infection. Hung among clothes, it spread a delicious scent. Nowadays we stick to the last use mostly and suspend the clove orange from a clotheshanger in a cupboard. It lasts for many years. We have one, aged seven, and it seems marvellously intact: light and dry and scented.

Catnip Mice

No one will be a more delighted recipient of an herbal gift than your cat, or any cat with whom you are on gift-giving terms. As Gerard pointed out more than three hundred years ago, cats find catnip "so pleasant unto them, that they rub themselves upon it, & wallow or tumble in it, and also feed on the branches and leaves very greedily."

Why cats are intoxicated by catnip is a mystery that modern science has so far failed to solve. But there it is. And commonly, there it is in the garden, a weed that is moderately difficult to keep within bounds, completely unnoticed by a cat until you crush a leaf. If it is not in your garden, you can probably buy a plant from a market or garden centre in the spring, or order seeds from a nursery. (Or, in a pinch, buy a package from your local pet store.)

Cut branches of the catnip on a dry day in September, tie them together in bunches, put the bunches in a paper bag and suspend from some convenient spot in the garage. When you want to use the dried leaves, strip them from the branches and crumble them.

It's best to make a mouse that is approximately real-life size, so that your cat can carry or toss it about, as fancy dictates. Use sturdy cotton or felt. Sew two mouse shapes together, leaving a small opening for the catnip stuffing; fill, then sew up completely. Your cat will never sneer at your artistic ability; it will be too busy wallowing and tumbling. How long this will go on depends partly on your sewing. A really keen cat can tear apart a weakly sewn catnip mouse in thirty minutes (but it will have been a good thirty minutes).

Christmas

I remember the first Christmas Day I passed in Canada — being laughed at because I wandered out on to the plains near Peterboro', and brought in a wreath of the boxleaved trailing wintergreen (which with its scarlet berries reminded me of the varnished holly with which we were wont to garnish the old house at home,) and hanging it over the mantel piece, and above the pictures of my host's parlor, in honor of the day. It seemed to me these green branches might be held as emblems to remind us that we should keep faith bright and green within our hearts.

Catharine Parr Traill
The Canadian Settler's Guide, 1854

Decorations

How like Mrs. Traill to happen upon the wintergreen, which for most of us would be hidden by snow in December. It is a charming little evergreen plant with glossy green leaves and bright red berries, which creeps about forest floors and nearby clearings from Newfoundland to Manitoba. Its more famous cousin, salal, lives in British Columbia, its fruit long valued by native peoples and its foliage used extensively by florists. Lucky British Columbia, for it has the holly as well.

Wreaths can be made from coathangers stretched into a round shape and then filled out with strips of foam material. Small holly branches are then stuck in or tied in place. However, this can be a tricky and prickly business, so you may want to settle for buying a fresh evergreen wreath from the market. Even if not in the same league as a holly wreath, it does look splendid on the front door. Nowadays one can also buy vine wreaths of all sizes. They last for years, and can be decorated with dried flowers, spices, Christmas tree ornaments — the possibilities are endless.

Christmas Trees

More important and central to the question of Christmas decorations is the tree. Choosing one is a passionate business, beginning with the variety — Scotch pine or spruce? We ourselves are divided on the subject, one of us claiming that she always had a Christmas cold when the family bought spruce trees; when they switched to Scotch pine she stopped sniffling through Christmas. The other claims heatedly that the traditional spruce tree with its dipping branches is far more receptive of ornaments, easier to decorate, prettier, really. It has to be admitted that the Scotch pine keeps its needles more tenaciously. Be sure to secure a freshly cut spruce tree, or you will be left with heaps of needles on the floor and something resembling a ghost tree. Shake the tree you are about to buy to see whether the needles are already dropping. If they are, put it down and look again.

Before bringing the tree into the house, chop a piece off the bottom. The new cut will ensure that the tree absorbs much more water. One of us has found a commercial stand that really works. The other, after many disappointments, has settled for a big crock and a supply of large round stones, hoarded from year to year, used to prop the tree in place.

Christmas Eve — Market Square

City of Christmas, here, I love your season,
where in the market square,
bristled and furry
like a huge animal
the fir trees lie
silently waiting buyers.
It's as if
they hold the secrets of a Christmas sealed —
as statues hold their feelings sealed in stone —
to burst in bells and baubles on their own
within the warmth and lightness of a house.

The sellers, bunched and bundled,
hold their ears,
blow lazy boas as they call their wares,
and children out of legends pulling sleds,
prop tall trees straight in search of symmetry
and haul their spikey aromatic wonder
home through a snowy world.
Almost the tree sings through them in their carols
almost grows taller in their torsos, is
perfectly theirs, as nothing ever was.

The soft snow falls,
vague smiling drunkards weave
balancing bulging parcels with their wings
they tip-toe where the furry monster grows
smaller and hoarier
and nerveless sprawls
flat on its mammoth, unimagined face.
While in far separate houses
all its nerves
spring up like rockets,
unknown children see
a miracle
and cry
to cut the ceiling not to lop the tree.

P.K. Page

During the long winter evenings the children would frequently gather before the fireplace and amuse themselves by popping corn and cracking nuts. The "pop" corn is a variety of corn with a small ear and small kernel, and is raised only for the purpose of popping. In the fall of the year it is taken off of the stalk, the husks pulled back and tied in a loop at one end of the ear; a number of ears are then bundled together and hung up till winter to dry. A small handful of corn after being shelled is put into a frying pan or spider, covered up and held over the hot coals in the fireplace. After constant shaking for a minute or two, the kernels swell and burst and fill up the pan with white feathery particles.

A "Canuck"
Early Pioneer Life in Upper Canada, 1905

Cranberry and Popcorn Chains

Few of us now make our own decorations for the tree, apart from the odd kindergarten contribution of misshapen paper chains and wobbly Santas with flyaway cotton batting beards, but a popcorn chain is a pleasant way to add a Victorian touch to a Christmas tree. Children can make them, too.

Using strong thread and a large needle, string three kernels of popcorn alternating with one cranberry until the chain is the length you wish. Push the needle through the soft white part of the popcorn rather than the hard kernel. Some people find that stale popcorn is easier to work with.

A Christmas Bouquet

For a handsome and inexpensive bouquet, buy a cheap poinsettia, cut off the red leaves and sear the ends with a candle immediately after cutting in order to seal in the juices. (This technique is also useful with poppies and iris.) Use the red leaves as cut flowers with white chrysanthemums in a vase, or float them in a glass bowl.

And don't throw your poinsettia out when the holidays are over. It will remain red for months and will then go happily into the garden for the summer.

Seed Catalogues

It is always well to save your own seeds if you can. A few large carrots should be laid by to plant out early in Spring for seed. Onions the same, also beets, parsnips, and some of your best cabbages. —Seeds will always fetch money at the stores, if good and fresh, and you can change with neighbours.

If you have more than a sufficiency for yourself do not begrudge a friend a share of your superfluous garden seeds. In a new country like Canada a kind and liberal spirit should be encouraged....

Catharine Parr Traill
The Canadian Settler's Guide, 1854

If she were living now, Mrs. Traill would have to revise her notes on collecting seeds. Do not bother to save the seeds of any hybrid flower or vegetable, for they will not breed true. Cucumber and squash seeds can produce unpleasant surprises, and jubilee marigolds produce nothing at all, a strange quality in marigolds, for they are usually vigorous self-seeders. Some plants still seed themselves lavishly — dill and many marigolds, shirley poppies and parsley, to name a few. Parsley requires patience because it is a biennial. You have to wait for the plants to bloom in their second year, and a third year until the seedlings appear.

The subject of seeds arises because by tradition January is the month when the seed catalogues arrive in the mail. At such a time they offer an almost too-seductive contrast to conditions actually prevailing in the garden.

The inexperienced gardener should start gently, with seeds easy to germinate and handle. Seed catalogues often have suggestions for a child's flower or vegetable garden — start right there. If such suggestions are lacking, begin by trying lettuce and radishes, then green beans, carrots and beets. Don't bother with tomato seeds at first; they need a considerable amount of expert care if they are not going to turn out spindly and hopeless. It is far better to buy the plants from a greenhouse, then put them in the garden. (And when doing this, keep in mind that small plants transplant more easily than large ones, which also take longer to get used to new circumstances.)

For an herb garden, dill and sweet basil germinate readily. Parsley is slower, and one can often buy small parsley plants at a moderate price. (They don't like being transplanted much, but if you soak the little plants with lots of water, root damage is minimized.)

As to flowers, petunias are tiresome to start from seeds, but marigolds, cosmos, asters and nasturtiums are easy. Nasturtiums are best planted where you mean them to grow, and this is true of most vegetables and herbs. Marigolds, cosmos and asters, among others, transplant easily, so it is tempting to give them a head start by planting them indoors about three weeks before transplanting them outdoors.

In planning the garden, the scale of operation should never be forgotten. Seed catalogues are intoxicating. There is a very real danger that you will buy enough to plant several acres, when in fact you have an apartment balcony. If you have practically no time and hardly any space, ignore seed catalogues. Buy some lettuce seeds in a supermarket, a couple of tomato plants from a garden centre in the spring, get some chives from a friend, and you have the makings of a salad.

If you do have a sizeable garden, seed catalogues contain many varieties of the same species, as well as many more species, than supermarket selections. Only in seed catalogues will you likely find the delightful annual shirley poppies, the unassuming mignonette with its wonderfully sweet perfume (useful for pot-pourri), statice and helichrysum for dried flower arrangements, calendula (a cheerful plant and useful herb), all of which are easy to grow. As you venture on into perennials, you may want to grow single hollyhocks, if you can find the seed.

As you browse through the catalogues, you should consider reading Katharine S. White's *Onward and Upward in the Garden.* An accomplished gardener and editor, she brings a fine critical mind to the business of reading seed catalogues.

Indoor Gardening

To banish the red spider.

Cut off the infected leaf. The leaf once attacked soon decays and falls off; but in the mean time the animals remove to another, and the leaf, from the moment of attack, seems to cease to perform its office; but persevere in the amputation, and the plants become healthy.

Mackenzie's Five Thousand Receipts, 1846

Now is the time to revive the house plants, no doubt shamefully neglected during the hectic Christmas season. They should be put in the bathtub and given a shower in cool water, about the temperature of an amiable spring shower. Leave the plug in the tub and let them soak in the water for about 10 minutes; remove the plug and let the water drain away, but leave the plants for another hour, enough time to let the water drain off their foliage.

As to fertilizing, there should be no hurry about this until the light grows stronger. The plants themselves are a good gauge of the right time. When in late February or early March they begin to show new growth, they should be given a restorative dose of fertilizer, preferably of an organic sort like Lakefish. For flowering plants, the approved formula is 5-10-5 (5% nitrogen, 10% phosphorus, 5% potassium), though there is no harm in using an all-purpose formula of 6-6-6. There *is* harm in dosing your plants too heavily with fertilizer — it can be dangerous to their health. Three or four times is quite enough between late February and late May, when you can put your house plants outside for their summer holiday.

Your plants likely won't be troubled by insect pests, if you look after them appropriately. But sometimes, particularly in late winter, there is trouble: white fly on the impatiens, or scale insect on the

citrus fruits. Buy natural insecticides with a soap base. (It's best to stick to natural insecticides and fertilizers, for they are less treacherous for amateurs — perhaps for everyone.)

If you have bulbs resting in the root cellar, they should now be ready for forcing. The paperwhites should be ready first, probably in December. They will be followed by the hyacinths, crocus early in January, and later in the month by daffodils. Tulips, at least some varieties, seem to be slower, and there is no need to rush them before February. When you remove the bulbs from their cool dark surroundings, bring them first into a cool bright place. After a few days they will be green, and you can bring them into the warmer living room or wherever else you wish to enjoy them.

House Plants

It has been a month since I gave up shaving
& already the houseplants are much more alert,
a pleasure to see such delicate strength —
it would be so easy to hurt their little stems
yet they stand so proud & fearless,
their leaves gently cocked
between the sun streaming through the windows
& that other sun streaming through my cloudy thoughts.

Of course when I think an unkind thought
the plants imperceptibly shudder
& when I open a can of pork & beans
or watch TV commercials
or holler at my wife
or contemplate suicide
the plants become aware of their perilous position
stranded on small islands of potted soil
in an ocean of human supremacy.

They know what a killer I am,
worse than the birds, insects, fungus & harsh weather
they'd be exposed to outside.
Being cut, smoked, trod on, eaten & tossed out
they can accept
& perhaps they know they can't really be killed
but it is much harder for them to accept
my boredom, my bombing of cities,
my incomprehensible evil,

& yet they are forgiving & spring to life
& they are so easily pleased
& even a simple thing like me forgoing
the daily torture of slicing off my facial hairs
has given them new hope,

& now the clouds have covered the sun
& the houseplants continue to shine.

David McFadden

You cannot force your bulbs twice. However, except for paperwhites, which are not hardy in Canada, most can be persuaded to bloom outdoors in the following years. Once they have flowered, remove the withered blooms, put the bulbs in a cool, bright room and water moderately until the leaves have turned yellow and dried up. In the spring (some say the fall) plant them outside in a convenient spot, and the following year (or two years later, depending on your authority) you will have a small mixed garden.

African violets, it should be remembered, do not like water on their leaves. They should not be given showers nor be put outside to be rained on in the summer. Experts may tell you to throw out your African violets after four years because they grow old and stalky. Don't believe it. Properly treated, they improve with age. Just keep splitting and replanting them. One friend has a grande dame of a plant that is fifteen years old — and smothered in blossoms.

Growing Sprouts and Cress

Late winter is a time when fresh greens are expensive or difficult to obtain, or both. Short of exploring hydroponics seriously, it is possible to grow sprouts without too much difficulty.

Alfalfa sprouts are the easiest, and seeds can usually be obtained from health-food stores. Place a handful of seeds in a large-mouthed jar. The mouth of the jar should be covered with coarse cheesecloth secured in place by a heavy elastic band. The seeds should be rinsed twice a day. Pour water through the cheesecloth into the jar, then allow it to drain out. Put the jar in a dry dark place such as the kitchen cupboard under the sink.

The alfalfa sprouts will be ready in about four days. They can be placed in the light for a few hours to be "greened off", then refrigerated to be used in salads or in sandwiches instead of lettuce. They are crunchy and nourishing.

Cress seeds, not to be confused with watercress, though they have a little of the same sharpness and bite, also germinate readily. If grown under a fluorescent light, they will sprout with alarming speed, within two or three days. (A batch of seeds planted late one Friday afternoon were showing signs of activity by Monday morning. That night they were coming up and by Tuesday morning there was a mass of little green shoots.) Sow them thickly on top of soil in pots or even on thoroughly damp wads of paper towels.

Try combining plantings of pepper cress (*Lepidum sativum*) with white mustard cress (*Brassica hirta*). To have the two cresses mature at the same time, plant the pepper cress first and the mustard four days later. In a week or less, there will be a mob of little green seedlings ready to eat. Traditionally they are eaten sprinkled on bread and butter with cheese. (Children will find it amusing in late winter to grow these little cress "farms".)

Radish seed can be planted and used the same way; it has an even more spirited flavour.

Blossoming Branches

In January, once there have been a few heavy frosts, cut branches of forsythia and bring them in from outside. Pound the ends of the stems well with a hammer to break down the fibres so that they will absorb water more readily.

Soak the entire branches in warm water for a few minutes, then arrange them in a vase in a sunny window. They will blossom in about ten days or less. At worst you can enjoy their fresh green leaves.

This technique also works with apple blossoms, although they take much longer, since they are further away from their natural season. The gnarled black branches are handsome in themselves while you wait. A Japanese vignette. Flowering quince and pussy-willows are other possibilities.

If you're forcing bug-prone flowering branches later in the season, it might be wise to spray them before bringing them indoors, or caterpillars may sprout along with the blossoms, as one unhappy mother discovered when she brought armloads of apple blossoms indoors for her daughter's spring wedding.

You ask me for seeds and bulbs of the flowers of this country. We have those for our garden brought from France, there being none here that are very rare or very beautiful. Everything is savage here, the flowers as well as the men.

Marie de l'Incarnation
Letters, August 12, 1653

The Kitchen

Fanny too has been busy making mince pies and arranging her Christmas feast, and declares that she will have no more to do with cookery for a twelvemonth.

Mary O'Brien
Journals, 1828–38

Gifts

Instead of giving a large amount of just one recipe, make up small jars of different relishes, flavourings, etc., and assemble a different tray for each friend.

As the hectic joys of December approach, with presents, parties and families to be prepared for, it is time to head for the cupboard to produce such herbal delights as mint or tarragon vinegar and basil or parsley jelly (see page 192).

Should you have been a domestic grasshopper and not filled your cupboard during the summer, all is not lost. There is still time to produce interesting gifts for your hostess, piano teacher or the friend who appears on your doorstep with an unexpected parcel. It's an agreeable way to exchange gifts. Some, who are dab hands with yeast baking (not us), will enjoy receiving a jar of jam or relish, or perhaps a small dish of chicken liver pâté (see page 90) from their ham-fisted friends, in exchange for a braided loaf of bread.

Flavoured Sugars

The Romans used sugar for medicine; honey was their sweetener. The medieval English, on the other hand, revelled in all sorts of sugars, plain and fancy, including violet and rose. You can make them, too, but for now, try these.

Vanilla Sugar: Put a vanilla bean in a jar, fill with granulated sugar and cover. Let it stand for at least three days.

Cinnamon Sugar: Mix 1/4 cup (50 mL) cinnamon with 2 cups (500 mL) granulated sugar. It's handy to have this ready-mixed on the shelf for making the perennial winter favourite, cinnamon toast, or for sprinkling on coffee cakes, streusel and apple pies.

Citrus Sugar: Grate 2 tbsp (25 mL) fresh lemon or orange rind into 1 cup (250 mL) granulated sugar.

Save small attractive jars to use as containers for gifts. Keep small boxes for holding nuts and candy and cookies. Keep an eye out at flea markets, garage sales and bazaars for interesting containers, too. Tie circles of sprigged cotton on top with a matching ribbon. (Remnants are frequently on sale.) A child who likes to do calligraphy can make labels.

Flavourings

Vanilla Extract: Put a vanilla bean in a small bottle and cover it with brandy. Let it stand for five days until the flavour permeates and then use.

Viennese Vanilla: For a subtle flavouring that is particularly good with whipped cream, mix 1/4 cup (50 mL) vanilla extract with 2 tbsp (25 mL) almond flavouring. Use in the same proportions as you would regular vanilla.

Peanut Brittle

If simplicity is your ideal, then this recipe should meet your specifications, as well as delight the recipients. For Christmas handouts (useful for Hallowe'en, too) combine a handful or two of freshly made popcorn with a couple of pieces of peanut brittle.

2 cups (500 mL)	granulated sugar
1 cup (250 mL)	blanched peanuts, coarsely chopped

Put the sugar in a heavy pot and stir constantly until it has completely turned to liquid. This will take about 10 to 15 minutes on a fairly hot burner. Remove from the heat and add the chopped peanuts. Stir until they are thoroughly coated. Pour the liquid candy into a well-buttered 9-inch (2.5-L) square pan. Let it cool slightly and then mark into squares. When the candy is cold, turn it out of the pan and break into squares, or in irregular pieces, as some people prefer. Makes about 1 1/4 lb (625 g).

Butterscotch

A little more time and care is required to produce this confection, but the rich and mellow flavour is adequate justification. Admirable for Christmas gifts, and a pleasing birthday treat that older children can make for parents who are not on diets.

1/2 cup (125 mL)	corn syrup
2/3 cup (150 mL)	brown sugar
1/3 cup (75 mL)	butter
2/3 cup (150 mL)	water
1 1/2 tsp (7 mL)	vanilla

Put the corn syrup, brown sugar, butter and water in a heavy pan. Bring to a boil without stirring, and boil over medium heat until the temperature reaches 280°F (140°C). If you do not have a candy thermometer, let the mixture boil until it becomes fairly thick, and then begin to test it to see if it has reached the soft crack stage. To test the candy for readiness, half fill a cup with cold water; then let a few drops of the candy liquid drop into the cup. When the liquid turns quite brittle in the cold water, it is ready. Use fresh cold water for each test.

When the candy is ready, remove it from the heat and add the vanilla, stirring it in very slightly. Pour it into a well-buttered 12 × 8-inch (3-L) pan. Let it cool until it is warm but not hard, then mark it into squares. Makes about 10 oz (300 g).

Shortbread

Although it is constantly available in Scotland, here we associate shortbread with Christmas, rolling it out quite thin, using seasonal cookie cutters and decorating it lightly with small cake decorations, coloured sugar and bits of glacé cherries. The result is festive but time-consuming. You may be satisfied with decorating the Christmas tree and baking the shortbread plainly.

1 cup (250 mL)	unsalted butter, softened
3/4 cup (175 mL)	sifted icing sugar
1/4 cup (50 mL)	cornstarch
1 3/4 cups (425 mL)	all-purpose flour

In a large bowl, cream the butter with an electric mixer until light. Add the sugar gradually, beating until it is absorbed. Combine the cornstarch and flour in a separate bowl. Add the dry ingredients to the butter mixture slowly, beating until the mixture is smooth. This should make a stiff dough.

Turn the dough onto a lightly floured board and knead slightly. Roll it out gently, then lift into a 9-inch (2.5-L) square cake pan. Pat it into place and bake at 300°F (150°C) for about 40 minutes, or until it just begins to change colour. Let it cool before serving. Cut into serving pieces with a sharp knife.

If, to please children of all ages, you are making decorated shortbread, you may find it easier to roll out the dough if you omit the cornstarch and use 2 cups (500 mL) flour. The rolled shortbread cookies, being thin, will take far less time to bake — 15 minutes may be enough to turn them a delicate golden colour.

Quick Relishes

You can make these as last-minute gifts, too, or to embellish Christmas feasts.

Pickled Herring

In Nova Scotia they call this Lunenburg specialty Solomon Gundy. Marie Nightingale in *Out of Old Nova Scotia Kitchens* suggests that it may be a corruption of Salmagundi, which various other cookbooks seem to consider a particularly berserk Salade Niçoise, featuring strips of chicken, grapes and hard-boiled eggs.

6	salt herring
3	large onions
2 1/2 cups (625 mL)	white vinegar
2 tbsp (25 mL)	pickling spice
1/2 cup (125 mL)	granulated sugar
6	bay leaves

Let the herring soak in cold water overnight in a large pan. Rinse the fish and squeeze to remove the water. Cut off the heads and tails and remove the skin, which tends to become chewy when pickled. Fillet the fish and cut in bite-sized pieces. Slice the onions and place in sterilized jars, alternating layers of herring and onion.

Heat the vinegar to the boiling point in a large saucepan, add the pickling spice and sugar and let simmer for about 10 minutes. Let the liquid cool, then strain and pour it over the herring. Place a small bay leaf in each jar. Store in the refrigerator and use as an appetizer or in salads after a few days. It keeps for several weeks. Makes 6 small jars.

Pickled Eggs

A brightly coloured French-Canadian variant of the old standby.

12	hard-boiled eggs
1 cup (250 mL)	canned beet juice
1 cup (250 mL)	cider vinegar
1	clove garlic
1	bay leaf
1 tsp (5 mL)	salt
1/4 tsp (1 mL)	pepper

While peeling the eggs, bring the beet juice, vinegar and spices to a boil in a small saucepan. Put the eggs in a large glass jar and pour over the juice. Cover the jar, let the eggs cool and chill for at least 24 hours (the longer, the better). Serve them whole, sliced in salads, or as an appetizer on wholewheat crackers with a touch of anchovy paste on top. They will keep in the refrigerator for at least two months.

Chinese Eggs:
Sir Francis Rose suggested this recipe to Alice B. Toklas. Try it — if you have lots of sherry lying around. You boil eggs for 5 minutes, shell them and simmer in sherry for an additional 5 minutes. Then you put the eggs in a covered casserole with butter and 3 large spoonfuls of soy sauce and simmer until they turn a dark brown. (More frugal cooks may wish to save the sherry and the soy sauce for further cooking in other dishes.) Serve warm as an appetizer.

Corn Relish

1 tbsp (15 mL)	cornstarch
1/4 cup (50 mL)	water
1	12-oz (341-mL) can corn, undrained
1/3 cup (75 mL)	granulated sugar
1/3 cup (75 mL)	white vinegar
1 tsp (5 mL)	turmeric
1	green onion, finely chopped
1/2 tsp (2 mL)	celery seed

Blend the cornstarch and water to a paste in a small saucepan. Add the remaining ingredients and mix well. Cook over medium heat, stirring occasionally. The mixture will begin to thicken just before it comes to a boil. Remove the relish from the heat, let it cool and store it in the refrigerator in a small covered jar. It is a good accompaniment for roasts, ham and chicken. Makes about 2 cups (500 mL).

Spiced Pineapple

An attractive side dish for a buffet supper, particularly if ham is involved. Serve it well drained and very cold.

2	14-oz (398-mL) cans pineapple chunks
3/4 cup (175 mL)	white vinegar
1 1/4 cups (300 mL)	granulated sugar
pinch	salt
8	whole cloves
2	cinnamon sticks

Drain the syrup from the pineapple. Put 3/4 cup (175 mL) syrup in a small saucepan and add the vinegar, sugar, salt, cloves and cinnamon sticks. Stir the mixture until blended and heat gently for 10 minutes. Add the pineapple and bring to a boil. Remove from the heat. After the pineapple cools, refrigerate the mixture in a covered container and let stand for one day. Makes about 3 cups (750 mL).

Potluck Dishes

We had a nice Christmas. We had an entertainment, or a social as they call it, here at our school house on Christmas Eve and it was quite a success. The school was crowded. It was for the children, who went free. All ladies who provided went free also. Outsiders and gentlemen paid 25 cts each, which money went to buy presents for the children. Most of the mothers baked something, I made 30 little rolls of pork, chopped fine and spiced, nice short crust; and 30 good currant buns. Some made one thing and some another; then these things were divided and little paper bags were filled and carried round, and a good cup of tea boiled in a big sap kettle on the stove.

Anna Leveridge
Your loving Anna: Letters from the Ontario Frontier, 1883–91

Since early days, winter has been a favourite time for parties in Canada. Travellers' accounts are full of faintly wistful descriptions of the Canadians merrily racing through the snow in their sleighs en route to yet another celebration. And we've all seen Krieghoff paintings.

We still entertain around Christmas and the New Year, but without the well-stocked larders of the *habitants* it can be a problem. The equally ancient tradition of the potluck dinner can be a boon, sharing as it does both labour and cost.

Stilton Pâté

Spread this rich, creamy mixture on crackers, and your guests will not complain. This also freezes well.

1/2 cup (125 mL)	Stilton cheese
1/2 cup (125 mL)	butter
1/2 cup (125 mL)	cream cheese
2	large cloves garlic, minced

Mash everything together in a small bowl until well blended, or blend in a food processor. Store the pâté in the refrigerator in a small covered container. Before serving on crackers or pumpernickel bread, allow it to soften slightly. Makes about 1 1/2 cups (375 mL).

Cheddar Port Dip

Somewhat similar to the Stilton pâté (and somewhat cheaper) is this mixture which can also be spread on crackers and used in sandwiches.

1/3 cup (75 mL)	sherry or port
1/2 cup (125 mL)	cream
1 tbsp (15 mL)	chopped chives or green onion
8 oz (250 g)	old Cheddar cheese, diced

Blend all ingredients on high speed in a blender or food processor until smooth. Store in small crocks in the refrigerator. Makes about 1 cup (250 mL).

Smoked Salmon Yogurt Dip

This lavish dip is simplicity itself. Serve it on crackers or pumpernickel bread.

1 cup (250 mL)	finely chopped smoked salmon
8 oz (250 g)	cream cheese
1 cup (250 mL)	unflavoured yogurt
	Juice of 1 lemon
pinch	cayenne pepper
2 tbsp (25 mL)	chopped fresh dill, optional

In a food processor or blender, blend together the salmon and cream cheese. Add the yogurt, lemon juice and cayenne and process until smooth. Add the chopped dill and blend briefly. Makes 2 1/2 cups (625 mL).

(If using a blender, you may have to do this in batches to ensure even mixing.)

Chicken Liver Pâté

Simple and always delectable, but don't keep it for more than a week. It is also good on an open-faced sandwich.

1 lb (500 g)	chicken livers
1	small onion, chopped
2	cloves garlic, chopped
1/2 cup (125 mL)	butter, softened
1/4 cup (50 mL)	sherry
1 tsp (5 mL)	salt
1 tsp (5 mL)	Dijon mustard

Cover the chicken livers with cold water, bring them to a boil and simmer gently until cooked, about 15 minutes, or until no pink remains. Drain off the water and save it for soup stock.

Put the chicken livers in a blender or food processor with the remaining ingredients and blend until smooth. Pour into a crock and chill for a few hours before using. Keep refrigerated. Serve with crackers or thinly sliced pumpernickel bread. Makes about 2 cups (500 mL).

Bean Salad

An admirable salad for a buffet. Part of the pleasure comes from the sheer good looks of the contrasting colours and shapes of the beans. You may prefer to use lesser quantities of baby lima beans and chickpeas, but for the sake of appearances, it's good to include some.

1 cup (250 mL)	granulated sugar
1/2 cup (125 mL)	water
1 1/2 cups (375 mL)	white vinegar
1	14-oz (398-mL) can sliced green beans
1	14-oz (398-mL) can sliced yellow wax beans
1	10-oz (284-mL) can baby lima beans
1	14-oz (398-mL) kidney beans
1 cup (250 mL)	chickpeas
3	stalks celery, thinly sliced
3	onions, thinly sliced
1	green pepper, thinly sliced
1	sweet red pepper, thinly sliced

Bring the sugar, water and vinegar to a boil in a small saucepan. Remove from the heat and let cool to tepid. Meanwhile, drain the green and yellow beans. Drain and rinse the lima beans, kidney beans and chickpeas.

In a large bowl mix all the vegetables together; add the sauce. Cover with a plate and refrigerate for 24 hours before using. Makes 8 to 10 cups (2 to 2.5 L).

Tourtière

This substantial meat pie is always served at the Réveillon, the family feast after the holiday midnight Mass in French Canada. Even if you have Christmas dinner instead, stick one of these (baked) in your freezer, pull it out Boxing Day morning to defrost and reheat it for a painless and delicious lunch.

1 lb (500 g)	ground pork
1/2 cup (125 mL)	water
1	onion, finely chopped
1	clove garlic, chopped
1/2 tsp (2 mL)	salt
1/2 tsp (2 mL)	dried thyme
1/2 tsp (2 mL)	dried sage
1/2 tsp (2 mL)	dry mustard
1/2 tsp (2 mL)	ground cloves
1/2 tsp (2 mL)	dried savory
1/4 tsp (1 mL)	pepper
1/4 tsp (1 mL)	celery seed
1	potato, boiled and peeled
	Pastry for a double-crust 9-inch (23-cm) pie

Simmer the meat and water in a medium saucepan for 45 minutes. Add the onion, garlic and seasonings and cook for 15 minutes longer. Mash the potato and add it to the mixture. Cool. Pour the filling into the unbaked pie shell and cover with pastry. Prick the crust with a fork to let the steam escape and bake at 450°F (230°C) for 10 minutes, then reduce heat to 350° F (180° C) and continue baking for 30 to 40 minutes, or until the pastry is golden-brown. Serve hot or cold with chili sauce (see page 30) or corn relish (see page 88). Serves 6.

The Christmas Feast

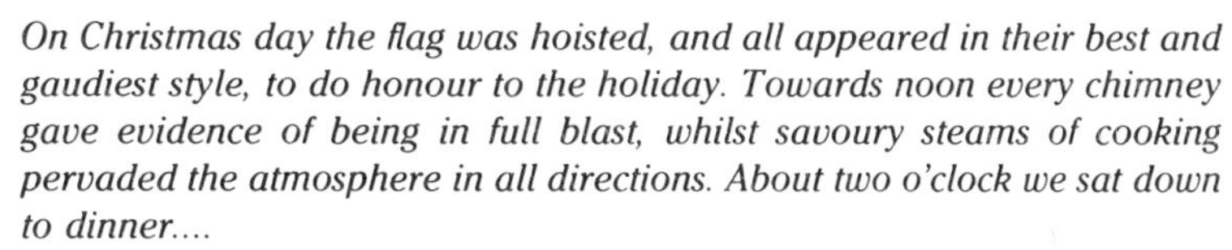

On Christmas day the flag was hoisted, and all appeared in their best and gaudiest style, to do honour to the holiday. Towards noon every chimney gave evidence of being in full blast, whilst savoury steams of cooking pervaded the atmosphere in all directions. About two o'clock we sat down to dinner....

The dining-hall in which we assembled [in Fort Edmonton] was the largest room in the fort, probably about fifty by twenty-five feet, well warmed by large fires, which are scarcely ever allowed to go out....No tablecloth shed its snowy whiteness over the board; no silver candelabra or gaudy china interfered with its simple magnificence. The bright tin plates and dishes reflected jolly faces, and burnished gold can give no truer zest to a feast.

Perhaps it might be interesting to some dyspeptic idler, who painfully strolls through a city park, to coax an appetite to a sufficient intensity to enable him to pick an ortolan, if I were to describe to him the fare set before us, to appease appetites nourished by constant outdoor exercise in an atmosphere ranging at 40° to 50° below zero. At the head, before Mr. Harriett, was a large dish of boiled buffalo hump; at the foot smoked a boiled buffalo calf. Start not, gentle readers, the calf is very small, and is taken from the cow by the Caesarean operation long before it attains its full growth. This, boiled whole, is one of the most esteemed dishes amongst the epicures of the interior. My pleasing duty was to help a dish of mouffle, or dried moose nose; the gentleman on my left distributed, with graceful impartiality, the white fish, delicately browned in buffalo marrow. The worthy priest helped the buffalo tongue, whilst Mr. Rundell cut up the beavers' tails. Nor was the other gentleman left unemployed, as all his spare time was occupied in dissecting a roast wild goose. The centre of the table was graced with piles of potatoes, turnips and bread conveniently placed, so that each could help himself without interrupting the labours of his companions. Such was our jolly Christmas dinner at Edmonton; and long will remain in my memory, although no pies, or puddings, or blanc manges, shed their fragrance over the scene.

Paul Kane
Wanderings of an Artist Among the Indians of North America, 1859

Christmas Eve comes. Some head to the store for last-minute gifts (the grasshoppers usually come out ahead, such is the unfairness of life, and find theirs on sale). Other members of the family are dispatched to pick up the fresh turkey and the ham from the butcher, and such forgotten necessities as Christmas crackers and more butter. Always, more butter.

Christmas Pudding

We do not make our own Christmas cake, preferring to buy a good-quality brand on sale on Christmas Eve. Making a Christmas pudding, however, is not quite so daunting. This Depression recipe calls for carrots and is much lighter than usual — a Christmas pudding for those who don't really care for it, but cherish the tradition.

1/2 cup (125 mL)	butter
1 cup (250 mL)	granulated sugar
1 cup (250 mL)	grated carrots
1 cup (250 mL)	grated potato
1/2 cup (125 mL)	raisins
3/4 cup (175 mL)	mixed glacé cherries and pineapple
1 cup (250 mL)	all-purpose flour
1 tsp (5 mL)	cinnamon
1/2 tsp (2 mL)	ground cloves
1/2 tsp (2 mL)	grated nutmeg
1/2 tsp (2 mL)	ground ginger
1 tsp (5 mL)	baking soda
1 tbsp (15 mL)	brandy

Small children, in our experience, detest Christmas pudding. One sensible grandmother took care to have Eskimo pies as a pleasing alternative.

In a large bowl, cream the butter and sugar together. Add the carrots and half of the grated potatoes and mix in. Toss the fruit with a little of the flour until lightly coated and combine with the ingredients in the bowl.

In a separate bowl, sift the remaining flour and spices. Dissolve the baking soda in the remaining potato and add to the dry ingredients. Add this mixture to the fruit and blend. Stir in the brandy. Pour the pudding into a greased 1-quart (1-L) mould. Cover tightly and steam for 3 hours.

Remove the pudding from the mould and let it sit at room temperature, lightly covered with waxed paper, for a day to mellow. Store the pudding in the freezer until needed.

When you are ready to serve the pudding, defrost it and steam, covered with foil, for about 30 minutes. To serve, heat brandy gently in a small saucepan that you can take to the table. Carry in the dessert, turn out the lights, pour the brandy over the pudding and set a match to it. (If the pudding itself is very hot, you may not need to heat the brandy, but it never hurts.) Keep spooning the dancing blue flames over the dish until they die down.

Serve the pudding with one or more sauces.

Hard Sauce

So sweet it can only be eaten once or twice a year, but who can resist it then?

2 cups (500 mL)	butter, softened
3 cups (750 mL)	icing sugar, approx.
3/4 tsp (4 mL)	grated nutmeg
1/3 cup (75 mL)	brandy

Cream the butter thoroughly with an electric mixer or in a food processor. Add the sugar slowly and beat until the sauce is creamy. Add the nutmeg and brandy. Chill overnight. Let the sauce soften a trifle before serving in a clear glass bowl, topped with a maraschino cherry, with the Christmas pudding. Makes about 4 cups (1 L).

Cumberland Rum Butter

This is an approximation of the famous Lakeland specialty. Very sweet and very good, in small doses.

1/2 cup (125 mL)	butter, softened
1/2 cup (125 mL)	honey
3/4 tsp (4 mL)	cinnamon
3/4 tsp (4 mL)	grated nutmeg
3 tbsp (45 mL)	rum

Blend all the ingredients until smooth in a blender or food processor. Store in a covered container in the refrigerator. Makes 1 cup (250 mL).

Grandma Perrin's Butterscotch Sauce

This sauce is less rich than Cumberland rum butter, but it complements the flavours of Christmas pudding in a very friendly way.

2 tbsp (25 mL)	granulated sugar
1 tbsp (15 mL)	butter
1 cup (250 mL)	hot water
1/2 cup (125 mL)	brown sugar
1 tbsp (15 mL)	cornstarch
1/2 tsp (2 mL)	vanilla

In a small pot, stir together the granulated sugar and butter over medium-high heat until the mixture becomes quite brown. Stop before it burns, but not much before. Remove from the heat and add the hot water and brown sugar. Return to the heat and stir until the mixture is smooth.

In a small cup mix the cornstarch with a few spoonfuls of cold water to make a thin paste; then add to the first mixture, stirring constantly. Bring to a boil, turn down the heat and cook for a minute or so until the sauce has thickened. Add the vanilla. Keep warm until ready to use.

This will make a little more than a cup of sauce, enough to satisfy a family of eight on their Christmas Day pudding. You may want to double the recipe to take care of the leftover pudding. Store in the refrigerator.

Fluffy Sauce

A last-minute sauce which is somewhat lighter than the others. Serve it over frozen strawberries, slightly warmed in the oven, and you have a winter version of Fraises Romanoff.

1 cup (250 mL)	whipping cream
4	egg yolks
1/2 cup (125 mL)	granulated sugar
1/4 tsp (1 mL)	salt
1/3 cup (75 mL)	sherry

Beat the whipping cream in a small bowl until stiff. In another bowl, beat the egg yolks with the remaining ingredients until very light and foamy. Fold this mixture gently into the whipped cream and serve at once over fruit or pudding. Makes about 2 cups (500 mL).

Syllabub

If your tastes don't run to Christmas pudding, try a light dessert like this syllabub. The quickest and simplest of milky desserts — and perhaps the best. The perfect finale to a rich meal.

1 1/4 cups (300 mL)	whipping cream
1/3 cup (75 mL)	lemon juice
1/4 cup (50 mL)	rum, sherry or whisky
3 tbsp (45 mL)	granulated sugar
1	egg white

Whip the cream until it stands in soft peaks. Gently fold in the lemon juice, liquor and sugar. Beat the egg white until stiff and fold into the cream. Pour into individual glass serving dishes and refrigerate for 24 hours. Serves 8.

Baked Ham

In many households, a baked ham is the traditional Christmas Eve dish. Get a large bone-in ham from the butcher, allowing plenty for leftovers. Put the ham in a large roasting pan, rind side up, and bake at 325°F (160°C), allowing approximately 20 minutes per pound. About 1 hour before you're ready to serve it, remove the ham from the oven and score the top in diamonds with a sharp knife. Glaze it with maple syrup, or rub it with dry mustard and ground cloves and drizzle honey on top. Or spread it with Cumberland rum butter (see page 95).

Roast Goose with Giblet Gravy

Roast goose used to be the choice for Christmas Day dinner in northern England. It makes a sumptuous alternative to the traditional North American turkey.

1	8- to 10-lb (4- to 5-kg) goose, with neck and giblets
	Stuffing:
1/4 cup (50 mL)	butter
1	medium onion, chopped
2	large stalks celery, chopped
1	large cooking apple, preferably Northern Spy, diced
4 cups (1 L)	soft breadcrumbs
1 tsp (5 mL)	salt
1/4 tsp (1 mL)	pepper
2 tsp (10 mL)	dried sage

Rinse the goose in cold water and allow it to drain.

Prepare the stuffing by melting the butter in a saucepan. Add the chopped onion and celery and cook for about 3 minutes, until the onion is translucent. Add the apple. Turn off the heat and put a lid on the saucepan.

Combine the breadcrumbs and seasonings in a large bowl. Add the onion-celery-apple mixture and mix together. Fill the goose cavity with the stuffing and sew up the opening.

Put the goose in a large roasting pan and bake at 325°F (160°C) for 25 minutes per pound. Do not baste it, for the goose comes well equipped with its own fat. Prick the skin from time to time, to encourage the fat to exit from the goose. Pour off the fat as it accumulates in the roasting pan.

If you find your goose is cooked before you are ready to serve it — the oven thermometer registers nearly 185°F (85°C), or the meaty part of the leg feels soft when you press it, or the drumstick wiggles easily — then turn the oven down to 200°F (90°C) for the balance of the cooking time. Roast goose, unlike turkey, does not readily become dry from overcooking. Serves 8.

Make a pâté of the goose liver by mashing it and adding a little chopped onion, soft butter, salt and pepper and perhaps a touch of sherry.

Goose grease has a delicate flavour and has always been greatly prized by English country people, according to Dorothy Hartley. It can be combined with lemon juice, finely chopped onion and parsley and used as a sandwich spread, used medicinally in a variety of ways, or applied to exposed skin to prevent chapping. It is also delicious when used to seal pâtés.

Giblet Gravy

After you have put the goose in the oven, begin preparing the gravy by rinsing the giblets and neck. Put them in a saucepan with a quartered onion, some celery tops and a carrot cut in chunks. Cover with cold water and bring slowly to a boil. Let it simmer while the goose is cooking. Turn off the heat about 30 minutes before you make the gravy.

Remove the goose from the oven, place it on an ovenproof platter and put it back in a 200°F (90°C) oven. Make the gravy in the roasting pan on top of the stove, pouring off any excess fat until you have about 1/2 cup (125 mL) goose grease (and pan drippings).

Add enough flour to make a smooth paste. Heat and stir, slowly adding the stock from which the giblets, neck and vegetables have been removed. Bring to a boil and let cook for at least 2 minutes. If it is too thick, add water to the gravy until it is the right consistency, stirring constantly to avoid lumps. Season to taste with salt and pepper.

Turkey Stock

On Christmas night, while the others do the dishes, the cook rewards herself with a few sloes in gin while preparing turkey stock from the remains. Cookbooks will give you stern instructions on making stock, but you can slide through life by putting the bones of the turkey carcase in a large saucepan and adding a roughly cut onion, a carrot and a couple of stalks of celery (including tops). For a large turkey carcase, increase the vegetables. Season with salt and pepper, cover with cold water, bring to a boil and let simmer gently for a couple of hours. Strain. Freeze what you don't need and keep a container of stock in the refrigerator for adding to soups and gravies. If you wish, save the vegetables and bits of meat from the bones, whirr them in the blender and add them to the stock, too.

Savoury Turkey Slices

Most families are full of enthusiasm for cold turkey on Boxing Day, but grow increasingly sullen as the week — but not the turkey — vanishes. Here is one way to disguise the remains.

1/3 cup (75 mL)	chopped lean ham or crumbled cooked bacon
1/3 cup (75 mL)	finely chopped onion
1/3 cup (75 mL)	chopped fresh parsley
1 cup (250 mL)	soft white breadcrumbs
1 tsp (5 mL)	finely grated lemon rind
1/4 tsp (1 mL)	curry powder
1	egg
1 tbsp (15 mL)	cold water
1 lb (500 g)	sliced cooked turkey
	Vegetable oil or butter

Mix the first six ingredients lightly together in a medium bowl. In a shallow dish, beat the egg with the water. Dip the turkey slices into the egg mixture and then coat with the savoury mixture. Cook the turkey slices in vegetable oil or butter, turning once, until the crumbs on each side are golden brown. Serve with steamed rice and a salad. Serves 4.

Soups

The best soups are made with a blending of many flavors. Don't be afraid of experimenting with them. Where you make one mistake you will be surprised to find the number of successful varieties you can produce. If you like a spicy flavor try two or three cloves, or allspice, or bay leaves. All soups are improved by a dash of onion, unless it is the white soups, or purees from chicken, veal, fish, etc. In these celery may be used. In nothing as well as soups can a housekeeper be economical of the odds and ends of food left from meals. One of the best cooks was in the habit of saving everything, and announced one day, when her soup was especially praised, that it contained the crumbs of gingerbread from her cake box! Creamed onions left from a dinner, or a little stewed corn, potatoes mashed, a few baked beans — even a small dish of apple sauce have often added to the flavor of soup.

My Pet Recipes: Tried and True
by the Ladies and Friends of St. Andrew's Church Quebec, 1900

Especially in the bleak days and nights of winter, there is nothing like a healthy and warming soup. A convivial neighbour enlivens January by holding lunchtime Soup and Sherry parties on Saturdays (later in the afternoon, it becomes harder to say). She offers a range of sherries (dry, medium and sweet) and serves two kinds of soup (usually one vegetarian and one fish), wholewheat bread and dry white wine. She ends with cheese and cheerful guests. The soup is kept hot in the kitchen in stainless-steel bowls set in large saucepans of hot water so they won't burn dry (or use a slow cooker if you have one). People go into the kitchen and help themselves.

Papa was often too tired to eat anything, though mamma always had a kettle of soup or porridge waiting for him.

He ought to eat, she said; there was no nourishment in bread and coffee. And soup was the mainstay. Boiling beef or brisket with potatoes made a fine dish, the broth thickened with flour or a dash of oatmeal, and sometimes stepped up with an onion or a turnip when the budget permitted such luxuries.

Laura Goodman Salverson
Confessions of an Immigrant's Daughter, 1939

Oxtail Soup

Oxtails have a rich, distinctive flavour that makes them particularly suitable for winter soups. Often they can be found in supermarket meat sections, surprisingly pricey. Look for the ones that have a large proportion of meat on the bone.

2 lb (1 kg)	oxtail pieces
1/4 cup (50 mL)	barley
3	carrots, cut in large pieces
3	stalks celery, including tops, cut in large pieces
3	medium onions, sliced
1	bay leaf
2 tsp (10 mL)	salt
1/2 tsp (2 mL)	pepper
1 1/2 cups (375 mL)	canned stewed tomatoes
	Juice of 1/2 lemon

Put the oxtails, barley, carrots, celery, onions, bay leaf and seasonings in a slow cooker and cover with water. Cook, covered, at low setting for at least 12 hours — until the meat has loosened from the bone. Remove the bay leaf and the oxtails and take the meat off the bones. Discard the bones, return the meat to the soup and add the stewed tomatoes. Put the mixture into the blender in batches and puree. Put the puree in a large saucepan, heat and add water until the soup is adequately thin, but not too thin. (Slow cookers are excellent for making soup, but on the small side. What tends to emerge is oxtail stew which, when blended, does need to be made less concentrated.)

Correct the seasonings and add lemon juice to sharpen the flavour. When the soup is thoroughly hot, serve. Serves 10 to 12.

You can also make this soup in a large pot on top of the stove. Simmer as slowly as possible until the oxtail meat comes easily from the bones (this will take less time than when you use a slow cooker). Then proceed as above.

Party Oxtail Soup

The unusual topping adds a mysterious flavour to this quick and delicious soup for the lazy.

2	10-oz (284-mL) cans oxtail soup
2	10-oz (284-mL) cans beef consommé
	Sherry to taste
1/2 cup (125 mL)	whipping cream
1 tsp (5 mL)	curry powder

Mix the soup *undiluted* in a large saucepan and heat gently. Just before serving, add sherry to taste. Whip the cream with the curry powder. Serve the soup in bowls and top with a spoonful of the cream. Serves 8.

Scotch Broth

	Meaty bones and pieces from roast leg of lamb or shoulder
8 cups (2 L)	cold water, approx.
1 tbsp (15 mL)	salt
8	whole peppercorns
1	bay leaf
1	whole onion, peeled
4	cloves
2 tbsp (25 mL)	butter
1/2 cup (125 mL)	finely chopped carrot
1/2 cup (125 mL)	finely chopped celery
1/2 cup (125 mL)	finely chopped turnip
1/2 tsp (2 mL)	dried marjoram
1/4 cup (50 mL)	barley

Place the meaty lamb bones in a deep pot. Add water to cover. Add the salt, peppercorns, bay leaf and onion stuck with cloves. Bring quickly to a boil. Skim off the foam, if any. Cover and simmer for about 2 hours, until the meat seems ready to come off the bones. Cool and skim off the top fat. Remove the bones and dice the meat clinging to it. Strain the broth into a bowl and reserve.

In the pot, heat the butter and cook the vegetables, stirring for about 5 minutes. Add the broth, diced meat, marjoram and barley. Simmer for 45 minutes, or until the soup is thickened. Serves 6.

If you have a problem skimming the fat off broth, refrigerate the broth first. The fat will solidify and can then be easily removed. Complete the soup the next day.

Winter Minestrone

2 lb (1 kg)	meaty beef bones
2 tsp (10 mL)	salt
2	bay leaves
8 cups (2 L)	cold water, approx.
2 tbsp (25 mL)	vegetable oil
2	cloves garlic, finely chopped
3	small onions, chopped
2	stalks celery, chopped
2	medium carrots, chopped
4 cups (1 L)	cold water
2 cups (500 mL)	finely shredded cabbage
2 cups (500 mL)	canned stewed tomatoes
1	19-oz (540-mL) can kidney beans or chickpeas, undrained
1/2 cup (125 mL)	pasta, broken in small pieces
	Grated Parmesan or Cheddar cheese

Place the meaty bones (plus a knucklebone and a couple of pieces of marrow bone if you can find them) in a slow cooker with the salt and bay leaves. Cover with the water (add a little more water if necessary to cover) and cook at low heat for 12 hours or until the meat is thoroughly loosened from the bones. Strain the stock.

In a large pot heat the oil. Add the garlic, onions, celery and carrots and cook for about 3 minutes or until tender. Add the strained stock, along with the cold water, cabbage, tomatoes and beans. Simmer, covered, for 1 hour. Add the pasta and simmer, covered, for 45 minutes. Taste, correct seasonings and serve with grated Parmesan or Cheddar cheese. Makes about 16 cups (4 L).

For Summer Minestrone, add 2 cups (500 mL) sliced fresh green beans and 1 cup (250 mL) green peas with the pasta.

Breads

A Moravian woman married to a Farmer near here brought me a loaf of bread so peculiarly good that I could not but enquire about it. She said that it was made with Rennet & Whey, without Yeast or Water & baked in wicker or Straw baskets which is the method taught at the Moravian School at Bethlehem in the States where she was educated. The bread was as light as possible & rich like cake.

Elizabeth Simcoe
Diary, 1792–96

Everyone has unfulfilled ambitions that they intend to get around to sooner or later. Ours is to read Proust, learn to speak French properly and come to grips with yeast bakery. Baking bread, by all accounts, is a mystic experience which saves one from psychiatrist's bills, fills the house with marvellous smells and is good exercise to boot. Some day. Meanwhile, we concentrate on various quick-breads, which are almost effortless, can be popped in the freezer and pulled out when people drop in for tea. "My, the house smells good," they say. "You've been baking bread. How do you find the time?"

Farmhouse Currant Loaf

A substantial bread that winds up tasting oddly of blueberries. A good accompaniment for soup and sherry parties, because the recipe makes two large loaves.

1	tea bag
4 cups (1 L)	currants
2 cups (500 mL)	brown sugar
2	eggs
4 cups (1 L)	all-purpose flour
4 tsp (20 mL)	baking powder

Pour 3 cups (750 mL) boiling water over the tea bag and let sit for 5 minutes.

Combine the currants and sugar in a very large bowl. Pour in the tea. Stir well and leave overnight to soak.

The next day, beat the eggs and add to the currant mixture. Sift in the flour and baking powder. Mix well (the batter will be fairly stiff) and divide between two 9 × 5-inch (2-L) buttered loaf pans. Bake at 325°F (160°C) for 1 1/4 hours or until a fork stuck into the bread comes out clean. The loaves are better kept for a day or so before eating. They will keep for 2 to 3 weeks well-wrapped in the refrigerator, or months in the freezer.

Carrot Bread

1 cup (250 mL)	granulated sugar
1/2 cup (125 mL)	vegetable oil
2	eggs
1 tsp (5 mL)	vanilla or Viennese vanilla (see page 85)
1 cup (250 mL)	coarsely grated carrots
1 1/2 cups (375 mL)	all-purpose flour
1 tsp (5 mL)	baking soda
1/2 tsp (2 mL)	salt
1/2 tsp (2 mL)	cinnamon
1/2 cup (125 mL)	chopped nuts, optional

Mix the sugar, oil, eggs and vanilla in a large bowl and blend well. Add the carrots. Sift the flour, baking soda, salt and cinnamon together and stir in. Add the nuts. Spoon into a greased 9 × 5-inch (2-L) loaf pan and bake for 1 hour at 350°F (180°C).

Old Fire Engine House Cakes

Ely must be one of the most satisfying of English cathedrals. Revisited time after time, there is always something new to discover after you have marvelled at the glories of the Octagon, the frozen beauty of the Lady Chapel and the black filigree of the wrought-iron gates. And after you have wandered about the cathedral, it is time to head across the Green to the Old Fire Engine House for cakes and a pot of English Breakfast tea. This variation is so close to the real thing that you'll almost feel you're back.

1 cup (250 mL)	self-raising cake and pastry flour
1/2 cup (125 mL)	butter, softened
1/3 cup (75 mL)	granulated sugar
2/3 cup (150 mL)	currants or raisins
1/4 tsp (1 mL)	grated nutmeg
1	large egg, well beaten
1/2 cup (125 mL)	milk or buttermilk (for a particularly light cake)

Self-raising flour does appear on the occasional supermarket shelf, although you may have to hunt for it. It's as the name suggests. You don't add any leavening or salt. English recipes frequently call for it.

Sift the flour into a medium bowl and work in the butter. Add the sugar, currants and nutmeg. Stir in the egg and enough milk to make a stiff batter. Put spoonfuls of the mixture into well-greased muffin tins or in small heaps on a greased cookie sheet and bake at 400°F (200°C) for 20 minutes. Makes about 24 small cakes. Serve with butter, or, as the Old Fire Engine House does, with a large bowl of whipped cream and a dish of strawberry jam. (These are best eaten within two days — rarely a problem — but after that they become good exercise for the teeth.)

Winter Vegetables

There are fields of white-headed Cabbage & Turnips, which are kept for the entire year....The Cabbages are left in the field after they have been pulled up, the head down & the stalk in the air; in this way they are preserved by the snow which comes & covers them to a depth of five or six feet, & they are only taken out as they are needed; the Settlers never fail to put some into the cellar as well. Neither of these vegetables goes into the Pot without the other, & nourishing soups are made of them, with a large slice of Pork. It is necessary, above all else, to have a great many Cabbages, because the People eat only the hearts, & the Pigs are given what is left; during the Winter it is their only food, & these gluttonous animals, of which there are a great number, are not satisfied with a small quantity.

Sieur de Dièreville
Relation of the Voyage to Port Royal, 1708

Few of us have root cellars nowadays, although owners of historic farmhouses in the country may still possess this evocative souvenir of the past. Most of us visit our supermarket weekly for specials on substantial winter vegetables such as cabbage. Broccoli, Brussels sprouts and cauliflower — all equally detested by children — are members of the same family. So, too, is the flamboyantly curly kale.

Winter Cabbage Salad

"If you lived on cabbage," remarked Diogenes to a young courtier, "you would not be obliged to flatter the powerful." "If you flattered the powerful," quipped the courtier, "you would not be obliged to live on cabbage."

1/2 cup (125 mL)	vegetable oil
3/4 cup (175 mL)	white vinegar
3/4 cup (175 mL)	granulated sugar
1 tsp (5 mL)	salt
1 tsp (5 mL)	celery seed
1 tsp (5 mL)	mustard seed
1	medium cabbage, shredded
1	medium onion, chopped
2	green peppers, chopped
2	carrots, shredded
1/2 cup (125 mL)	pitted and chopped green olives

In a medium saucepan, combine the oil, vinegar, sugar and spices. Bring to a boil and then let cool to lukewarm.

Combine the vegetables in a large bowl. Pour the lukewarm mixture over the vegetables and let sit for a while before serving. Keeps in the refrigerator for at least two weeks. Makes 12 cups (3 L). To serve, lift from the liquid and drain slightly. Add cream salad dressing before serving.

Rumbledethumps: The Scots have such splendidly comic names for mundane dishes. Despite its prosaic ingredients, this dish as described by Christopher North is surprisingly good: "Take a peck of purtatoes, and put them into a boyne [large pot] — at them with a beetle — a dab of butter — the beetle again — another dab — then cabbage — purtato — beetle and dab — saut [salt] meanwhile — and a shake o' common black pepper — feenally, cabbage and purtato throughither — pree [taste], and you'll fin' them decent rumbledethumps." Translated — you take equal amounts of boiled potatoes and cabbage, and add chopped chives or cooked onions to taste. Put it into a casserole, cover with grated cheese and brown it in the oven at 350°F (180°C) for about 15 minutes.

Red Cabbage Relish

1	medium red cabbage, shredded
1/2 cup (125 mL)	cider vinegar
	Salt and pepper
1/2 cup (125 mL)	granulated sugar
1	large onion, chopped
2 tbsp (25 mL)	butter
1	large apple, peeled and chopped
2 tbsp (25 mL)	red currant or apple jelly

In a large saucepan, combine the cabbage, vinegar, salt, pepper and sugar and simmer gently until the cabbage is soft, about 1 1/2 hours.

In a small frying pan, cook the onion gently in the butter for about 3 minutes or until softened, then add the apple. Fold the apple-onion mixture into the cabbage and stir in the jelly. Store in clean jars in the refrigerator. Makes about 4 cups (1 L).

Little White Turnips

These often appear in supermarkets in winter. Buy the smallest ones you can find. Peel and slice them and put them in a saucepan with a little water to cook for 10 minutes, then cook them gently in butter in a frying pan. Sprinkle with salt, pepper and oregano and cook until golden-brown, turning frequently. Add more butter if necessary.

Pork Chops Normandy Style

Pork and cabbage have a natural affinity, and both are particularly heartening in winter.

8	green onions, chopped
1/4 cup (50 mL)	chopped fresh parsley
	Salt and pepper
1/4 cup (50 mL)	melted butter
8	large pork chops
1 cup (250 mL)	cider
2 tbsp (25 mL)	Calvados, optional

Mix the onions, parsley, salt, pepper and melted butter together in a small bowl. Spread half of the mixture over the pork chops. Grill for 15 minutes under the broiler. Gently turn the chops over and spread the rest of the mixture on top. Grill for another 15 minutes. Put the chops in a serving dish and keep warm. Quickly drain off the excess fat from the pan and pour the cider into the pan juices. Boil for 2 minutes. Add the Calvados if using, then pour the cider sauce over the chops. Serves 8.

Turnip Apple Casserole

You may think turnips and apples strange bedfellows, but in fact the combination is so good that it is likely to seduce most, if not all, hardened turnip-haters. Use this casserole to accompany roast pork or turkey.

Add 1/2 cup (125 mL) shredded raw turnip and a large spoonful of crumbled blue cheese to your cole slaw, and garnish with black olives and cherry tomatoes.

1	medium turnip
1/4 cup (50 mL)	butter
	Salt and pepper
2 cups (500 mL)	sliced, peeled apples, preferably Northern spies
1/2 cup (125 mL)	brown sugar
2 tbsp (25 mL)	all-purpose flour

Cut the turnip into pieces and peel. Cook in a small amount of water until tender, about 1 hour. Remove from the heat, add half the butter, salt and pepper and whip with an electric beater until light and smooth. Let cool.

Combine the apples with half the brown sugar. Butter a 2-quart (2-L) casserole. Put a layer of turnip in the bottom, then a layer of sliced apple; repeat, completing with a layer of turnip on the top.

Combine the flour, remaining butter and remaining brown sugar together and sprinkle over the top of the casserole. Bake uncovered at 350°F (180°C) for 1 hour. Serves 6.

Oatmeal

That breakfast...was one that will not be forgotten while I live....We had real porridge and cream, coffee with veritable sugar and milk, and authentic butter, light rolls made of actual flour, unquestionable bacon and potatoes, with jam *and* toast *— the really, truly things — and we had as much as we could eat! We behaved rather badly — intemperately, I fear — we stopped only when forced to do it, and yet both of us came away with appetites.*

Ernest Thompson Seton
The Arctic Prairies, 1911

Granola

How many of us take the time, even on weekends, to indulge in such a splendid breakfast nowadays? The Loyalist Highlanders who settled in eastern Ontario after the American Revolution brought their large horn spoons with them from New York to eat their porridge. What would these kilted stalwarts have thought of today's favoured oatmeal breakfast?

7 cups (1.75 L)	coarse rolled oats
1 cup (250 mL)	wheat germ
1/2 cup (125 mL)	sesame seeds
1/2 cup (125 mL)	sunflower seeds
1/4 cup (50 mL)	brown sugar
1/2 tsp (2 mL)	salt
1 cup (250 mL)	shredded unsweetened coconut
1/2 cup (125 mL)	honey
1/2 cup (125 mL)	hot water
1/2 cup (125 mL)	vegetable oil
1/2 tsp (2 mL)	vanilla

Mix the dry ingredients in a large shallow roasting pan. Mix the honey and water, stir in the oil and vanilla and add to the dry mixture. Bake at 325°F (160°C), stirring every 20 minutes or so until the oats are crisp and pale gold (about 1 1/4 hours). Cool and store in a plastic container in the refrigerator or freezer. Add fruit (raisins, currants, chopped dried apricots) to taste when serving. Makes about 10 cups (2.5 L).

Scottish Oat Scones

Some people wax ecstatic over croissants and coffee. Others are known to indulge in peanut butter toast. But what could be better than these scones, topped with jam, honey or Cumberland rum butter (see page 95)?

1 1/2 cups (375 mL)	all-purpose flour
1/4 cup (50 mL)	granulated sugar
1 tbsp (15 mL)	baking powder
1 tsp (5 mL)	cream of tartar
1/2 tsp (2 mL)	salt
1 3/4 cups (425 mL)	quick-cooking rolled oats
1	egg
1/3 cup (75 mL)	milk
2/3 cup (150 mL)	melted butter
1/2 cup (125 mL)	raisins or currants, optional

The oat scones may be frozen and served warm in various ways. For breakfast, cut the pieces in half and toast them under the broiler.

For savoury oat scones, omit the raisins, reduce the sugar to 1 tbsp (15 mL), add 1/2 cup (125 mL) grated Cheddar cheese and 1 tsp (5 mL) dried dill or other herbs. Serve hot with soup and a salad.

Sift the flour, sugar, baking powder, cream of tartar and salt into a medium bowl. Add the oats and mix together.

In a separate bowl, beat the egg slightly. Add the milk and melted butter. Add the liquid ingredients to the dry ingredients and mix until they are moistened. Stir in the raisins. (If the dough seems dry, add a touch more milk.) Shape the dough into a ball and pat it out onto a floured surface to form an 8-inch (20-cm) circle. Place on a well-greased cookie sheet and mark the top to form eight wedges.

Bake at 425°F (220°C) for 12 to 15 minutes or until golden-brown.

Herring in Oatmeal

Should a Scottish husband recommend this splendid dish to his innocent Canadian bride, she should remember that there is a difference between fine oatmeal and Canadian oats — otherwise she runs the risk of producing Herring in Porridge.

4	herring
2 tbsp (25 mL)	all-purpose flour
	Salt and pepper
1/4 cup (50 mL)	milk
1/2 cup (125 mL)	fine oatmeal
3 tbsp (45 mL)	lard

To make your own fine oatmeal, grind rolled oat flakes in the blender for a few seconds.

Scale, clean and split the herring. Season the flour with salt and pepper. Dip the herring in the flour, brush with milk, then roll in the oatmeal, pressing on well to give a good coating. Fry in very hot lard, turning once, until browned. Serve with fresh oatcakes, grilled tomatoes, sliced lemon and parsley. Serves 4.

A genuine Oatcake recipe,
courtesy of the
Corporation of Glasgow —
Education Department.

1/2 lb. Fine Oatmeal
1 dessertspoonful Dripping Lard, or Butter
1/4 teaspoonful Salt
Cold Water

Method

1. Rub the shortening into the meal.
2. Add salt and enough water to make a firm dough.
3. Turn out, knead well, press into a round.
4. Roll out thin, taking care to keep edges neat.
5. Cut in four or eight; rub with meal, turn and rub other side.
6. Shake off loose meal, bake one side on a moderately hot girdle [old-fashioned round iron plate much used in Scotland for cooking on the stove] till corners begin to curl up. Do not turn.
7. Toast other side before the fire or under the gas.

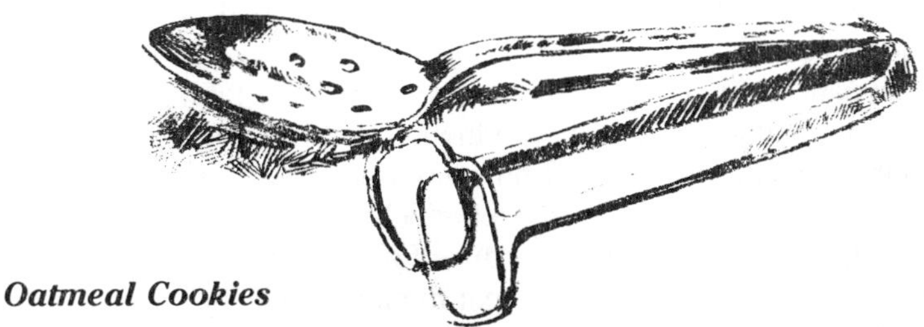

Oatmeal Cookies

1 cup (250 mL)	brown sugar
1 cup (250 mL)	granulated sugar
1 cup (250 mL)	shortening
2	eggs
1 tsp (5 mL)	vanilla
1 1/2 cups (375 mL)	all-purpose flour
1 tsp (5 mL)	salt
1 tsp (5 mL)	baking soda
3 cups (750 mL)	quick-cooking rolled oats
1/2 cup (125 mL)	finely chopped walnuts
1/2 cup (125 mL)	dessicated unsweetened coconut

In a large bowl, thoroughly cream the sugars and shortening. Add the eggs and vanilla and beat well.

Sift together the flour, salt and baking soda and add to the wet ingredients along with the rolled oats, nuts and coconut. Mix well. Shape into four rolls about 10 inches (25 cm) long and 1 inch (3 cm) in diameter. Wrap in waxed paper and chill in the refrigerator until the dough is very stiff. This may take 3 to 4 hours.

Slice the cookies thinly — about 1/4 inch (5 mm) thick. Bake on greased cookie sheets at 350°F (180°C) for 10 minutes. Makes about 100 cookies.

Citrus Fruits

Here is an interesting account of the origin of the word "marmalade." It is said that Mary Queen of Scots, when a prisoner in Loch Leven Castle, was so ill and depressed that she entirely lost her appetite, and nothing could tempt her to eat. At this time a Scotch confectioner invented a new preserve, an orange jam, and sent a sample to the imprisoned queen. This she liked so much that in honor of her he called his new jam "Marie Malade," which has since been contracted into marmalade.

The Early Canadian Galt Cook Book, 1896

Marmalade

The story, alas, is apocryphal, according to C. Anne Wilson's *The Book of Marmalade: Its Antecedents, Its History and Its Role in the World Today*. Others have claimed that marmalade was invented by Janet Keiller or by the Portuguese. The Greeks had their *Melomeli*, made from Cydonian apples (quinces) and honey, and used by physicians as a cure for indigestion. So did the Romans, but our marmalade comes from the Portuguese *marmelo* (quince again). Their *marmelada* was a stiff quince paste, served with cheese.

Why, in February, do we feel impelled to make marmalade? Is it an atavistic fear of scurvy, that dreadful scourge of the early settlers in Canada until the Indians taught them to drink spruce beer (see page 163)? Or is it the presence of Seville oranges in the stores?

The classic marmalade is made with Seville or bitter oranges, available in late January but especially February. These will never replace sweet oranges at the breakfast table, but they do make a marmalade with a particular tang. About 2 pounds (1 kg) of fruit will yield nine 6-oz (175-g) jars. Use the Seville oranges either by themselves or in combination with sweet oranges, lemons or grapefruit.

Cut the oranges in half, squeeze and strain the juice into a preserving kettle. To augment the supply of pectin, save the orange pips, put them in a small bowl, cover with 1 cup (250 mL) warm water and let sit overnight. Cut the orange peel (with the pith) as finely as possible, using either scissors or a very sharp knife, then add to the juice. Measure the peel and juice. For each cup, add 1 cup (250 mL) water. Let soak overnight — at least 12 hours.

In the morning, simmer the mixture of orange juice, peel and water gently in a covered pot for at least 1 1/2 hours, or until the peel is tender. Before this is quite ready, simmer the pips in their soaking water for about 15 minutes, then strain the fluid into the orange juice and peel mixture.

Measure the mixture again. For each cup, add 1 cup (250 mL) granulated sugar. Heat and stir until the sugar is dissolved. Then stir and boil until the marmalade reaches the gel point — this will take approximately 30 minutes. Pour into hot sterilized jars and seal at once, using Mason lids or paraffin.

Broiled Grapefruit

Grapefruit, which bears the apt name *Citrus paradisi*, is just fine as it is, but this versatile dish makes a pleasant change and can be served as a first course or as a dessert.

2	grapefruit
2 tbsp (25 mL)	brown sugar
4 tsp (20 mL)	butter
2 tbsp (25 mL)	brandy

Cut the grapefruit in half and loosen each segment of the pulp with a small sharp knife. Sprinkle the halves with the sugar, dot with butter and add the brandy.

Broil until the sugar bubbles, about 7 minutes, but keep an eye on it. Serves 4.

Orange Surprise

Three homesick little Canadians, who had been dragged around one Roman ruin too many, cheered visibly when served this simple yet appealing dessert in an Italian restaurant in Colchester.

Carefully cut off the top of an orange, reserving it to use as a lid. Gently scoop out the pulp. Fill the orange shell with orange sherbet or ice cream and cover. Wrap the orange in foil and put it in the freezer. Remove about 30 to 45 minutes before serving. For Adult Orange Surprise, put a spoonful of Cointreau in the bottom of the shell before filling. Serves 1.

To liven up frozen orange juice, squeeze the juice of an orange into every cup.

Slightly thawed orange juice mixed with the standard amount of water and zizzed in the blender for a few seconds is delicious.

For a refreshing drink, combine equal portions orange juice and soda water.

For a different flavour when making fruit pies, cut the fruit into orange juice rather than lemon juice to prevent it from turning brown. Use orange juice instead of water when making applesauce.

If you have an orange tree (well worth the trouble and expense for its enchanting mixture of blossoms and fruit, use both the peel and the bitter fruit (it's really a calamondin) in sweet breads and in gin and tonic.

Key Lime Pie

This pie takes seconds to make. It is usually eaten in seconds, too, with appreciative murmurs. For lemon meringue pie, use fresh lemon juice instead.

4	eggs, separated
6 tbsp (90 mL)	granulated sugar
1/2 tsp (2 mL)	cream of tartar
1	300-mL can sweetened condensed milk
1/2 cup (125 mL)	fresh lime juice
1	baked 9-inch (23-cm) pie shell

For the meringue, beat the egg whites until stiff, then gradually blend in the sugar and cream of tartar, beating until the mixture is firm enough to hold its shape. Set it aside and, without washing the beaters, beat the egg yolks until they are thick and pale yellow. Add the condensed milk and lime juice. Beat until thick. Pour the mixture into the baked pie shell and spread the meringue over the pie. Bake at 350°F (180°C) for 15 minutes, or until the peaks of the meringue have turned golden-brown.

Chinese New Year

This important celebration, at the end of January or in early February, is always a time for family reunions and visits with friends and relations. The children look forward to it, too, because their parents and grandparents slip money, in special red envelopes, under their pillows. A typical greeting on the envelope reads, "Wishing that you will have everything going your way and bright days ahead of you."

The ancestors are remembered by having a place set at the table at the New Year's Eve dinner, with flowers and dishes. Everyone eats rice cakes (Nien Gau) and enjoys the firecrackers.

If you aren't lucky enough to be attending a New Year's dinner, Chinese restaurants often have special buffets, or you can cook a simplified Chinese dinner for yourself to brighten up the season. It may take several of you to help with the stirring, chopping and frying.

Eggflower Soup or Soup of the Gods (Dan Hwa Tang)

While enjoying Mongolian Hot Pot (a kind of fondue from the Steppes), the guests, not all experts with their chopsticks, kept dropping bits of spinach and beef into the bubbling chicken broth. "This would make a good soup," someone remarked. The hostess smiled seraphically, and produced small porcelain bowls and ladles at the end.

4 cups (1 L)	beef broth
2	eggs
2 tsp (10 mL)	vegetable oil
2 tbsp (25 mL)	soy sauce
1 tsp (5 mL)	white vinegar
	Pepper
2	green onions, chopped

Bring the broth to a boil. Beat the eggs and oil together while you wait. Pour the mixture slowly and steadily into the broth and stir in the rest of the ingredients. Bring to a boil again and serve. Serves 4 to 6, depending on the size of your bowl.

Fried Rice (Chao-Fan)

1/4 cup (50 mL)	vegetable oil
2 tbsp (25 mL)	chopped onion
1/2 cup (125 mL)	diced bacon
2 tbsp (25 mL)	frozen green peas
2	eggs, beaten
4 cups (1 L)	cooked rice
1 1/2 tsp (7 mL)	salt

Heat half the oil in a wok or frying pan. Stir-fry the onion and bacon until brown, then add the green peas (don't bother to defrost them) and stir 1 minute. Pour in the beaten eggs and stir quickly until they are in small pieces. Remove the mixture from the pan and keep warm. Heat the remaining oil and cook the rice until it is just brown. Sprinkle it with a spoonful of water, add the salt and reduce the heat. Stir until the rice is thoroughly heated. Add the egg mixture and serve. Serves 4 as a main dish or 6 as a side dish.

Sweet and Sour Spareribs

3 tbsp (45 mL)	vegetable oil
2 tbsp (25 mL)	grated fresh ginger
1 1/2 lb (750 g)	spareribs, cut in 1 1/2-inch (4-cm) pieces
1 tbsp (15 mL)	sherry
2 tbsp (25 mL)	white vinegar
3 tbsp (45 mL)	granulated sugar
1/4 cup (50 mL)	soy sauce
1/3 cup (75 mL)	boiling water

Heat the oil in a large frying pan. Add the ginger and spareribs and stir-fry for 2 minutes. Add the remaining ingredients all at once and mix well. Cover and simmer for about 1 hour or until the meat is tender and the sauce has thickened. Serves 6 with rice and a salad.

Bean Sprouts

Chinese folktales tend to end not with "so they lived happily ever after," but "and they all lived in harmony together." A significant difference. This desire for harmony is applied to Chinese cooking, too. Care is taken to have the ingredients cut into harmonious shapes, so the celery should be cut along the grain in thin strips to blend with the long thin bean sprouts.

1 tbsp (15 mL)	vegetable oil
1 lb (500 g)	fresh bean sprouts
4	stalks celery, cut in thin strips
1 tbsp (15 mL)	grated fresh ginger
1/4 cup (50 mL)	soy sauce

Heat the oil in a frying pan or wok. Put the bean sprouts in the pan and heat them gently. Add the celery and cook for 3 minutes. Sprinkle with the grated ginger and soy sauce. Serves 4 or 5.

Cress

One problem with growing cress, even on the window ledge (see page 82), is how to use it. In addition to using it in salads (try a combination of cress, Chinese lettuce, green onions and mandarin oranges) and sandwiches (we like a handful of cress sprinkled on egg-salad sandwiches), try these.

Chicken Breasts with Cress

1/2 cup (125 mL)	all-purpose flour
	Salt and pepper
8	single chicken breasts, boned
3 tbsp (45 mL)	vegetable oil
1/2 cup (125 mL)	butter
1/3 cup (75 mL)	white wine or dry white vermouth
1/3 cup (75 mL)	chicken stock
1/4 cup (50 mL)	chopped cress
	Lemon slices for garnish

Boned chicken breasts may be bought — for a price — but it is much more economical to bone them yourself. Usually the breasts come halved. Take a small, very sharp knife and, starting at the top end, slice as close to the bones as possible. The flesh slides away quite easily.

Never mind that the first efforts produce somewhat ragged results; it does get easier. And don't forget to save the skin and bones to make stock.

Combine the flour, salt and pepper. Dredge the chicken breasts lightly in the flour.

Heat the oil and 1/3 cup (75 mL) butter in one large or two smaller frying pans. Add the chicken breasts and cook gently for 6 minutes on each side. Put them in a serving dish and keep them warm in the oven.

Add the wine and stock to the juices in the pan, stir and bring to a boil. Boil for 1 minute. Add the cress and remaining butter and stir until blended. Pour the sauce over the chicken and garnish with lemon slices. Serves 8.

Cress Butter

Scrape the butter into a small plastic tub and keep it covered in the refrigerator for dotting on steaks or chops. You don't need to bother with rolling and slicing it; just scoop it out when needed.

4	cloves garlic
4	shallots
2 tbsp (25 mL)	chopped cress (pepper cress is especially good)
pinch	salt
1/2 cup (125 mL)	butter, softened

Process or chop by hand the garlic, shallots, cress and salt. When finely chopped, add the butter and mix. Makes about 1/2 cup (125 mL).

Detail

The ruined stone house
has an old apple tree
left there by the farmer
whatever else he took with him
It bears fruit every year
gone wild and wormy
with small bitter apples
nobody eats
even children know better
I passed that way on the road
to Trenton twice a month
all winter long
noticing how the apples clung
in spite of hurricane winds
sometimes with caps of snow
little golden bells
And perhaps none of the other
travellers looked that way
but I make no parable of them
they were there and that's all
For some reason I must remember
and think of the leafless tree
and its fermented fruit
one week in late January
when wind blew down the sun
and earth shook like a cold room
no one could live in
with zero weather
soundless golden bells
alone in the storm

Al Purdy

The Cellar

Get up, guid wife, and shake your feathers,
You needna think that we are beggars,
For we have only come to say,
Please give to us our Hogmanay!

We are but bairns come to play,
Get up and give us our Hogmanay.

William MacEvery Brown
The Queen's Bush, 1932

Hogmanay is the Scottish word for New Year's Eve, once the primary holiday in Scotland, far surpassing the importance of Christmas. An expatriate Scot still has vivid memories of being tossed out-of-doors shortly before midnight in order to be an appropriate "first-footer". It was important for good luck in the year ahead that the first person over the threshold should be a tall, dark-haired man bringing a small gift to the household, often shortbread. Mysteriously, too, the first-footer would often carry a piece of coal.

Party Eggnog

A dram of single malt whisky would be the approved drink at Scottish celebrations, but this rich concoction is useful for holiday parties.

6	eggs, separated
1/2 cup (125 mL)	granulated sugar
1 1/2 cups (375 mL)	brandy, rye or Scotch
1/2 cup (125 mL)	rum
2 cups (500 mL)	whipping cream
2 1/2 cups (625 mL)	milk
	Grated nutmeg

Early on the day of the party, or the day before, beat the egg yolks with an electric mixer until they are thick and lemon-coloured. Gradually beat in the sugar, then slowly stir in the brandy and rum. Cover and refrigerate. Just before serving, fold in the stiffly beaten egg whites, whipped cream and enough milk to thin as desired. (Some like it thick, some thin.) Top with grated nutmeg. Our source made four times this amount for 20 people and had just the right amount. That's country living for you.

Herbal Teas

One...Indian tonic had nine ingredients: burdock root, wintergreen (leaves and berries) nettle root, thistle root, poplar bark, ironwood heart, black and red cherry bark and tag alder. These were brewed into a kind of tea and given effectively as a tonic. In the warm weather the addition of half a cup of brandy helped to preserve it (from the elements), although it was observed more men suffered the need of a good tonic at this season than at any other.

Dorothy Sliter
The Friendly Village, 1967

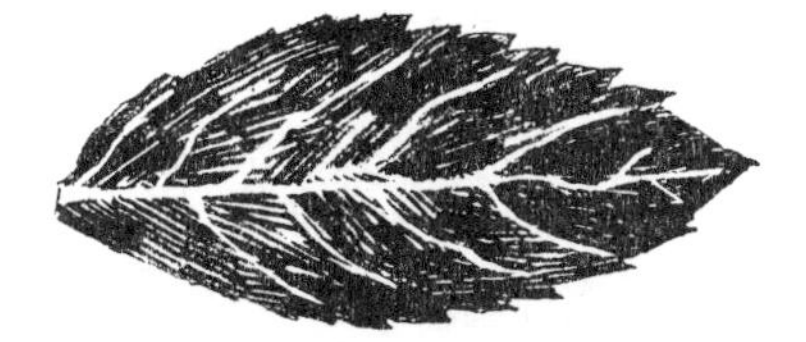

Herbal teas have been growing rapidly in popularity as an alternative to coffee and tea. They have a long history of usefulness for medicinal purposes, and for that very reason perhaps ought to be viewed with caution. There is no great gain to be made in leaping from an excess of caffeine into some other excess.

There are, of course, herbs and herbs, and most of those suitable for making tea may be enjoyed in moderate quantities. Safest and most pleasurable are the mints. "All Mints," wrote Culpeper in the seventeenth century, "are astringent, and of warm subtle parts; great strengtheners of the stomach." Traditionally mint tea was given to settle upset stomachs. Both peppermint (*Mentha piperata*) and spearmint (*Mentha spicata*) are excellent. Use one heaping teaspoonful of the dried herb for each cup of boiling water; let steep for about 10 minutes. If desired, the tea may be sweetened with honey and seasoned with a few drops of lemon juice.

Dr. Samuel Twining, director of the Twining Tea Company, advises on cleaning teapots: "The trick to keeping your teapot clean is to never use a detergent but to use what we call bicarbonate of soda [baking soda]. Two dessertspoonfuls in some hot water will gently clean your teapot without leaving a stain or an aftertaste."

Hot Lemon

Mrs. Septimus Barrow contributed this hearty suggestion as a cure for a cold (*My Pet Recipes*, 1900): "Bake a lemon till soft, take out all the inside, and mix with as much sugar as it will hold. Strain and stand till cold when it will jelly." In this age of convenience, we might prefer to mix 1 tsp (5 mL) sugar or honey with 1 tbsp (15 mL) lemon juice in a cup. Fill with boiling water and drink.

No. 224. Balm, Mint, and other Teas.

These are simple infusions, the strength of which can only be regulated by the taste. They are made by putting either the fresh or the dried plants into boiling water in a covered vessel, which should be placed near the fire for an hour. The young shoots both of balm and of mint are to be preferred, on account of their stronger aromatick qualities. These infusions may be drunk freely in feverish and in various other complaints, in which diluents are recommended. Mint tea, made with the fresh leaves, is useful in allaying nausea....

The Cook Not Mad, 1831

Aniseed Milk

This Dutch favourite is only for those who enjoy the flavour of licorice. European grocery stores often sell aniseed cubes, which you just drop into the milk, dissolve and serve hot or cold.

1 cup (250 mL)	milk
1 tsp (5 mL)	honey
1/4 tsp (1 mL)	ground anise, approx.

Mix and heat in a small pan. Serves 1.

Sack Posset

This rich and soothing medieval concoction will convert the most hardened Ovaltine addict, but be careful to serve it at once after you have added the sherry, or it will curdle.

1 1/2 cups (375 mL)	milk
1/4 cup (50 mL)	granulated sugar
1 1/2 tsp (7 mL)	all-purpose flour
1/2 tsp (2 mL)	grated nutmeg
1	egg
1/3 cup (75 mL)	sherry

Blend all the ingredients except the sherry and cook over low heat until thick enough to coat the back of a spoon. Add the sherry carefully and serve at once. Makes ample for 2.

Hot Toddy

A brother-in-law with a cold, given this stern Scottish brew, retired to his bed and slept for twelve hours. "If you want to enjoy it," said our source, "dress it up with a little lemon juice. If you just want to get rid of your cold, take it straight."

1/4 cup (50 mL)	Scotch
1 tsp (5 mL)	granulated sugar
1/4 cup (50 mL)	lemon juice, optional

Mix the ingredients in a glass or mug with a silver spoon in it (to prevent cracking). Pour in very hot, not boiling, water from a tea kettle (not from the tap). Stir and serve. Serves 1.

I often used to put mint leaves into my tea to correct the taste of the foul swamp-water.

The Earl of Southesk
Saskatchewan and the Rocky Mountains, 1875

Spring

My Garden

A little blade of grass I see,
Its banner waving wild and free,
And I wonder if in time to come
'Twill be a great big onion;
We cannot tell, we do not know,
For oft we reap and didn't sow;
We plant the hairy coconut,
With hope serene and sturdy — but
We cannot tell, for who can say,
We plant the oats and reap the hay,
We sow the apple, reap the worm,
We tread the worm and reap the turn:
Too much, too much for us this thought,
With much too much exertion fraught;
In faith we get the garden dug —
And what do we reap — we reap the bug.
In goodly faith we plant the seed,
Tomorrow morn we reap the weed.

Paul Hiebert

Introduction

The Carolingians had a name for it. They called March "Mud Month", and many a distraught mother hurls the same epithet at the school holiday that looms menacingly in the middle of the month, while pacifying the troops with cookies and Easter-egg making. But March is also the month for excursions to the maple syrup bush, and for watching the house plants perk up in the extra sunlight.

Before we know it, the snow really has gone, and we can start to poke about outside, remembering the old Chinese saying: "If you would be happy for a week, take a wife; if you would be happy for a month, kill your pig; but if you would be happy all your life, plant a garden."

Restlessly, we plant the seeds indoors, while keeping an eye out for the first tiny green spears that betray the coming of the chives. Soon the other wild greens spring up on all sides, including the dandelions and violets that produce such interesting spring soups and salads.

Then the delectable moment of the first local asparagus and the early rhubarb sitting on the market stalls beside the tempting pots of tulips and daffodils. The woodruff flourishes mightily in the garden, and we wonder if *this* year we will be able to attempt the fabled Maibowle.

The Canadian spring is transient and full of surprises. Sometimes it seems more like a series of April Fool's days than a season, for we are alternately battered by wet snowstorms and enchanted by perfect summer days. Impossible to know where you're at, unless you listen for the wild geese honking and see them flying north. Goldfinch also make plain the season, changing from demure winter grey into an iridescent yellow, and singing like the wild canaries they really are.

But still and all, it is an exhilarating time of year. Even the sober Champlain was so captivated by its speedy charms that he wrote what must be one of the earliest and best descriptions of this hopeful season.

On the eighth of the said month [May] the cherry-trees began to open their buds and unfold their leaves.

About the same time small flowers, flax-grey and white [probably the Hepatica], were springing from the soil: these are the spring primroses of those localities.

On the ninth, the raspberries began to bud and all kinds of herbs to come out of the ground.

On the tenth or eleventh the elder bush showed its leaves.

On the twelfth white violets were seen in flower.

On the fifteenth the trees were in bud, the cherry-trees covered with leaves, and the wheat was over a span in height.

The raspberry bushes put forth their leaves; the chervil was ready to cut; and in the woods the sorrel could be seen two inches high.

On the eighteenth the birches opened their leaves, the other trees following them closely: the oak had its buds swelling, and the apple-trees we had transplanted from France, as well as the plum-trees were budding; the leaves on the cherry-trees were quite large; the vines were budding and flowering; the sorrel was ready to cut.

Samuel de Champlain
Voyages, 1620-29

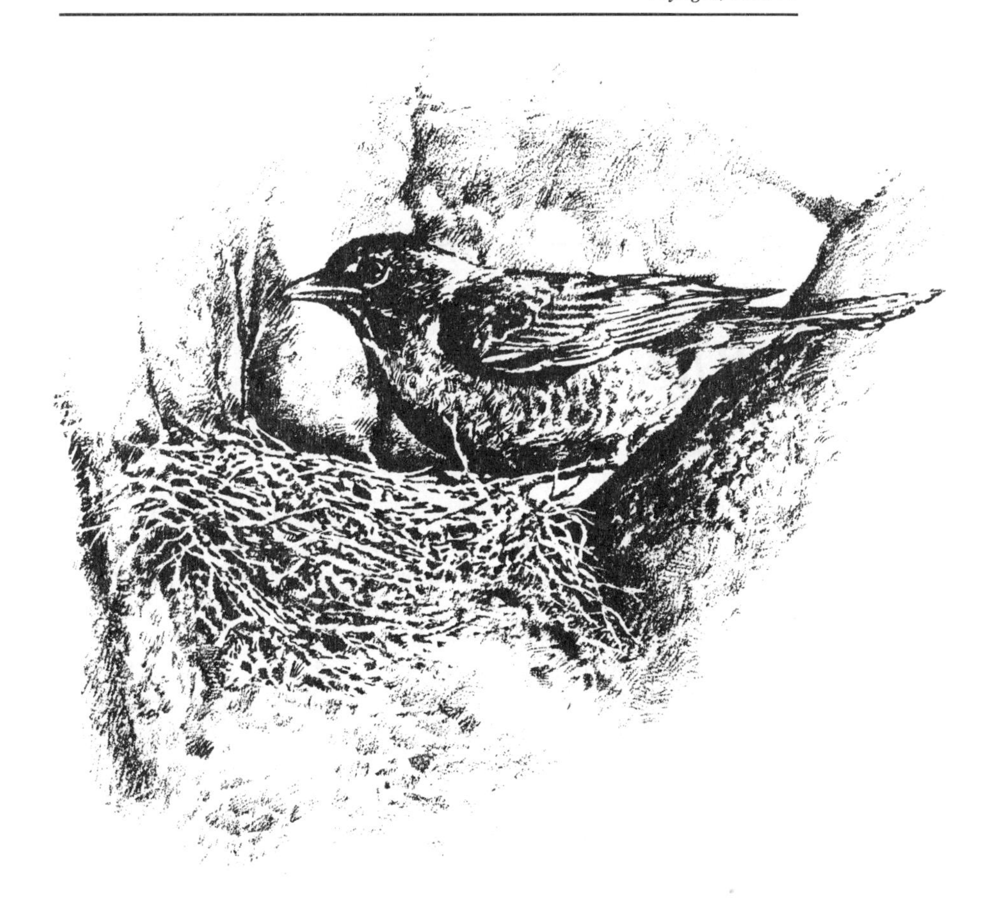

The Garden

In Spate

Another winter done, brooks
go shouldering through the fields
with their icy trash.

Among the trees
they hurry past one's eye.

No pools to brood in, flat
water where it is low.

Roads get hurt.
Fields dont show much hurt.

George Johnston

House Plants

After the indoor spring of forced bulbs dwindles, and before the hurly-burly of the outdoor garden begins, is a good time to hunt down a few exotic plants — a change from the ubiquitous geranium (only truly satisfactory in a very sunny window), ivy and African violet. Rather than buying these plants at exorbitant prices, drop in on plantophile friends, taking snippers with you.

Here are a few of our favourites. Nearly indestructible, they will flourish even with benign neglect.

Clivia miniata: This spectacular plant grows like a weed in South Africa, where it is known as the Kafir lily. Several years of patience are needed before the striking orange blossoms first appear in spring and summer, but the dark-green, strap-like leaves are a handsome sight in themselves for the rest of the year. The clivia is one of those admirable plants with cast-iron constitutions. It will have few problems if you supply bright indirect light and let it rest — that is, water it very sparingly between October and the first appearance of the flower stalk, when you should begin to water and feed it more frequently. It appreciates having its leaves washed. As time passes you will need ever-larger containers for the giant roots that heave through the surface (clivia have been known to break through earthenware pots). No need for cuttings here. The clivia obligingly creates little clivia by itself. It can move outside into a semi-shady spot in the summer.

Euphorbia splendens: Another useful plant for those with black thumbs. A Victorian favourite, the "crown of thorns" produces sharp thorns, green leaves and an abundance of elegant miniature red flowers for weeks in the spring. This unlikely relation of the poinsettia, left to its trouble-free self in a sunny window, will grow to a great age and become as splendidly gnarled as an old apple tree. Like the poinsettia, it is poisonous, but it is so well armed with thorns that it seems unlikely children will want to munch on it. Take cuttings a few inches long and allow the juices to dry for forty-eight hours, then insert them in sandy soil. (Use the same technique for the jade plant, which through the years will become a majestic presence. When pruning, pot the clippings as gifts or for barter.)

Bitter aloe: Sometimes known as the first-aid plant. It is said that the Roman legions carried aloe with them for wounds. The aloe now turns up frequently in supermarkets. The fleshy, dagger-shaped leaves contain a juice that really does soothe minor cuts and burns. Just cut the surface with a fingernail or break off a small piece. (One small niece nearly wore out an entire plant.) It is easily propagated, for little aloes spring up beside the mother plant. It enjoys a sunny window, but will survive in bright indirect light.

Decorative Shrubs

When the cold weather was over, towards the end of March the best disposed among us set themselves who should best till the soil, and make gardens wherein to sow seed and reap the fruit thereof. This happened most seasonably, for during the winter we were much inconvenienced by our lack of garden herbs. When each of us had finished his sowing it was a marvellous pleasure to see them grow and increase day by day, and a still greater contentment to make the abundant use of them which we did; in so much that this commencement of good hope made us almost forget our native country, especially when the fish began again to seek the fresh water and to come in such abundance into our brooks that we knew not what to do with them.

Marc Lescarbot
History of New France, 1609

If you have a backyard large enough to support a shrub or two, consider planting red currant, black currant and gooseberry bushes. Currants and most gooseberries have a neat growing habit and an attractive appearance. Their flowers are neither here nor there, but their fruit is a spectacular asset in the kitchen, for nowadays these useful fruits are either unobtainable or prohibitively expensive. The fruit matures in July, at about the same time as raspberries. Currants are very easy to pick, though gooseberry bushes are prickly. One learns to take care. Compared to tending strawberry beds, looking after currant and gooseberry bushes is a snap, a non-event. Compared to both strawberries and raspberries, they occupy extremely little space in relation to their yield.

One word of warning: currants and gooseberries should not be planted within 1,000 feet of white pine trees, for the bushes may be host to the white pine blister rust. A single exception to this caution is the rust-resistant Consort black currant.

A little over thirty years ago, we planted two each of red currant, black currant and gooseberry bushes. The black currant and gooseberry bushes have had to be replaced once, but the red currant bushes are still marching on. It is true that they are now old and gnarled and less productive, but they have taken steps to provide for their future by layering themselves — low branches, touching the ground, have thrown out little root systems, and these have developed into new bushes. At the outset of our career in currants, we did try to follow the mind-boggling pruning instructions, but somehow we lapsed, and since the currant crops continued abundant, we felt confirmed in our policy of neglect. The new gooseberry bushes yielded nine quarts a few years ago, at a time when the only local supermarket that was selling them was charging three dollars a quart.

Nor are we forced to share our bushes with the birds to the same extent as we have had to share strawberries and raspberries. We used to be faithful in throwing a net over the bushes about the time they were ripening, following the advice of an English gardening book which observed that birds disliked tangling their little feet in the net. But sometimes we have neglected even this task, and without too dire results. The gooseberries are generally less attractive to birds because we tend to pick them when they are still green — not too appealing to the birds, but excellent for jams and pies.

Currants are not fussy bushes in any kind of way. They can be planted singly, for pollination is not a problem. The best time to start them is in the spring, when the ground can readily be cultivated. Allow about five feet between the bushes — a little more for the black currants, which grow taller. Both currants and gooseberries prefer moist clay soils, so on lighter soils they will profit from mulching — peat moss, grass clippings or partly composted leaves spread around the base of the bush to help retain moisture — and watering. Not surprisingly, their yield will be higher if they are grown in full sunlight, although they adapt quite reasonably to partial shade.

There are many other possibilities for growing edible plants, bushes and trees in the garden. Japanese quince, often planted as a garden shrub, begins with flame-coloured blossoms and ends in edible fruit — knobbly and green, full of pectin and useful for jelly and jam. It is a cousin of the true quince, a tree not commonly cultivated any more, whose fruit was used in the earliest of marmalades, before Seville oranges were even thought of. Far easier to find these days are flowering crabapple trees. The fruit of these can be gathered in September to make an attractive crabapple jelly. Then, too, there are high-bush cranberries, whose merits were discerned by the ever-acute Catharine Parr Traill over one hundred years ago:

The high bush-cranberry, or single American Guelder-rose, is a very ornamental shrub in your garden; it likes a rich moist soil and a shady situation. The flowers are handsome in Spring, and every period of ripening in the fruit, is beautiful to see, from the pale orange tint, to the glowing scarlet when fully ripe, and, after the frost has touched them, to a light crimson. The berry when fully ripe is almost transparent. The flat, hard seeds in this juicy fruit make it unsuitable for jam, but as a jelly nothing can be finer, particularly as a sauce for venison or mutton. The native soil of the high bush-cranberry is at the edge of swamps, or near rivers and lakes, where the soil is black and spongy; but they also thrive in shady flats in dry ground in our garden.

Catharine Parr Traill
The Canadian Settler's Guide, 1854

The high-bush cranberry can be used in jellies, syrups and juices. It is very tart, however, and best gathered late, about the time the frosts begin, for use in sauces and jellies. We have several high-bush cranberry bushes in our back garden. One variety, the European guelder rose, is very picturesque, both in spring with its white blossoms and in fall with its red fruit. It maintains its fruit through the winter into the following spring, when the birds seem to find the berries particularly attractive.

As to fruit-bearing plants, it seems madness to bother with strawberries (unless you are very fond of weeding) when they are so readily available at pick-your-own farms. Rhubarb is another story, very easy and trouble-free, occupying very little space in relation to its yield. This vigorous plant presents the first fruits of the spring, flourishes in full sunlight and, if the flower head is cut off, can be consumed into summer. The leaves are another story, poisonous because of the oxalic acid they contain; they are best cut off when you gather the stalks, and left at the base of the plant to form a useful mulch.

Choose a rhubarb variety with a bright-red stalk; it used to be called strawberry rhubarb, but now seems to go under the name of crimson cherry. Plant it about 4 inches deep in the spring in ground that is well cultivated. Allow about 2 feet between the plants. In the first year let the plant become established and do not gather the stalks. In fact, never gather the stalks completely; the plant is a grand producer, but functions best if you thin it, rather than crop it entirely.

Finally, a word might be said in favour of the Jerusalem artichoke, a kind of sunflower that blooms in September, and whose tuberous roots can be dug like potatoes after the first frost. It is a very invasive, aggressive sort of plant, growing about 10 feet tall, so you have to make up your mind as to whether you have a corner of the garden that you wish to give to this particular good cause.

Tubers, though not easy to find commercially, can be planted either in the fall or spring. Cut each tuber into several pieces and plant them about 3 inches deep in cultivated soil. They take a little time to get started in the spring, but then they really take off. They are a nutritious vegetable, superior to potatoes in that respect, but much more disagreeable to peel. They can be used fresh in salads, and for soups the small ones can be washed and scrubbed, not peeled, and later sieved. They combine nicely with leeks, but are overwhelmed by onions. The larger ones are delicious peeled, steamed until tender, then served with a cheese sauce.

Starting Seeds

There are advantages to growing one's garden from seeds. Seed catalogues provide a much wider choice of varieties than even the best of nursery gardens; and for the same amount of money you will get a far larger supply of plants from a package of seed than you will by buying plants already started. However, there are difficulties. Seedlings require a good deal of attention, particularly when they are started indoors. And yet the problematic character of the Canadian spring — so often too little and too late — makes it tempting to start at least some seeds early. But not too early. If you attempt to gain too great a march on the season, you will need to transplant the seedlings from their initial containers, which they will soon outgrow. And the larger they grow indoors, the slower they will be to adapt to outdoor conditions.

So although it is sensible and easier to reserve the main planting of seeds to the outdoors when the danger of frost is over and the garden can be easily cultivated, there is some advantage in giving a few of the annuals a head start. Try easy ones like lettuce and marigolds first. Lettuce, if started indoors, may actually produce leaves large and numerous enough for June sandwiches. Plant the seeds indoors no more than a month ahead of the earliest possible planting outdoors. (If the frost-free season begins about mid-May, then plant indoors in mid-April, or even a little later.)

The egg-shaped halves of Styrofoam egg cartons make useful containers for starting seeds. Fill with planting soil and plant seeds according to the directions on the package. Sprinkle very small seeds on top of the soil; larger ones should be buried to a depth about three times their diameter. The containers should have water added to them until the soil is thoroughly damp; then cover each container with plastic wrap and place in a warm and sunny window. The sun is not strictly essential at this stage, except that it does provide the heat which, together with the moisture, encourages the seeds to get going. If the weather is co-operative, the seeds should be up in a very few days. At this point remove the plastic wrap. From now on the seedlings must be watched closely, for the small containers dry out quickly. They are likely to need water daily, especially on sunny days.

As soon as the weather permits, put the seedlings outdoors during the warmest and brightest hours of the day, from late morning to early afternoon. Steadily lengthen the period of exposure to outdoor conditions. They will grow sturdily this way, although they may need more water. If they are kept cooped up in the house, they will be spindly, and will wilt on sudden exposure to the outdoors. If the seedlings grow very quickly, you may have to transplant them into small peat pots before it is safe to put them directly in the garden.

If you have planted your seeds too thickly — and which of us does not — then the roots of the seedlings will grow together. At the time of transplanting, soak the container thoroughly with water, then tug the little plants gently apart. As long as some root remains with the plant, all should be well. In transplanting the seedlings, be sure to leave adequate space between the plants. Consult the directions on your seed packages.

For a time after transplanting into the garden, the small plants must be closely watched. The soil around them needs to be kept moist until their root systems develop. (They will always need water, but they are particularly vulnerable when small.) Curiously enough, we have found that the seedlings started at home come on faster than the larger plants one buys. These tend to sit around thinking about growing for some time before actually doing it.

Hardening Off

Hardening Off House Plants

House plants, too, find that the outdoors takes a bit of getting used to. Accustomed to sunlight being filtered through windows (increasingly dirty windows), they respond to full sunlight the same way we do. They get a sunburn. They need to advance to a position in the garden by stages, beginning perhaps by taking up a fairly shady position on a porch. In fact, they probably should never be put in full sunlight, and will require a sheltered spot in the garden. African violets are even fussier. They don't mind going outdoors, but draw the line at being rained on.

So much depends on the kind of house plant you are dealing with. If you have been harbouring geraniums, impatiens, ivies and fuschias, then perhaps you have the makings of window boxes or half-barrel plantings. Very likely they will have grown too large and rangy for the purpose, so in mid-April you might want to take slips and plant these outdoors when they have developed roots. Of course, all these plants may be put straight into a well-cultivated and partly shady garden, the soil enriched by compost or well-rotted manure. If the geraniums are too tall and spindly, plant them with the root and most of the stems covered by earth. Leave just the growing tips of the various branches — about 8 to 10 inches — above the soil level. From the several branches you will soon have several geraniums, each growing straight up.

House plants like jade, clivia, crown of thorns, Norfolk pine, Christmas cactus, hibiscus and many others will benefit from a summer holiday in a well-cultivated shady garden. It may be that the back porch is the only shady part of your garden, and if this is so, then the plants will have to remain in their pots. They can be repotted with fresh soil; at the least they should be given some fertilizer, preferably organic. And always you will have to make sure that they are regularly watered, remembering that pots dry out particularly fast in hot weather.

Hardening Off Tender Plants

It is easy to buy tomato plants in the middle of May, but rash to plant them outside so early unless one lives in the very mildest part of Canada. They are very susceptible to frost, and don't even like cold weather much. The trouble with postponing the purchase of tomato plants is that by the first of June, they are well and thoroughly picked over. Therefore it seems preferable to roll with the tide of commerce, buy tomato plants (or cucumber, equally tender) early and bring them home to enjoy sunshine by day and the indoors by night. They must be watered assiduously, for they are heavy drinkers, and maybe they will need to be replanted into peat pots to allow for growth. This is troublesome, but far better than exposing them to cold weather, from which they will be slow to recover.

As to the potted herbs that have been sulking indoors most of the winter because of lack of light, reviving timidly in the spring sunlight, they will delight in going to the sunniest part of your garden. The bay tree, the rosemary, tarragon and lemon verbena will now begin to show you what they can really do. (Though it is tempting to discard the parsley now going to seed, and start again with fresh seeds or plants.) Whatever else you've been trying to grow in the kitchen window — chives, thyme, sage — should be liberated into the garden as soon as the danger of frost is over. They will be like kids let out of school for the summer holidays.

Pioneer Gardens and Wildflowers

More and more people are coming in touch with old-fashioned pioneer gardens like the ones the early settlers kept, noting their simplicity and restfulness. At the same time, as natural habitats diminish, more and more people are attracted to native wildflowers for their individuality and charm. (Is this some kind of reaction to high-tech culture?)

Wildflowers are undeniably appealing. They always have been. To read John Geikie's century-old list of beauties is to be inflamed by a desire for possession: "What shall I say of the wild flowers which burst out as the year advanced? In open places, the woods were well nigh carpeted with them, and clearings that had, for whatever reason, been for a time abandoned, soon showed like gardens with their varied colors. The scarlet lobelia, the blue lupin, gentian, columbine, violets in countless variety, honeysuckles, flinging their fragrant flowers on long tresses from the trees, campanula, harebell, balsams, asters, calceolarias, the snowy lily of the valley, and clouds of wild roses, are only a few from the list. Varieties of mint, with beautiful flowers, adorned the sides of streams or the open meadows, and, resting in a floating meadow of its own green leaves...whole stretches of the great white water-lily rose and fell with every gentle undulation."

Of course, he does rather stack the deck, emotionally speaking, by summoning up the beauties of spring, summer and fall in one charged paragraph. Violets are over before wild roses begin, and both are firmly in the past when it's time for wild asters. Nor does it follow that because all these things are lovely in their own natural habitat, they can readily be plunged into an urban garden.

With wildflowers, therefore, one must proceed cautiously, starting with the purchase of Roger Tory Peterson's *Field Guide to Wildflowers* or the Audubon Society's *Field Guide to North American Wildflowers* or both. It also helps to see wildflowers in their natural setting (conservation areas are often ideal for this) to judge whether they will suit your garden; and unless you are a superb gardener, you should avoid any that you know to be rare and difficult. Many wildflowers are tough and adaptable, but even they can be wiped out by excessive picking or by too many enthusiasts digging up too many roots.

As usual, Catharine Parr Traill had a good sense of the practical, and her list of wildflowers for the garden needs only a few revisions today:

White Trillium (Trillium Grandiflorum)
Nature has scattered with no niggardly hand these remarkable flowers over hill and dale, wide shrubby plain and shady forest glen. In deep ravines, on rocky islets, the bright snow white blossoms of the Trilliums greet the eye and court the hand to pluck them. The old people in this part of the Province call them by the familiar name of Lily. Thus we have Asphodel Lilies, Douro Lilies, &c. *In Nova Scotia they are called Moose-flowers, probably from being abundant in the haunts of Moose-Deer.*

Rock Columbine (Aquilegia Canadensis)
The wild Columbine is perennial and very easily cultivated. Its blossoms are eagerly sought out by the bees and humming birds. On sunny days you may be sure to see the latter hovering over the bright drooping bells, extracting the rich nectar with which they are so bountifully supplied. Those who care for bees, and love humming birds, should plant the graceful red-flowered Columbine in their garden borders.

In its wild state, it is often found growing among rocks and surface stones, where it insinuates its roots into the clefts and hollows that are filled with rich vegetable mould; and thus, being often seen adorning the sterile rocks with its bright crown of waving blossoms, it has obtained the name in some places of ROCK COLUMBINE.

Herb Robert (Geranium robertianum or foetid geranium)
...is said to have been introduced from Britain, but is by no means uncommon in Canada, in half cleared woodlands and by waysides attracting the eye by its bright pink flowers, and elegantly cut leaves, which becomes bright red in the fall of the year. This pretty species is renowned for its rank and disagreeable odour when handled.

Catharine Parr Traill
Canadian Wild Flowers, 1868

White trillium, rock columbine and herb Robert are all tough, feasible plants for the garden. They like sun in the spring when they are going to flower, but will settle for shade during the rest of the growing season. They can therefore be planted near deciduous trees or shrubs, for they will have gathered up all the necessary sunlight before the tree and shrub leaves come out. How to get hold of these perennials? It's easiest to get them from a friend who wants to reduce a superabundance to some reasonable limits. Wildflowers can get out of hand. There are also commercial sources, both nurseries for plants and catalogues for seeds.

There are many possible additions to Mrs. Traill's list for a spring wildflower garden. To the white trillium, rock columbine and herb Robert could be added the Virginia bluebell (*Mertensia virginica*) and Dutchman's breeches (*Dicentra cucullaria*), a delicate and distant cousin of bleeding heart that is adaptable to gardens. And perhaps most especially the common blue violet (*Viola papilionacea*). These are usually easy to come by, for people with violets, like those with kittens, are eager to share. Violets are best for easy-going gardeners with understanding neighbours. Despite their fragile appearance, they like to creep about and, given the right damp shady conditions, you may find yourself with a violet meadow instead of a lawn (though you can eat the vitamin C-packed leaves in salad all summer long). Trilliums, on the other hand, stay still, although the clumps get larger.

As to pioneer gardens, some of the inhabitants of these early cultivated gardens have escaped over the years and now ramble freely about the countryside, at least as freely as is possible in these days of diminishing countryside. Look for the old-fashioned day lily (*Hemerocallis fulva* if orange, and *Hemerocallis flava* if yellow). It is tough, spreading and enduring, and anyone living in an old farmhouse is likely to be endowed with a rich inheritance. Or try the creeping bellflower (*Campanula rapunculoides*), a charming plant with violet-blue bells that blooms through July and into August, pretty much the same period as the day lilies. Queen of the meadow (*Filipendula ulmaria*) is another garden escape, blooming in the middle of the summer with clusters of tiny feathery and fragrant blossoms, pink to cream. This perennial has an ancient herbal history, for it was sacred to the Druids and was also Queen Elizabeth's favourite strewing herb.

Then, too, there is the musk mallow (*Malva moschata*), delicately pink or white, originating in old gardens, but found in fields and roadsides. It can be hard to transplant, even early in the season, and seems to spread itself at least in part by seeds. Bee balm or Oswego tea (*Monarda didyma*) is also a garden escape, much beloved by hummingbirds wherever they find it, and used by our ancestors as a substitute for tea. It is a tough perennial, easy to transplant and willing to spread.

Finally, passing swiftly over the old-fashioned mauve phlox and the ever-cheerful golden glow, there is the globe thistle (*Echinops ritro*), the sturdy inhabitant of at least one pioneer garden and currently advertised as "blue burst" in one Manitoba seed and plant catalogue. At least 3 feet tall, blooming in the middle of the summer, globe thistles are exactly what the hummingbirds want and need after they have finished with the bee balm. And not just hummingbirds — monarch and white admiral butterflies and innumerable varieties of bees also rejoice in them. They are useful for dried flower arrangements, but who could bear to gather them before the birds and insects have had their fill?

If you have trouble finding these old-fashioned flowers, ask the gardener at your nearest pioneer village how he got his specimens. (Indeed, pioneer villages might go beyond selling freshly baked bread, and sell off their excess perennials in the spring and fall.)

In conclusion, it's worth issuing the plea not to pick or dig up native wildflowers in their natural site, the way we all used to be in the habit of doing. It's too late in the day for that. There are too many of us and too few of them. Friends, nurseries and seed catalogues ought to provide all the normal appetite requires. And real enthusiasts can turn to the North American Native Plant Society (PO Box 84, Station D, Etobicoke, Ontario, M9A 4X1), which operates a seed exchange.

The Kitchen

The New Kitchen

From seed the green beginnings
open
tingle
butterfly the air

and the little carrot swells
down and around,
the root-hairs feel
into the damp dark, the root-beats carry
out the clay pot with its pores
down the wooden table
into the floor and around,

the tiny carrot
fierce in its pot
rings the whole kitchen, rings
the whole yellow kitchen
round

Marvyne Jenoff

Leeks

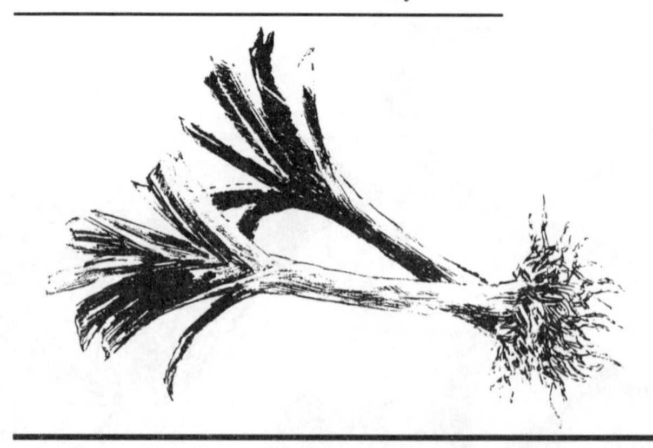

As David is the patron saint, so the leek is the emblem of Wales, although it has a long history before that, dating back to Ur. The Welsh wear bits of it in their hats on March 1 to celebrate the victory of King Cadwallader over the Saxons in 640 A.D. (the Welsh wore leeks in their caps as identification).

Leeks Vinaigrette

Leeks are mean to clean, and you risk comments about grit in the salad if you are not careful. On the other hand, if you buy them complete with their earth and roots attached, they'll be fresher. Jane Grigson suggests carefully removing the coarse green part (save it for soups and stews), then standing the leeks, root end up, in a jug of water to soak, letting the grit float out. If there still seems to be dirt, make a slit up the side of the leek and rinse.

3	leeks, white part only, cleaned and thinly sliced
2 tsp (10 mL)	capers, chopped
2 tbsp (25 mL)	lemon juice
1/4 cup (50 mL)	olive oil
1/2 tsp (2 mL)	granulated sugar
1 tsp (5 mL)	Dijon mustard
1	clove garlic, minced
	Salt and pepper
1 tbsp (15 mL)	chopped fresh parsley
1 tbsp (15 mL)	chopped cress

In a small bowl, toss the leeks and capers. Put the lemon juice, olive oil, sugar, mustard, garlic and herbs in a jar, cover and shake vigorously. Pour the dressing over the leeks and mix well. Chill for 2 hours in the refrigerator. Serves 2 as a vegetable or 4 as a relish, and will keep for several days. Any leftovers make a spirited addition to an egg salad sandwich.

The prevalence of leeks in country cooking suggests the truth of the saying that "leeks are the poor man's asparagus." But they are not inexpensive here. Indeed, in North America, asparagus might be considered the poor man's leek.

Scalloped Potatoes with Leeks

The Scots are also devoted to leeks, as witness cock-a-leekie soup. The Irish have a St. Patrick legend about them, and in the north of England there are working men's clubs where they hold leek shows, ending "with a great boil-up of the prize-winning vegetables into a soup for all...." And, of course, they are a staple of French cooking.

This pleasing combination is a fine accompaniment for baked peameal bacon.

3	medium potatoes, thinly sliced
3	leeks, white part only, finely chopped
	Salt and pepper
1 1/2 cups (375 mL)	light cream
3/4 cup (175 mL)	grated Gruyère cheese

In a buttered 2-quart (2-L) casserole, layer one-third of the potatoes, then one-third of the leeks. Sprinkle with salt and pepper. Repeat until you have three layers of potatoes and leeks. Pour in the cream and spread the Gruyère over the top of the casserole. Bake at 350°F (180°C) for 1 hour, or until the potatoes are tender and the cheese topping is crusty and brown. Serves 4.

Baked Peameal Bacon: For a dinner party, put a whole peameal bacon — 6 to 8 lb (3 to 4 kg) — in an open pan. Fill the pan with cold water up to the bottom of the fat line on the meat. Cook, uncovered, at 325°F (160°C) for 3 1/2 hours. Pour off the water and serve the bacon with hot applesauce (see page 48). The cold meat will be excellent for dinner the next night, or for sandwiches or omelettes. Serves 6 to 10.

Maple Syrup

19th (March, 1794) This is the Month for making Maple Sugar, a hot Sun & frosty nights cause the Sap to flow most. Slits are cut in the bark of the Trees & wooden troughs set under the Tree into which the Sap — a clear sweet water — runs. It is collected from a number of Trees & boiled in large Kettles till it becomes of a hard consistence. Moderate boiling will make powder sugar but when boiled long it forms very hard Cakes which are better. I saw a number of Trees slit today as I rode with Mr. McGill to his farm.

Elizabeth Simcoe
Diary, 1792-96

There's no denying that maple syrup is expensive. It is more economical to buy it in larger rather than small amounts; the only problem is that when you open a container, it must be kept in a refrigerator.

Perhaps the best thing to do is to buy a gallon, heat the syrup to 170°F (83°C), then divide it up among hot sterilized Mason jars. In the unlikely event that this leaves you with too much maple syrup, present small jars as gifts. Very welcome they are.

Maple syrup can also be packed in freezer containers with an inch of headspace and frozen. To use later, defrost for 30 minutes and shake well before serving. As an alternative, it is said that there is an even easier way of dividing up the gallon can. Just pour the syrup into unwashed whisky or brandy bottles. The small amounts of liquor remaining in the bottles will preserve the maple syrup.

Maple syrup can be used in many ways: as a glaze for baked ham (with cider vinegar and Dijon mustard), on baked squash, to enliven baked beans, on baked apples and pancakes, and as a luxurious sauce (heat gently and add rum to taste) for ice cream, custard or cottage puddings. For a simple icing, beat together 4 oz (125 g) cream cheese, 1 tbsp (15 mL) cream, 1 tbsp (15 mL) maple syrup and 1 tsp (5 mL) vanilla.

Maple Walnut Pie

3	eggs, lightly beaten
1/2 cup (125 mL)	brown sugar
1/4 tsp (1 mL)	salt
1 cup (250 mL)	maple syrup
1/2 tsp (2 mL)	vanilla
1 cup (250 mL)	chopped walnuts
1	unbaked 9-inch (23-cm) pie shell
1/2 cup (125 mL)	whipping cream, whipped

Mix the eggs, sugar, salt, maple syrup, vanilla and walnuts together in a medium bowl. Pour the mixture into the pie shell. Bake for 10 minutes at 450°F (230°C), then for 30 minutes at 350°F (180°C). Chill and cover with a thin layer of whipped cream.

Maple Syrup Pie

This light and delicate pie is a complete contrast to the rich maple walnut pie. Indeed, you could even omit the pie crust, put the mixture into a 1-quart (1-L) casserole and serve it as a mousse, accompanied by oatmeal cookies (see page 109) to provide a little crunch.

1 tbsp (15 mL)	unflavoured gelatine
2 tbsp (25 mL)	cold water
1/4 cup (50 mL)	milk
3/4 cup (175 mL)	maple syrup
1/4 tsp (1 mL)	salt
2	eggs, separated
1 cup (250 mL)	whipping cream
1 tsp (5 mL)	vanilla
1	baked 9-inch (23-cm) pie shell

Soak the gelatine in the cold water for about 5 minutes to soften. Heat the milk, maple syrup and salt in the top of a double boiler until warm. Add the well-beaten egg yolks slowly. Cook and stir for 5 minutes. Add the gelatine and stir until dissolved. Cool the mixture in the refrigerator until it is about room temperature.

Beat the egg whites until they are stiff and fold into the maple mixture. Whip the cream until it begins to thicken; add the vanilla and whip until the cream forms fairly stiff peaks. Add half to the maple mixture, folding it in carefully.

Pour the mixture into the pie shell and top with the remaining whipped cream. Chill thoroughly in the refrigerator, for 4 to 6 hours, before serving.

Bananes d'Erable

We made this once for twenty-five guests, hoping for a dramatic effect. As the host carried the large silver platter into the darkened room, the blue flames, flickering merrily, leapt from the bananas and raced up and down his arms. Hastily he set the tray down, whereupon the flames danced across the table. It was an unforgettable moment.

6	fairly ripe bananas
1/4 cup (50 mL)	maple syrup
1/4 cup (50 mL)	butter
1/2 tsp (2 mL)	grated nutmeg
1/2 cup (125 mL)	rum

Peel the bananas and arrange them on an oven-to-table baking dish. Sprinkle with maple syrup, dot with butter and grated nutmeg and bake at 350°F (180°C) for 20 minutes. Just before serving, pour over the warmed rum and flame. Do not serve this dessert on a flat tray. Serves 6.

Maple Syrup Fudge

One of the joys of a trip to the Gaspé, apart from the magnificent scenery and the historical resonances, is the roadside stalls that offer homebaked bread, *tarte aux bleuets* and fudge.

Always make candy with a long-handled wooden spoon, so that you don't burn yourself with the hot mixture.

2 cups (500 mL)	maple syrup
3/4 cup (175 mL)	light cream
1/4 cup (50 mL)	butter

Bring all ingredients to a boil in a large saucepan (to avoid the danger of the candy boiling over the sides) and cook, uncovered, until the candy thermometer records 234 to 239°F (112 to 115°C), or a drop forms a soft ball in cold water. Cool, without stirring, to 110°F (43°C). Beat until creamy, pour into a buttered 8-inch (2-L) square cake pan and let cool slightly. Cut into squares before the candy hardens. If the mixture doesn't set, put it in the refrigerator to harden. Makes 1 lb (500 g).

Maple Sugar Sweeties

When sugaring off, take a little of the thickest syrup into a saucer, stir in a very little fine flour, and a small bit of butter, and flavor with essence of lemon, peppermint, or ginger, as you like best; when cold, cut into little bricks about an inch in length. This makes a cheap treat for the little ones. By melting down a piece of maple sugar, and adding a bit of butter, and flavouring, you can always give them sweeties, if you think proper to allow them indulgencies of this sort.

Catharine Parr Traill
The Canadian Settler's Guide, 1854

For a modern version of this recipe, heat the maple syrup gently to 234°F (112°C) and then let it cool as above without stirring. Add a few drops of lemon essence, ginger or peppermint. Beat the candy until it is light and fluffy. Let it harden and cut into squares.

One day William made his visitors some taffy, which they ate with great delight. He boiled a small pot of syrup or molasses down till it was in a state of consistence to "sugar off", when he poured it out upon a wider surface of clean snow; and then, so soon as it was cool enough to be handled, oiling his hands with some clean fat, he manipulating it very much as a shoe or harness-maker manipulates his wax, pulling it out, folding it together, and pulling it out again. By this means the gritty feeling passed away and it became stringy, and possessed the taste and all the attributes of taffy. The Young ladies were hugely delighted with it.

John Carroll
My Boy Life, 1882

Pioneer Flavourings

Along with their hopes, their luggage and their Bibles, the pioneers usually brought with them a handy compendium for guidance in the woods, such as *Dr Chase's Recipes or Information for Everybody, an Invaluable Collection of about One Thousand Practical Recipes* for use by merchants, grocers, saloon keepers, physicians...and families generally. *Mackenzie's Five Thousand Receipts in all the Useful and Domestic Arts* is another treasure-trove of information about "Agriculture, Bees, bleaching, brewing, calico printing, carving at table..." The fourth American edition, published in 1846, sustained and informed one Huron County family, whose descendant cannot resist sharing a few of the recipes:

General's Sauce

To make this sauce properly, infuse all the following ingredients for twenty-four hours, on ashes in an earthen pot, if possible which must be very very well stopped; viz. split six shallots, a clove of garlic, two laurel leaves, thyme and basil in proportion, truffles, tarragon leaves, half an ounce of mustard seed, bruised, six small pieces of Seville orange peel, a quarter of an ounce of cloves, as much mace, half an ounce of long pepper, two ounces of salt; squeeze in a whole lemon, and add half a glass of verjuice, five spoonsful of vinegar and a pint of white wine; let it settle, and sift it very clear. This may be kept, bottled, a long time, and it will serve for all sorts of meat and fish — but it must be used in moderation.

There is a bracing, rollicking air to:

Admiral's Sauce

Chop an anchovy, capers, and seven or eight green rocamboles [a species of leek; Spanish garlic]; simmer them on the fire with a little salt, pepper, grated nutmeg, and butter rolled in flour; when ready, add a lemon squeezed.

"The People" partook of simpler fare:

Sailor's Sauce

Chop a fowl's liver with two or three shallots, and a couple of truffles or mushrooms; simmer these in a spoonful of oil, two or three spoonsful of gravy, a glass of white wine, a little salt and coarse pepper; simmer it about half an hour, and skim it very well before using.

But where did they get the truffles? Perhaps the settlers read of such unobtainable ingredients as Seville oranges or tarragon in the same wistful frame of mind with which we read of exotic fish or unimaginable cheeses in Elizabeth David.

To dress a military omelette

Make a ragout of stewed sorrel, with a little parmesan cheese rasped and mixed with bread crumbs; make two omelettes, put this ragout between, and garnish the dish round with fried bread, standing up like a paste border; which may be done by dipping the edge of each bit in whites of eggs to make them stick; pour a little melted butter over it, and strew bread crumbs and parmesan cheese as before; give colour in the oven, or with a hot shovel.

Traveller's Rabbit

It often happens, that in travelling, the materials for a rabbit may be had when there is nothing else in the house the gourmand can eat. In this case, if there is no blazer or chafing dish, an excellent substitute is formed in a moment, by two soup plates, separated from each other by pieces of a bottle-cork placed on the rim of the lower one, which should contain any kind of spirits. Put your cheese into the top one, fire the spirits with a slip of paper, and set your rabbit on the corks; it answers as well as the most expensive heater in Christendom. — Probatum est.

On reading further in this admirable work, one discovers that parsons were allowed lemon-peel, pickled cucumbers and catsup for their sauce, while nuns feasted on veal and ham, mushrooms, white wine and "a dozen of pistachio-nuts whole". Misers, as might be expected, contented themselves with chopped onions, mixed with a little vinegar.

Rice Cheesecakes

Boil 4 ounces of rice till it is tender, and then put it into a sieve to drain; mix with it 4 eggs well beaten up, half a pound of butter, half a pint of cream, 6 oz. sugar, a nutmeg grated, a glass of brandy or ratafia water. Beat them all well together, then put them into raised crusts, and bake them in a moderate oven.

Fish

The first Fish to be caught, comes in the Springtime, & is a variety of Smelt, not quite so good as that of France, although it will pass as a substitute, & one is glad enough to have it to eat. That which follows is the Flounder, & the Rivers are completely filled with it; it is no better than elsewhere, but it is at least fresh, & if it could be caught during Lent when there is nothing but salt Fish to eat, one would be only too thankful to get it. I know how much I suffered from having salt or dried Cod at every meal, which had, moreover, to be eaten with oil, because of the lack of butter. Although butter is made in the Country [Acadia] it is not good & each Settler keeps only a very small supply, preferring to use the milk.

Then comes the Gaspereau [alewife], & more than is wanted is taken as it goes up the Rivers to spawn in fresh water; it is like a Mackerel, the difference being that it is much smaller & far less palatable. The roofs of the houses, which are of wood, are covered with them, so that they may dry in the Sun.

The Shad follows, & such a quantity is caught that more than half is wasted; it is eaten fresh while it lasts, & salted for provision; each Man fills barrels with it, but these Fish are so oily that they do not always keep well in brine.... The Sturgeon, the Bass, the Eel & the Sardine are also common.

Sieur de Dièreville
Relation of the Voyage to Port Royal, 1708

One sighs on reading the Sieur de Dièreville's description of Nature's watery bounty, although he doesn't seem particularly grateful for it. It is hard to grow accustomed to fish being a luxury, a discovery quickly made when browsing through the fish section at the supermarket or visiting a fish store. Dreams of inexpensive fresh fish direct from the harbour on Maritime camping trips quickly fade, for the fishermen seem as elusive as their catch. And now we must worry about mercury, too. Never mind. These recipes are worth the risk.

Cod au Gratin

Cod brought the Basque fishermen to the Grand Banks even before Columbus. The "beef of the sea" is still a favourite dish in Newfoundland and along the St. Lawrence. One visiting professor was fed this delicacy three times in three days—twice as an appetizer and once as a main dish. He liked it so much that he now makes it for himself in Ontario.

1 lb (500 g)	cod fillets, frozen and thawed, or fresh
1 1/2 cups (375 mL)	milk
3 tbsp (45 mL)	butter
1/4 cup (50 mL)	all-purpose flour
1/2 tsp (2 mL)	salt
	Pepper
1/3 cup (75 mL)	grated old Cheddar cheese

Simmer the cod gently in the milk, being careful not to let the milk boil. Turn the fish once during this simmering period. When the fish is cooked enough to flake, after about 15 minutes, remove it from the milk, saving the liquid. Flake the fish, carefully removing all the bones, and then place the fish flakes in the bottom of a buttered 2-quart (2-L) casserole.

To make the sauce, melt the butter in a saucepan, blend in the flour, salt and pepper and gradually add the reserved milk. Stir and cook until the sauce is thick enough to coat the back of a spoon. Spread the sauce evenly over the fish in the casserole. Cover with grated cheese and bake at 350°F (180°C) for 15 minutes. Broil for a minute or two until the cheese is browned. Serves 6.

Our source swears that her grandfather was not teasing when he told this story. Apparently, during the Depression, as part of a government program to assist farmers, salt cod was sent to the Prairies. The farmers considered it inedible and used the cod like shingles to patch the roof.

Baked Whitefish

1/2 cup (125 mL)	finely chopped onion
2 tbsp (25 mL)	butter
5	mushrooms, sliced
3/4 cup (175 mL)	breadcrumbs
1 tbsp (15 mL)	chopped fresh parsley
	Salt and pepper
1	whole whitefish—about 2 lb (1 kg)

Cook the onion in the butter. When it begins to become translucent, add the sliced mushrooms and cook 3 minutes longer. Remove from the heat and add the breadcrumbs and seasonings.

Rinse the fish with cold water and check to see that the cavity is thoroughly clean. Pat it dry with a paper towel. Leave on the head since it helps retain moisture in the fish during baking.

Fill the cavity with dressing; then sew the two sides together. Place the fish on a broad, ovenproof platter. Bake, uncovered, at 350°F (180°C) for 45 minutes, basting the fish from time to time with a mixture of half melted butter and half hot water. Serves 3 to 4.

It is difficult to convey to an outsider the charm of the word "whitefish". Any northerner will tell you that it is the only fish that is perfect human food, the only food that man or dog never wearies of, the only lake food that conveys no disorder no matter how long or freely it is used.... It would be hard to imagine a less imaginative name than "white" fish for such a shining, burning opalescence. Indian names are usually descriptive, but their name for this is simply "The Fish".

Ernest Thompson Seton
The Arctic Prairies, 1911

We have had a great many whitefish. They are caught here from October till April. In summer they go into deeper water; they are most exquisitely good & we all think them better than any other fresh or salt water fish, they are so rich that sauce is seldom eaten with them, but it is a richness that never tires it is of so delicate a kind. They are usually boiled, or set before the fire in a pan with a few Spoonfuls of water & an anchovy which is a very good way of dressing them.

Elizabeth Simcoe
Diary, 1792-96

Seafood Salad

For a cheerful light dinner, easy to prepare and consume, this seafood casserole is definitely right: hot, crunchy and tasty. There is no need to do more than serve it with crusty rolls and a tossed green salad.

1	medium green pepper, finely chopped
1	medium onion, finely chopped
3	stalks celery, finely chopped
1	6 1/2-oz (184-g) can crab, flaked
1/2 cup (125 mL)	frozen shrimp, thawed
1/2 tsp (2 mL)	salt
	Pepper
1 tsp (5 mL)	Worcestershire sauce
1 cup (250 mL)	mayonnaise
1 cup (250 mL)	breadcrumbs
3 tbsp (45 mL)	melted butter

Mix together the vegetables, crab, shrimp, seasonings and mayonnaise and put in a buttered 12 × 8-inch (3-L) casserole. Combine the breadcrumbs and melted butter and spread evenly over the top of the casserole. Bake at 350°F (180°C) for 30 minutes. Serves 6.

Herring Soup

Take eight gallons of water, and mix it with five pounds of barley-meal. Boil it to the consistence of a thick jelly. Season it with salt, pepper, vinegar, sweet herbs, and to give it a gratifying flavour, add the meat of four red herrings pounded.

Mackenzie's Five Thousand Receipts, 1846

Fish Chowder

This is a good basic chowder, to which, feeling frisky, we once added small whole mushrooms, leftover green peas, sliced frozen okra and Creole seasoning. If we'd had any shrimp, we would have added them, too.

1 lb (500 g)	fish fillets, fresh or frozen and thawed
2 tbsp (25 mL)	butter
1/4 cup (50 mL)	finely chopped onion
1 cup (250 mL)	finely chopped carrots
1/4 cup (50 mL)	finely chopped celery
1/4 cup (50 mL)	all-purpose flour
1/2 tsp (2 mL)	salt
	Pepper
pinch	paprika
2 cups (500 mL)	chicken stock
3 cups (750 mL)	milk

Cut the fish into 1-inch (2.5-cm) cubes. In a large saucepan, melt the butter, and cook the onion, carrots and celery until the onion is translucent. Blend in the flour, salt, pepper and paprika. Gradually add the stock and milk. Cook, stirring constantly, until the sauce thickens, but do not let it boil. Add the fish and simmer until the fish flakes easily with a fork — about 5 minutes if the fish is fresh and 10 minutes if it is frozen. Serve with a Caesar salad and crusty rolls. Serves 5 to 6.

Shrimp Rémoulade

While others fantasize about the Turks and Caicos Islands becoming our tropical province, we vote for somehow getting hold of New Orleans once more. After all, it was founded by one of Quebec's famous d'Iberville brothers, Jean-Baptiste Le Moyne, and the Cajun culture stems from those Acadians who landed in the bayous after the Expulsion.

1/4 cup (50 mL)	olive oil
2 tbsp (25 mL)	lemon juice
1	small onion, finely chopped
1/4 cup (50 mL)	chili sauce
2 tsp (10 mL)	Dijon mustard
1 tbsp (15 mL)	horseradish
1/2 cup (125 mL)	shrimp, fresh or frozen and thawed

Mix all the ingredients except the shrimp in a small bowl. Add the shrimp and chill in the refrigerator for about 4 hours. Serve the shrimp with the marinade in small bowls as an appetizer, on a bed of lettuce or, sloppily but deliciously, on crackers. Serves 4 as an appetizer.

The bass is an excellent fish — firm, white and sweet at table, and very lively on the hook; leaping out of the water like a salmon. They are good either boiled or fried — at breakfast or dinner, and make an admirable curry. During our stay on the shores of Lake Ontario, I caught some thousands of them, and ate them constantly without satiety.

Surgeon Henry
Trifles, ca. 1831-33

Bass

Inland Canadians may often think mournfully of the august luxuries that coastal Canadians receive from the oceans, but there are small treasures lurking in little lakes, too, and fresh bass are among them. They may be caught by fishing with bamboo poles from a dock, the line armed with a hook and the hook baited with a worm, or with much more complicated casting equipment. Usually the best results for amateurs occur early in the season and early in the evening.

After you have caught your fish, clean it. The head must be removed, and the insides. Then, slowly and carefully, remove the skin. Wash the fish carefully, salt lightly and refrigerate overnight if you are serving it for breakfast. In the morning, lightly flour the fish and cook it in lots of butter, about 5 to 7 minutes on each side, depending on the thickness of the fish.

Serve at once with buttered toast — it makes a memorable breakfast. (Some will argue that brook trout, dealt with in the same way, are superior.)

Eating Fish

Here is how I eat a fish
— Boiled, baked or fried —
Separate him in the dish,
Put his bones aside.

Lemon juice and chive enough
Just to give him grace,
Make of his peculiar stuff
My peculiar race.

Through the Travellers' Hotel
From the sizzling pan
Comes the ancient fishy smell
Permeating man.

May he be a cannier chap
Altered into me
Eye the squirming hook, and trap,
Choose the squirming sea.

George Johnston

Spring Break

Airports may sincerely believe that all Canadian schoolchildren fly south during the March break, but it simply isn't true. The remaining hordes are visiting overcrowded zoos and museums, and on rainy-sleety-snowy days (who knows what form bad weather will take in March?) are drumming their heels with impatience. So it's prudent to have a few in-house activities arranged.

Stained-Glass Windows

An old-fashioned English idea that produces something edible and charming.

Ingredients:

Pastry: Use either the scraps left over from making a pie, or make enough for one pie crust. (This will be enough to amuse several children.)

Hard candy: The English call this boiled sweets. They are like our Lifesavers, only larger, and they must be of various colours. (If you use Lifesavers, you will spend much of your time peeling off the foil, and it will be very expensive.)

Line a cookie sheet with aluminium foil; then grease the foil with butter. Wrap about half a dozen candies of every colour, each colour in its own waxed paper. Weigh down on each one with a rolling pin, or hammer gently with a small hammer, and crush into fragments.

Roll out the pastry so that it can be cut into strips. First cut strips about 1/2 inch (1.5 cm) thick and place on the foil, shaping into the outline of a Gothic window, about 3 inches (8 cm) wide and 6 inches (15 cm) high. Press the joints together securely, adding a drop of water to help the pieces stick together. Next make a simple criss-cross pattern within the outline, using pieces of pastry about 1/4 inch (5 mm) wide. (Small hands may prefer to settle for wider

diameters.) Attach these pieces to the window frame, again using a drop of water to help the pastry stick together. Press the edges firmly together where they cross within the frame.

Carefully pour a thin layer of candy fragments into each window pane, arranging colours so that they will make attractive contrasts. Break up more candies if necessary.

Bake at 400°F (200°C) for 10 to 12 minutes, or until the candy melts and bubbles and the pastry is golden-brown.

Let cool completely, and then remove the aluminium foil. The stained-glass windows will look surprisingly pretty; almost, but not quite, too good to eat.

Easter Eggs

Easter is sure to be lurking somewhere in the vicinity of spring break, so colouring and decorating eggs is an appropriate activity. This may be a simple or complicated endeavour, depending on the age, patience and artistic enthusiasm of the people involved.

At the simplest level, clean white eggs are boiled in water containing 3 tbsp (45 mL) vinegar and 1 tsp (5 mL) food colouring to each 2 cups (500 mL) water. When they are hard-boiled, the eggs must be removed from the coloured water and chilled. They are then ready for further decoration: watercolours or markers can be used to make geometric patterns or funny faces. Coloured sticky paper can be cut in appropriate shapes, yarn attached initially with a little glue and wound around the egg, and much else.

For more elaborate decorations, it is best to evacuate the contents from the egg. This is time-consuming and messy, but worthwhile for serious decorators. (Use the contents for scrambled eggs.)

With a darning needle, make a small hole in the pointed end of the egg and a larger one at the wide end. Blow gently through the smaller end, and eventually the contents of the egg will be evacuated through the larger end.

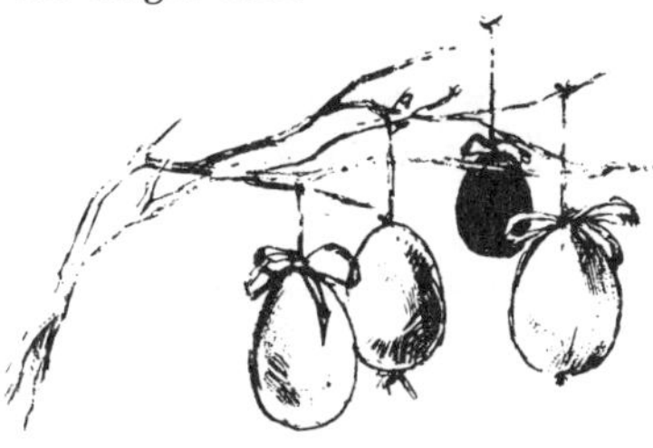

The emptied eggs are, of course, lighter, and can be used to decorate an Easter tree — a reasonably shaped bare branch planted in any kind of large pot. Hang the light, decorated eggs with pieces of coloured yarn knotted at one end and threaded through the holes. You can spray the eggs with varnish or shellac if you like, but they will last without being treated. This festive arrangement might enlarge with the years and ages of children, beginning with a very small branch and few eggs. The best eggs could be saved to make possible a larger branch the following year, and so on. Up to a point.

Peppermints

St. Patrick's Day frequently coincides with spring break. Children will enjoy making these gentle candies, though not all children will enjoy the flavour.

1 1/2 cups (375 mL)	granulated sugar
1/2 cup (125 mL)	boiling water
6	drops peppermint flavouring
	Green food colouring

Put the sugar and water in a large saucepan and stir with a wooden spoon until the sugar dissolves. Boil the mixture until the syrup forms a hard ball in cold water, or it reaches 250 to 260°F (121 to 130°C) on a candy thermometer. Add the peppermint and food colouring and beat until creamy. Drop by spoonfuls onto waxed paper and cool.

Scented Geraniums

No kitchen window sill is complete without at least one scented geranium to supply both fragrance and flavour. The flower is insignificant, but the plant flourishes under most circumstances and roots readily, so beg a cutting from a friend.

In the summer, this easy-going plant moves happily outdoors, but you must bring it in for the winter. To release the scent, rub a leaf with your fingers. Instant smelling salts.

There are many varieties. The most common are rose, lemon, peppermint and apple. Coconut and pine are harder to come by. The leaves can be used for pot-pourri, to scent drawers or bath water, or for tea. Add them to stews and gravies in place of bay leaves, or to lemonade, punch or rice puddings.

Geranium Custard

The flavour of this custard is so refined that it almost seems necessary to be adorned with lavender and old lace while eating it.

3	eggs
1/4 cup (50 mL)	granulated sugar
1/4 tsp (1 mL)	salt
2 cups (500 mL)	milk
1 tsp (5 mL)	vanilla
1 or 2	geranium leaves

Beat the eggs in a large bowl and combine with the sugar and salt. In a small saucepan, heat the milk until small bubbles begin to form around the edge of the pan, but do not let it boil. Stir the milk into the egg mixture with the vanilla. Place a small piece of geranium leaf in the bottom of each of six custard cups and pour in the custard. Set the cups in a shallow pan filled with 1 inch (2.5 cm) hot water. Bake at 325°F (160°C) for about 1 hour, or until a knife inserted in the custard comes out clean. Serve warm or cold, with warm maple syrup on top (add rum to taste). Serves 6.

Geranium Cream:
Put a geranium leaf in 1 cup (250 mL) whipping cream and let it stand in the refrigerator for several hours. Remove the leaf, then whip the cream as usual, but omit the vanilla.

Wild Grape Jelly and Rose Geranium Bars

Children may groan, "not leaves in the cake again," but scented geranium adds a delicate and unmistakable essence to baking. (Just place a leaf in the bottom of the pan. If you chop it up, it's too hard to remove later.) The young leaves have the strongest flavour.

1/2 cup (125 mL)	granulated sugar
1/2 cup (125 mL)	shortening
1	egg, beaten
1 tsp (5 mL)	vanilla, preferably Viennese vanilla (see page 85)
1 1/2 cups (375 mL)	all-purpose flour
1 tsp (5 mL)	baking powder
3/4 tsp (4 mL)	cinnamon
1/4 tsp (1 mL)	ground cloves
1/2 tsp (2 mL)	salt
2	rose- or lemon-scented geranium leaves
1/2 cup (125 mL)	wild grape or apple jelly
	Icing sugar

Cream the sugar and shortening together in a medium bowl. Add the egg and vanilla. Add the sifted dry ingredients and blend well. Place the geranium leaves in the bottom of an 8-inch (2-L) square pan and cover with half the dough. Spread generously with the jelly and pat the remainder of the dough on top. Bake at 400°F (200°C) for 30 minutes. Let cool a bit before cutting into squares. Sprinkle lightly with sifted icing sugar. Makes about 2 dozen.

Use a sifter for icing sugar. This gets rid of lumps and also produces an attractive snowy effect.

Easter Pie

The bill of fare consisted of some excellent soup [in those days soup was a matter of course, for dinner as well as for supper], a cold pie, called an Easter pie, and served, on account of its immense size, on a board covered with a napkin or small white cloth, according to its proportions. This pie, that Brillat-Savarin might have envied, was composed of a turkey, two chickens, two partridges, two pigeons, the back and thighs of two hares, the whole covered with slices of fat bacon. The force-meat on a soft thick bed, on which these gastronomic treasures lay, and which also covered the upper part, was made from the two hams of [pig].... Large onions interspersed, and spices, completed the dish. But a very important part was the cooking, which was the more difficult as, if the monster burst, it lost fifty per cent of its attractiveness. To prevent so deplorable an event, the under-crust, which also covered about three inches in depth of the culinary monster's sides, was not less than an inch thick. This crust, impregnated with the gravy from all these meats, was a delicious part of this unique dish.

Aubert de Gaspé
Les anciens Canadiens, 1863

Chives

Strewing herbs, much used in the Middle Ages, were not a quaint custom but a necessity in an age where bones were flung on the floor for the dogs and vile smells were everywhere. Thomas Tusser lists 21 "Strowing Herbes", including "Cousleps and paggles[?], Daisies of all sorts, Tanzies and Winter saverie". He suggests "Herbes, Branches and Flowers" for windows and pots, too, including "Daffadowndillies, Holiokes, Larkes foot and Lillium cum valium" — a particularly tranquil flower.

Soon after Easter, with any luck, you will find the first batch of chives in the garden. You can grow them indoors (see page 174), but they will not compare in flavour with the outdoor ones. A kind of culinary strewing herb, this gentle relation of the onion — in Old French, *petit poireau* — has been used for centuries all over the world. The Chinese knew of its benefits as far back as 3000 B.C. It is reputed to be good for much of what ails you, including indigestion and high blood pressure. Chives add spirit to baked potatoes topped with sour cream, to scrambled eggs and omelettes, or to soups and salads. The small purplish flowers can also be used, although we never feel inclined to do so. They have the same taste as the green part.

Chive Spread

This is good in sandwiches or on crackers. It also makes a spirited dip for raw broccoli and cauliflower. For an unusual if untidy hors d'oeuvre, put a spoonful on a lettuce leaf and wrap it up.

1 1/2 cups (375 mL)	coarsely chopped chives
8 oz (250 g)	cream cheese, cut in pieces
2/3 cup (150 mL)	mayonnaise

Combine all ingredients in a blender or food processor and blend until smooth. Refrigerate. Makes about 2 1/2 cups (625 mL).

Mayonnaise

Use this in the chive spread, or anywhere else that a good basic mayonnaise is required.

1 tsp (5 mL)	salt
1 tsp (5 mL)	dry mustard
1 tsp (5 mL)	granulated sugar
2 tbsp (25 mL)	white vinegar
1	large egg or 2 egg yolks
1 1/2 cups (375 mL)	vegetable oil
1 tbsp (15 mL)	fresh lemon juice

Combine the salt, mustard, sugar and vinegar, stirring until smooth. Add the egg and beat well. Add the vegetable oil slowly, about 1/4 cup (50 mL) at a time, beating each instalment thoroughly. Repeat until all the vegetable oil has been added. Do not hurry this business of adding the oil, or the mixture will separate. The mayonnaise should be thick enough to hold its shape. If the mixture does separate, beat another egg in a separate bowl. Begin to add the unsatisfactory mayonnaise to it, very slowly, beating after each 1/4 cup (50 mL), until thoroughly smooth.

Stir in the lemon juice before storing the mayonnaise in a covered jar in the refrigerator. Makes about 1 3/4 cups (425 mL).

For a quick and unusual grilled cheese sandwich, top two slices of bread with whatever cheese is on hand (Cheddar never fails) or cheese spread. Spread the outer sides of the bread generously with lemon chive butter. Cook gently in a frying pan until golden-brown.

Lemon Chive Butter

This useful butter adds flavour to most vegetables, fish and steak.

1/4 cup (50 mL)	butter, softened
1/2 tsp (2 mL)	grated lemon rind
3/4 tsp (4 mL)	lemon juice
1/4 tsp (1 mL)	freshly ground pepper
2 tbsp (25 mL)	finely chopped chives
1 tsp (5 mL)	finely chopped parsley

Cream the butter in a small bowl, add the other ingredients and mix well. Dot the butter on fish to be baked in oven. Allow no more than 1 tbsp (15 mL) per serving.

To use on steak, add 1/2 tsp (2 mL) dry mustard to the mix. Just before serving the steak, dot with small bits of the savoury butter. Makes about 1/4 cup (50 mL).

Chive and Cream Cheese Sandwiches:
Try cream cheese and ham on brown bread with a generous helping of snipped chives and cress. Another bracing mixture is liverwurst and goat cheese with chives and cress.

For tea parties (if such events still exist), spread cream cheese on thinly sliced white bread. Place a mandarin orange slice in the middle and arrange the chives so that they look like flower petals.

Pommes Canadiennes

8	medium to large potatoes
1/2 cup (125 mL)	lemon chive butter (see page 151)
2 tbsp (25 mL)	chopped fresh parsley
	Pepper

Bring a large pot of salted water to a rolling boil. Peel the potatoes and scoop out little balls with a melon-baller. You will have a fair bit of waste potato. (Boil the scraps and make mashed potatoes for the freezer.) Drop the balls into the water and parboil for 5 minutes.

Melt the butter in a large cast-iron frying pan. Do not let it brown. Drain the potatoes well and add them to the pan. Turn them over until they are well coated with butter, then cover and cook over high heat for 15 minutes. Be sure to keep shaking them. They should become crisp and golden-brown. Sprinkle with chopped parsley or more chives. Very good with chicken. Serves 6.

Ham and Chive Casserole

3	small potatoes, thinly sliced — about 2 cups (500 mL)
1	medium onion, finely chopped
1 cup (250 mL)	grated Cheddar cheese
1/2 cup (125 mL)	chopped chives
	Pepper
1	slice ham, 1/2 inch (2 cm) thick — about 1 lb (500 g)
1 1/2 cups (375 mL)	canned stewed tomatoes

Spread the thinly sliced potatoes over the bottom of a 1 1/2-quart (1.5-L) buttered casserole. Sprinkle with the chopped onion and half the cheese. Sprinkle half the chives and the pepper. Cover with the ham slice. Spread the stewed tomatoes over the ham. Top with the remaining chives and remaining cheese. Bake at 350°F (180°C) for 1 hour. Serves 4.

Baked Eggs

A nursery or invalid dish, too often overlooked. It is simple and delicious.

2	mushrooms
1 tbsp (15 mL)	chopped chives
1	egg
	Salt and pepper
1 tbsp (15 mL)	milk or cream
1/4 tsp (1 mL)	butter

Slice the mushrooms into a custard cup. Sprinkle in the chives and break the egg on top. Season with salt and pepper and top with the milk or cream. Dot with butter and bake at 350°F (180°C) for 15 to 20 minutes, or until the egg has set. Serves 1.

Spring Greens

The great advantage of cooking with dandelions, violets and chives is that there is no shortage of supply — they can be used without compunction. One hesitates with the rarer plants. There *are* recipes for wild ginger and wild leeks, but you will not find them here.

Once people discover the gentle pastime of cooking off the land with leaves and flowers, they become, to put it politely, enthusiasts. How else is one to understand the inevitable recipe for elderflower fritters, a ghastly greenish mess that one family still remembers all too vividly. (Elderflower wine, on the other hand, has much to recommend it.) Beware, too, of airy remarks that tansy may taste a trifle bitter until you get used to it. Some flavours such as scented geranium and nasturtium are truly a delight. For others, the old phrase "a mess of greens" is all too apt.

There are other risks. Most people are wary of deadly nightshade, but foxglove can be injurious to your health, please don't eat the daffodils, and brewing up a relaxing cup of fool's parsley will cause paralysis and asphyxiation. Be very sure that you know what you are eating.

the Dandelion is frowsy & raggedy
his blossom is yellow, his leaf is jaggedy
his name implies you may well keep distant
but he isn't fierce, though he is insistent
his greens are edible & from the flower
you may brew some wine if you like it sour

Phyllis Gottlieb

Dandelion Greens

Dandelion greens, if they are to be used for a salad, should be gathered early, certainly before the plants bloom and probably by the beginning of May. They taste a bit like endive, and their numbers are legion, although you should take care not to gather them from areas that have been sprayed with poison.

The back lawn is a good place to begin. It is probably easiest to remove the whole plant with a dandelion digger, shake it free of soil, wash carefully and then snip off the leaves. It is a pesky business, for bits of dead grass must be removed. The dandelion greens will stay fresh longer if you gather the whole plant, but real enthusiasts who want to dig up the roots in the fall to make dandelion coffee (see page 164) will gather individual and youthful leaves, the "jaggedy" ones, as Phyllis Gottlieb puts it — a time-consuming occupation.

Dandelion Salad

4 cups (1 L)	lightly packed young dandelion leaves
3	slices bacon
1	small onion, finely chopped
1 tsp (5 mL)	brown sugar
1 tbsp (15 mL)	white vinegar
2 tbsp (25 mL)	unflavoured yogurt or sour cream
1/4 tsp (1 mL)	pepper

Wash the dandelion leaves carefully and let them drain. Place in a bowl.

Cook the bacon slices in a frying pan until they are thoroughly cooked. Remove them from the pan and drain on a paper towel. In the bacon fat, briefly cook the onion. Add the brown sugar and stir until dissolved. Remove from the heat and add the vinegar. Let cool for about 10 minutes, then add the yogurt and stir. The dressing should be about room temperature.

Sprinkle crumbled bacon over the leaves and grind pepper on top. Add the dressing and mix carefully. Serves 4 as a side salad.

For those who like very little to come between them and the taste of fresh spring greens, a simpler dressing may be preferred:

4 tsp (20 mL)	fresh lemon juice
2 tbsp (25 mL)	olive oil
	Salt and pepper

Mix all together and add to the dandelion leaves. Then toss.

Spring Spinach: After carefully washing your spinach, add clea dandelion and violet le to taste, along with cho chives, salt and pepper a sprig of fresh rosema two, or 3/4 tsp (4 mL) dried rosemary and a generous lump of butte Cook gently in a cover pot until the spinach is wilted.

Try the dandelion greens au gratin, in place of celery in potato salad, in omelettes and scrambled eggs and in soup. The season passes all too quickly, so make the most of them.

Dandelion buds cooked in butter are reputed to taste like mushrooms, but we could not bring ourselves to test this theory. People also suggest tossing them in the salad.

Before Mrs. Simmons left, she explained and showed how to secure and dry dandelion roots to make coffee. In lifting potatoes, when a dandelion root is seen, it is pulled carefully, or, if scarce among potatoes, dug up carefully in the fall so as to get the entire root. The roots are washed, dried in the sun and stored away. As wanted for use, a root or so is chopped small, roasted in a pan until crisp, then ground and made like ordinary coffee.

Robert Sellar
True makers of Canada: the narrative of Gordon Sellar, who emigrated to Canada in 1825, 1915

Violets

The excellence of the violet is as the excellence of El Islam above all other religions. (Old Eastern proverb)

The Persians and the Romans enjoyed violet wine. In the Middle Ages, violet garlands were strewn on the floor to discourage fleas.

The Tudors and Stuarts made conserves from them. "Violet Leaves, at the entrance of spring fried brownish and eaten with Orange and Lemon Juice and Sugar is one of the most agreeable of all the herbaceous dishes," wrote John Evelyn in 1699.

Modern tastes may find "cooking with violence" (as a neighbour thought he heard us say) better restricted to less exotic dishes. The young leaves make a useful addition to a green salad. The flowers can be added for colour if you wish. They are edible. Some would have you make soufflés, jams and ice cream out of the petals, but on the whole, we prefer looking at them in what used to be the lawn.

Violet Vinegar

This has a delicate colour and flavour and is good mixed with mayonnaise for salads and fish dishes.

Fill a small jar with violet petals. Pour over white vinegar, cover and let it sit on a sunny shelf for 2 weeks. Strain.

Crystallized Violets

One of us, feeling like a murderer, sacrificed the first few violets of spring to try this and the results were a sticky mess.

It's best to be neat-handed for this "simple" recipe, but the resulting floral sweet is surprisingly good. You can do it with roses, too.

Wash and dry your violets carefully, removing the stems and green, but keeping the flower intact. Stir an egg white with a fork and dip the flower in, covering it completely. Or you can paint it with a small paint-brush. Then sprinkle the flower with fruit sugar. Repeat. Put the flower on a tray covered with waxed paper and dry it in the sun, in a warm dry spot or in a 150°F (65°C) oven for 15 minutes, or until hardened. Store them in an airtight container between layers of waxed paper and use for decorations. The crystallized flowers should keep for months.

Sorrel

This is a vigorous perennial herb that is ready to use in May. It looks a little like spinach, but has a very acid taste. Indeed, on first tasting it, you may well wonder whether the best thing to be done with it is to dig the plant under. Do not yield to this impulse, but gather a couple of handfuls of leaves to use in soups and sauces.

Sorrel Soup

You will probably want to make this bright and lively soup more than once in the spring. Make sure you keep the seed stalks cut off so that the sorrel leaves will remain tender.

2 cups (500 mL)	sorrel leaves
2 tbsp (25 mL)	butter
1/2 cup (125 mL)	chopped onions or chives
4 cups (1 L)	chicken stock
2	egg yolks
1/2 cup (125 mL)	whipping cream
	Salt and pepper

Wash the sorrel leaves, drain them, cut off the tough stalks and discard, and slice the leaves into strips or chop roughly.

Heat the butter in a large pot. Cook the onions until translucent (if using chives, cook them for 1 minute). Add the sorrel, cover the dish and simmer for 3 minutes, or until tender. Add the chicken stock and simmer for 10 minutes.

Beat the egg yolks, add the whipping cream and mix well. Add a little of the hot soup gradually to the egg-cream mixture so that it does not curdle; continue adding soup slowly until about 1 cup (250 mL) has been added. At this point the egg-cream mixture can all be added back to the soup. Add salt and pepper to taste. Heat, but do not boil, and serve. Serves 6.

To make a flavourful sorrel spread, omit the cream from the sorrel sauce. Let the cooked sorrel leaves cool, and then to 2 tbsp (25 mL) leaves add 2 tbsp (25 mL) cottage cheese and 1 tbsp (15 mL) mayonnaise. Use as a spread for open-faced sandwiches, which can then be topped by thin slices of cheese or ham.

Sorrel Sauce

This sauce is admirable with fish, particularly those of an oily nature, such as whitefish, mackerel, bass, trout or tuna.

2 cups (500 mL)	tightly packed sorrel leaves — about 8 oz (250 g)
2 tbsp (25 mL)	butter
	Salt
2 tbsp (25 mL)	whipping cream

Wash and drain the sorrel, then cut off the tough stalks and discard. Chop the leaves coarsely. Melt the butter in a heavy pot and add the sorrel. Cover and cook over low heat for 3 to 5 minutes, or until tender. Add salt to taste and the cream. Heat gently for 2 minutes, stirring until it is well mixed. Makes 3/4 cup (175 mL).

We were out six days and nights, with very little provision, living chiefly on the scrapings of the inner bark of trees and wild roots, particularly onions, which grow in great abundance, and are not disagreeable to the palate. Hunger reconciles us to every thing that will support nature, and makes the most indifferent food acceptable. From my own woful experience I can assert, that what at any other time would have been unpleasant and even nauseous, under the pressure of hunger is not only greedily eaten, but relished as a luxury.

John Long
Voyages and Travels, 1768-88

Various less well-known weeds can be rooted out and eaten as free greens in the spring when lettuce tends to appear at prices that would make a highwayman blush, again with the proviso that you are armed with a guidebook to be sure of what you are eating, and that you can face such remarks as: "Socrates drank hemlock and look what happened to him."

Lamb's quarters *(Chenopodium album)*, called pre-historic spinach by one writer, is also known ingloriously as pigweed, white goosefoot or fat hen. It is not eaten much nowadays, although it has been handy in times of famine and was consumed in Europe during the Second World War. Mrs. Traill knew it, and no doubt it will soon be rediscovered and sold in gourmet stores.

There are several species of spinach, one known here by the name of lamb's quarter, that grows in great profusion about our garden, and in rich soil rises to two feet, and is very luxuriant in its foliage; the leaves are covered with a white rough powder. The top shoots and tender parts of this vegetable are boiled with pork, and, in place of a more delicate pot-herb, is very useful.

Catharine Parr Traill
The Backwoods of Canada, 1854

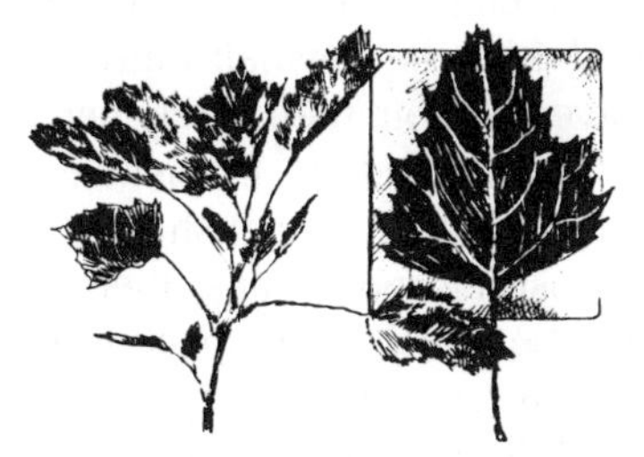

Garlic mustard *(Alliaria petiolata)*, otherwise known as sauce-all-alone, poor man's mustard or jack-by-the-hedge, can be added to a white sauce for fish, or used in salads and cooked greens.

Samphire

Word of fiddleheads has escaped the Maritimes, but not of that remarkable treat, "Sandfire Greens." (Samphire also grows in the marshes of Norfolk. Bright green and smelling of the sea, it is sold in the fish stalls of the Cambridge market.)

Eighteenth-century settlers in Moncton, New Brunswick, survived "mostly on Herbs which they gathered in the Marsh in the Spring &c." (samphire, goose tongue greens and cow cabbage). Should you be in the Maritimes in spring and find some of these delectable greens, cut off the roots and wash well, then cook them for about 10 minutes in slightly salted water. Drain and serve with plenty of melted butter. The mound of green branches may make guests apprehensive, but once they have tasted the samphire, they won't care how it is eaten. What does it taste like? It hints at asparagus that has gone to sea, but really has a unique flavour all its own.

Fiddleheads, incidentally, are not restricted to the Maritimes. In *A Taste of the Wild,* Blanche Pownall Garrett describes them as "unopened ferns, harvested from their blackened roots in the marsh while they are still all wrapped up in themselves in tight green circles." This sounded familiar. We rushed out and hungrily inspected our feathery ostrich ferns. Alas, there weren't enough of them, so we let them be and cannot speak from experience. The bracken fern and ostrich fern are also reputed to be edible during the short two-week fiddlehead season between mid-May and late June, depending on where one lives. Mrs. Garrett advises cooking the buttons in boiling salted water for about 10 minutes, and serving them with Hollandaise sauce or with wild onions in a salad.

Asparagus

Ragout of asparagus
Scrape one hundred of grass clean; put them into cold water; cut them as far as is good and green, chop small two heads of endive, a young lettuce, and an onion. Put a quarter of a pound of butter into the stew pan, and when it is melted, put in the grass with the other articles. Shake them well, and when they have stewed ten minutes, season them with a little pepper and salt; strew in a little flour, shake them about, and then pour in half a pint of gravy. Stew the whole till the sauce is very good and thick, and then pour all into the dish. Garnish with a few of the small tops of the grass.

Mackenzie's Five Thousand Receipts, 1846

In May come the fleeting pleasures of asparagus. Don't be tempted by the imported bundles sold early in the supermarket. They will be both expensive and tasteless. Wait for the first delicate spears grown locally.

Modern tastes prefer smaller amounts and a simpler treatment than that suggested by Mackenzie. One of the best ways is to serve the cooked asparagus by itself as a first course, with bowls of melted butter. Take a spear in your fingers, dip it in the butter and eat. Messy, but delightful.

Try it, too, with Hollandaise sauce.

Asparagus au Gratin

2	bunches asparagus — about 1 lb (500 g)
3/4 cup (175 mL)	mayonnaise
1	small clove garlic, minced
1/4 cup (50 mL)	freshly grated Parmesan cheese
	Pepper

Cut the tough ends off the asparagus stalks. Peel the stems partway up with a vegetable peeler, if you wish.

The best way to cook asparagus is to steam it so that the stalks stand vertically, with the tender shoots at the top. A Pyrex coffee percolator is useful for this purpose. The asparagus will need about 10 minutes.

Remove the stalks when tender and place them on an ovenproof platter that has been generously spread with butter.

Mix the mayonnaise, garlic, cheese and pepper, then spread on top of the cooked asparagus.

Place under a preheated broiler for about 2 minutes, or until the topping is thoroughly brown. Serve at once. Makes 4 to 5 servings.

Asparagus Omelette

5	thin asparagus stalks
2	eggs
2 tbsp (25 mL)	water
	Salt and pepper
dash	Tabasco sauce
1 tbsp (15 mL)	butter
1	green onion, chopped
2 tbsp (25 mL)	sour cream

Steam the asparagus and drain, keeping it warm in a small dish. Break the eggs into a small bowl and add water, salt, pepper and Tabasco sauce. Beat with a fork or a whisk (never an electric beater, because it is too energetic) for 30 seconds.

Melt the butter in the omelette pan over a fairly high heat. Just as it stops foaming, but before it turns brown, add the eggs. Reduce the heat slightly and let cook for a few seconds until the eggs begin to set. Then tip the pan and gently lift around the edges to allow the uncooked egg to flow under the cooked part. When there is only a small amount of liquid on top, place the asparagus on half of the mixture, sprinkle with green onion, salt and pepper and top with the sour cream. Cook for a few seconds longer. The omelette should be creamy, but not liquid. Very carefully, slide a large spatula halfway under the omelette, lift and fold over into a half-moon shape. Slide the omelette gently off the pan onto a plate and serve at once with toast, a green salad and a glass of white wine. Serves 1.

Omelettes are as infinite as Cleopatra in their variety, and entire books are written about them. You can fill them with slivers of chopped ham, all sorts of grated cheeses, finely chopped green onions or leeks, mushrooms, bacon and spinach, shrimp. We draw the line at the salami and onion ring filling we read about, but this is an area, like soup, where the possibilities are endless if you have a restless disposition in the kitchen.

If you mix all the ingredients, including the eggs, together in a bowl, pour them into the pan with heated oil to cook until partially set, then sit the pan (as far away from the heat as possible) under the broiler for 5 to 10 minutes or until set, you have a frittata.

Asparagus Tart

Another attractive lunch dish that can be served warm or cold, depending on your philosophy of quiche temperatures.

12 oz (375 g)	asparagus
1 cup (250 mL)	sour cream or unflavoured yogurt
	Salt and pepper
1	egg
4	green onions, chopped
1	unbaked 9-inch (23-cm) pie shell
1/2 cup (125 mL)	grated Cheddar cheese
2 tbsp (25 mL)	butter

Steam the asparagus for 7 minutes or until nearly tender. Let cool for about 10 minutes, then cut into 1-inch (2.5-cm) pieces. Mix the cream, salt, pepper and egg together in a small bowl. Place the onions evenly in the bottom of the pie crust. Arrange the asparagus evenly on top. Pour in the egg and cream mixture, sprinkle with cheese and dot with butter. Bake at 425°F (220°C) for 10 minutes, then at 325°F (160°C) for 20 to 30 minutes, or until a fork inserted comes out clean. Serves 6.

Asparagus and Mushrooms: A useful recipe for a small amount of asparagus. Cut the asparagus crosswise as thinly as you can. Slice an equal amount of mushrooms. Place both vegetables in a frying plan with melted lemon chive butter (see page 151), a few slices of fresh ginger and a few sprigs of chopped parsley. Cover and cook gently for about 5 minutes, or until the asparagus is tender.

Rhubarb

This is rhubarb time. Again, don't be tempted by imports; wait for it. And again, thin (but not scrawny) stalks tend to have more flavour than the thick.

The twenty-fourth of May
's the Queen's birthday,
'f you don't give us a
holiday, we'll all run away.

The most natural way to serve rhubarb at the very first of the season is stewed. Wash the stalks, then cut them in 1-inch (2.5-cm) pieces. Put them in a saucepan with a little water — just enough to cover the bottom of the pan. Bring to a boil and reduce the temperature so that the rhubarb simmers very slowly. Cook it until tender and let it cool a little. Then add sugar to taste.

Remember never to use rhubarb leaves, which contain oxalic acid and are poisonous.

Later in the season, when fresh strawberries are just beginning to be available but are still rather pricey, add a few fresh berries to the rhubarb at the same time that you are adding the sugar.

Rhubarb Relish

This fresh and agreeable relish is a good accompaniment to a wide range of meat dishes.

8 cups (2 L)	fresh rhubarb, cut in 1/2-inch (2-cm) pieces
1 cup (250 mL)	chopped onions
1 cup (250 mL)	white vinegar
2 1/2 cups (625 mL)	granulated sugar
1/2 tsp (2 mL)	ground ginger
1 tsp (5 mL)	cinnamon
1/2 tsp (2 mL)	ground cloves
1 tbsp (15 mL)	pickling salt

Combine all the ingredients in a large pot. Bring to a boil and simmer for 40 to 60 minutes, stirring more frequently as the mixture thickens, until it is as thick as applesauce. Pour into hot sterilized jars and seal. Makes about 6 cups (1.5 L).

Rhubarb Tapioca

Tapioca has had a bad press for the past generation or so, perhaps because it was a component in too many boarding school puddings. Sentiment does seem to be changing, and this pudding, combining as it does the bright and thrusting rhubarb with milder-mannered tapioca, should give it a push in the right direction.

3 1/2 cups (875 mL)	rhubarb, cut in 1-inch (2.5-cm) pieces
1 cup (250 mL)	granulated sugar
1/3 cup (75 mL)	quick-cooking tapioca
2 cups (500 mL)	boiling water
pinch	salt

Put the rhubarb in a buttered 2-quart (2-L) casserole. Sprinkle 3/4 cup (175 mL) sugar over the top. Cover and bake at 350°F (180°C) for 15 minutes.

While the rhubarb is baking, combine the tapioca and water in the top of a double boiler, cooking and stirring for about 15 minutes, or until the tapioca is transparent. Add the remaining sugar and salt and stir until dissolved. Pour the tapioca mixture over the rhubarb. Bake, uncovered, for about 30 minutes, or until the rhubarb is tender. Served either warm or cold, accompanied by plain table cream. Serves 6.

Add rhubarb to apple crumble to pick up tired apples — and what Canadian apple is not a bit tired by the time spring arrives?

To add zest to stewed rhubarb later in the season, add a few sprigs of chopped fresh mint and a few squeezes of lemon. Or top the rhubarb with meringue and brown it in the oven (see page 112). Around strawberry social time (do these still exist?), rhubarb vanishes from the stores and markets. If you have your own in the garden, you may neglect it for a time as rival fruits appear, but it is still useful for strawberry rhubarb jam (see page 186) or blueberry rhubarb jam (see page 215).

Rhubarb Custard Pie

Rhubarb pies sing of the coming of spring, of the beginning of a new gardening season. This pie, modulated a little by egg and vanilla, sings in dulcet tones.

1 cup (250 mL)	granulated sugar
1	egg
1 tbsp (15 mL)	all-purpose flour
2 tbsp (25 mL)	butter, softened
1 tsp (5 mL)	vanilla
2 1/2 cups (625 mL)	fresh rhubarb, cut in 1/2-inch (1.5-cm) pieces
1	unbaked 9-inch (23-cm) pie shell, plus pastry for lattice top

In a large bowl, mix the sugar, egg, flour, butter and vanilla together. Stir in the rhubarb until the sugar mixture is fairly evenly distributed. Place in an unbaked pie shell and cover with a lattice of pastry. Bake at 425°F (220°C) for 10 minutes, then reduce the heat to 350°F (180°C) and continue baking for about 30 minutes, or until the rhubarb is tender and the crust is set. If the crust seems pale, turn on the broiler until it browns, watching the pie carefully. Let cool before serving.

The Cellar

Spruce Beer

It is difficult, if not impossible, to find this staple tipple of our ancestors, who, like Captain Vancouver, constantly held forth about its virtues: "...about the outskirts of the woods [near Prince William's Sound] we procured a little wild celery, and the spruce beer that was here brewed far exceeded in excellence any we had before made upon the coast" (*A Voyage of Discovery to the North Pacific Ocean and Round the World*, 1790).

Occasionally a soft drink version — also called spruce beer — can be found in Quebec supermarkets, and very good it is, too, although some have described it as tasting like soapy dishwater.

You can make it for yourself, following this recipe given in Canada's first cookbook.

No. 205. For brewing Spruce Beer.

Take four ounces of hops, boil half an hour, in one gallon water, strain it, then add sixteen gallons warm water, two gallons molasses, eight ounces essence spruce dissolved in one quart water, put it in a clean cask, shake it well together, add half pint emptins, let it stand and work one week, if very warm weather less time will do; when drawn off, add one spoonful molasses to each bottle.

The Cook Not Mad, 1831

Cowards that we are, when it comes to brewing, we have purchased not one, but two packages of spruce essence from a wine-making supply store (which come with rather more complete instructions) and given them to beer-making friends in the hope that they would be inspired to try it and give us some. No luck, so far.

Canadian Cobbler

Half fill a soda-water glass with pounded ice, and add half a small lemon sliced, a dessert-spoonful of sugar and two glasses of sherry. Mix well together and drink through a straw. Time to make, a few minutes. Probable cost, 3d., exclusive of the sherry. Sufficient for one person.

The Dictionary of Cookery, London, ca. 1870

This, it turns out, is a discovery. Astonishingly light and refreshing, like the Maibowle (see page 165), it should be treated with caution. Serve jugs of this at summer (cold) soup and sherry parties, and you'll have a riot on your hands.

Although somewhat puzzled as to what size the two glasses of sherry should be, we pragmatically used sherry glasses and did just what the instructions said.

Dandelion Coffee

A famous recipe, which we could not leave out:

As to tea and sugar, they were luxuries we would not think of, although I missed the tea very much; we rang the changes upon peppermint and sage, taking the one herb at our breakfast, the other at our tea, until I found an excellent substitute for both in the root of the dandelion....

During the fall of '35, I was assisting my husband in taking up a crop of potatoes in the field, and observing a vast number of fine dandelion roots among the potatoes, it brought the dandelion coffee back to my memory, and I determined to try some for our supper. Without saying anything to my husband, I threw aside some of the roots, and when we left work, collecting a sufficient quantity for the experiment, I carefully washed the roots quite clean, without depriving them of the fine brown skin which covers them, and which contains the aromatic flavour which so nearly resembles coffee that it is difficult to distinguish it from it while roasting.

I cut my roots into small pieces, the size of a kidney-bean, and roasted them on an iron baking-pan in the stove-oven, until they were as brown and crisp as coffee. I then ground and transferred a small cupful of the powder to the coffee-pot, pouring upon it scalding water, and boiling it for a few minutes briskly over the fire. The result was beyond my expectations. The coffee proved excellent — far superior to the common coffee we procured at the stores....

The time of gathering in the potato crop is the best suited for collecting and drying the roots of the dandelion; and as they always abound in the same hills, both may be accomplished at the same time. Those who want to keep a quantity for winter use may wash and cut up the roots, and dry them on boards in the sun. They will keep for years, and can be roasted when required.

Susanna Moodie
Roughing It in the Bush, 1852

Sweet Woodruff (Asperula odorata)

Another strewing herb, once used to stuff mattresses, and in drawers to drive away moths, sweet woodruff is not as well known as it should be. A handsome ground-cover, with white star-like flowers, it flourishes in the shade and spreads in a gratifying way. It is reputed to share some of the heartening qualities of borage — Pliny, in the first century wrote, "I, Borage, bring always courage" — and should be taken with caution lest it bring on an excess of high-spiritedness. Its faint scent of new-mown hay increases with drying. For some reason, authorities give the quaint instruction that it should be dried in a covered china or earthenware bowl for two days before use. Put it in pot-pourri, in tea or, if you are feeling particularly medieval, hang a bunch in the house on a hot day.

Maibowle

So called because sweet woodruff is most highly flavoured during its flowering time in May. We have yet to test this recipe for the traditional German favourite (not enough woodruff in the garden), but our source speaks highly of it.

For a much simpler version, put a couple of sprigs of washed woodruff in a bottle of Rhine wine, recork and let sit for one week. Or steep the woodruff in cider or apple juice for several hours.

2	large bunches woodruff — about 1 cup (250 mL) packed
3/4 cup (175 mL)	granulated sugar
	Juice of 1 orange or lemon
3	750-mL bottles dry white wine
1	750-mL bottle Champagne or mineral water

Remove the woodruff flowers and stems. Wash the leaves and squeeze the water out gently. Place the woodruff, half the sugar and the juice in a large bowl with one bottle of wine, cover and let sit in a cool place for 2 hours. Strain, add another bottle of wine and the rest of the sugar.

Let sit another 2 hours. Strain again and add a third bottle of wine. Just before serving, add a bottle of Champagne or mineral water.

Wild Strawberry Leaf Tea

The most delicate of infusions. At first you may think you are drinking hot water, but once the palate adjusts, this subtle tea can be appreciated.

Pour boiling water on a generous handful of wild strawberry leaves and let stand for 7 minutes (regular strawberry leaves will not be the same). Serve clear, with honey if you like it sweetened.

Summer

Late August

This is the plum season, the nights
blue and distended, the moon
hazed, this is the season of peaches

with their lush lobed bulbs
that glow in the dusk, apples
that drop and rot
sweetly, their brown skins veined as glands

No more the shrill voices
that cried Need Need
from the cold pond, bladed
and urgent as new grass

Now it is the crickets
that say Ripe Ripe
slurred in the darkness, while the plums

dripping on the lawn outside
our window, burst
with a sound like thick syrup
muffled and low

The air is still
warm, flesh moves over
flesh, there is no

hurry

Margaret Atwood

Introduction

Summer in Canada. A golden time. Generally, you know where you stand. If it's cold, rainy and miserable when you wake up, chances are that's how it will be all day, and you can plan accordingly. Sunny and warm? Pack your picnic with confidence and sally forth.

The cold and rainy days have their own pleasures. This is the time for puzzles and clothespeg dolls, card games and cups of cocoa by the fire. And everyone naps in the afternoon with a clear conscience — wonderful sleeps, with the rain pattering soothingly on the roof. Then the sun bursts forth and we venture out, hoping for a good sunset.

Summer is also a harvesting time, from which come innumerable jams and jellies, relishes, pickled baby vegetables and dried herbs. In between swimming and canoeing, of course. There are excursions to Kettle Point, to Kakabeka Falls, to Grand Manan — whatever is the local beauty spot. And we take our picnics with potato salad, cold chicken and devilled eggs. Or complete hams.

Summer is a time for all sorts of get-togethers: strawberry socials, pancake breakfasts, church harvest suppers, barbecues in the park. In the Maritimes, lobster suppers and clambakes are the order of the day; Ontario leans to corn- and wiener-roasts with pop, potato chips and marshmallows toasted on willow twigs held perilously over driftwood fires. Nellie McClung portrays a Manitoban picnic; a friend, reminiscing about university years in Alberta, remembers a whole pig being roasted in a pit, or even — how appropriate — in an oil drum cut in half. And in lucky British Columbia, they have whole salmon to toss on the coals.

Lying in a hammock by a shimmering lake, vaguely swatting the occasional passing fly, we can only agree with Mary O'Brien's tribute to her new land: "If our necessaries run short, this is at least the region of luxuries. If our wheat crops does not equal those on the Street [we're fairly certain she means Yonge Street — that's what it was called, stretching as far as it did], yet our streams swarm with trout, which nobody has time to catch, our meadows have raspberries and strawberry beds, and our woods abound with May-apples and with a great variety of beautiful plants." (*Journals*, 1828-38)

The Garden

A Palimpsest

Two years ignored,
The whole yard went to seed.

Nothing watered, pruned,
or pulled away.

Beds overrun,
borders blurred.

Hopeless, we said,
empty after these are gone.

So much we didn't know.

Under the choking weeds
the yellow iris had survived.

Behind the tall grasses
rhubarb grew wild.

Chives beside the door,
mint by the fallen gate.

All along the broken porch
each dead stalk torn away

would send up overnight
a sharp green leaf

against the ruin.

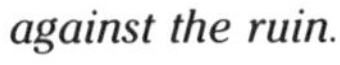

Susan Zimmerman

Small Vegetable Gardens

We have cleared quite a bit of ground and planted quite a few seeds and plants, so if we have not much else we expect to have a quantity of vegetables. The soil is very rich and easily worked. We have got in a nice patch of peas, some onions, cress, radishes, lettuces, beets for pickling, parsnips, carrots, and a great many cabbage plants. We are now preparing for potatoes....And we have tomatoes, cucumbers, and watermelons to plant yet. I begin to like gardening. It is nice to know the land you cultivate is your own.

Anna Leveridge
Your loving Anna: Letters from the Ontario Frontier, 1883-91

There is a satisfaction in growing your own food, whether it is lettuce for a few salads or the year's supply of vegetables (we relearn, for one thing, how vegetables ought to taste). It is comparable only to finding and gathering food in the wild, and far less time-consuming. A vegetable garden does absorb quite a lot of time and attention, however, from the very beginning of the season when one must begin to calculate the right time to dig and plant, right through hoeing, watering and weeding and into gathering the harvest. In fact, the amount of labour involved makes vegetable gardening an admirable family activity, one of the relatively few activities left that doesn't involve the use of machines. Quite young children are capable of planting seeds, learning how to weed, and even gathering lettuce and picking beans. They are likely to respond to the drama of planting and harvest, and to feel rather less excitement and interest in the interval between these two events. Parents may share these feelings, but know the necessity of rising above them. Steady application is necessary to assure that there is a harvest, but the harvest is very worthwhile.

The scale of operations depends entirely on resources and time. One of the essential resources is sun, which even easy-going herbs and certainly all vegetables require in abundance. If you have a shady garden or apartment balcony, adjust your sights to the feasible. Stick to geraniums, impatiens, begonias, fern and ivies, and

perhaps a pot of parsley. If you have a sunny apartment balcony — south or west in exposure — then you can begin gardening in a small way with potted herbs. These will require careful watering, for small pots dry out quickly in the summer sun and heat. If there is space and inclination, try planting lettuce in shallow clay pots, with gravel at the bottom for drainage, and a good-quality potting soil above. There are numerous varieties, but Great Lakes head lettuce works well. You needn't wait for the head — just gather lettuce leaves from the time they are large enough for a small sandwich, picking always the outside leaves, and leaving the centre parts to grow. Radishes also grow with enthusiasm and ease.

Depending on the size of the balcony, other vegetables can be added to the basic collection of herbs, lettuce and radishes. Dwarf varieties of tomatoes, such as patio or Florida petite or tiny Tim, are adaptable to pot culture.

Much more can be done in a sunny backyard garden, but still it is best to move from the basic and easy — adding green beans before pressing on to the demanding and sometimes simply space-consuming items like green peas, melons and cucumbers, not to mention corn, cauliflower and potatoes.

Gardens should be carefully dug with a spade in the spring (as soon as the soil is dry enough to be worked), hoed to break up lumps of earth, then raked smooth. If the soil is heavy, a top dressing of peat moss may be usefully applied, and well-rotted manure is always an asset. All soils will benefit from compost, and every large garden should have a compost heap, where grass clippings, weeds, dead leaves and any miscellaneous vegetable matter are allowed to rot. The pile should be kept damp, and turning it from time to time facilitates the process of decomposition.

Perhaps a word more should be said about the production of compost, though it is not a process that requires skilled handling (forest floors are constantly engaged in it, and they do not receive the least instruction). The problem in urban gardens is that if you let the grass clippings and leaves pile up on the lawn, the grass will be choked out. Far too many solve this problem in the worst possible way: they gather up all the dead vegetation from their garden, put it in plastic bags and out for the garbage. They thus deprive their garden of its replenishing nutrients, of compost richer than manure; and they contribute to the vast overproduction of garbage in our communities. Gardens then become less productive, and their owners are tempted to dose them with chemical fertilizers. To do this competently, it is necessary to get into soil analysis, which altogether is much more complicated than composting dead vegetation in the first place.

A compost heap is messy? Something depends on the eye of the beholder which, if it is well educated, will regard a compost heap as a natural part of a garden. However, for neatness freaks and for the impatient, commercial composters can be bought — metal drums that can be filled with vegetation and hurried into the production of compost. In ordinary compost heaps, production can be encouraged by feeding it with material that has been chopped fairly fine by the lawn mower, by sprinkling the heap with a layer of wood ashes from your fireplace, and with a layer of soil from time to time. Twigs and branches compost more slowly than leaves and grass clippings. Perhaps they could be used for kindling in the fireplace, and make their appearance in the compost heap in the form of wood ashes.

Herbal Gardens

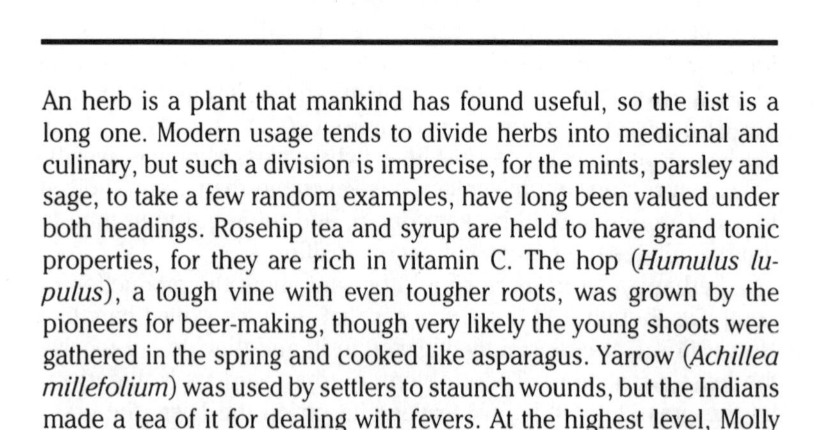

An herb is a plant that mankind has found useful, so the list is a long one. Modern usage tends to divide herbs into medicinal and culinary, but such a division is imprecise, for the mints, parsley and sage, to take a few random examples, have long been valued under both headings. Rosehip tea and syrup are held to have grand tonic properties, for they are rich in vitamin C. The hop (*Humulus lupulus*), a tough vine with even tougher roots, was grown by the pioneers for beer-making, though very likely the young shoots were gathered in the spring and cooked like asparagus. Yarrow (*Achillea millefolium*) was used by settlers to staunch wounds, but the Indians made a tea of it for dealing with fevers. At the highest level, Molly Brant advised sweet flag as a remedy for Governor Simcoe's cough.

You can grow herbs at home with a modest expenditure of effort, whether home is an apartment with a sunny window in winter and a balcony in summer, or an ordinary house with a garden. Herbs can be tucked in with the flowers or vegetables. Where space is available, they may be given their own terrain.

Most herbs like sun and lots of it, although the mints will tolerate a certain amount of shade. They are usually undemanding in the matter of soils, though when you are growing herbs in pots, it is well to lighten clay with a bit of sand, and enrich the whole with compost or well-rotted manure. If you have bought a root of rosemary or French tarragon (for rosemary is not grown readily and French tarragon not at all from seed), remember to bring them in before the frosts become severe. They are sturdy perennials but cannot manage the Canadian winter. The same is true of scented geranium; and in many parts of Canada, lavender will not winter, nor will thyme. Perennial herbs like the mints and sage will usually survive. Chives and sorrel are also very tough. Parsley, a biennial, usually does survive the winter, only to concentrate its energies the second year on producing seeds, not foliage.

Fresh herbs taste best, but it is unrealistic to expect to have them in sufficient quantities the whole year round. Not for us the lavish banks of wild rosemary spilling down a Siena hillside, nor the thirty-foot bay tree growing in the garden. Never mind, we can still treasure our miniature bay trees or pots of rosemary on the window-sill during the winter, gathering leaves with discretion.

Outdoor herbs should be harvested and dried, preferably just before the plant comes into bloom, when the flavouring oils are strongest. (Actually, sage and thyme both seem to retain flavour in their leaves after blooming, or perhaps they regain it quite fast.) Sage, savory, the mints and thyme dry easily. The old-fashioned way is to hang them in bunches in a dry place, which looks picturesque if you have the space and don't mind a bit of dust. If you do not, then spread the herbs on cookie sheets, put them in an oven turned to the lowest setting and leave them until they are thoroughly dry. If you are doing a considerable pile, they may need to be turned during the drying process. When the herbs are dry, the leaves should be stripped from the branches and stored in clean, dry, air-tight containers.

The flavour of some herbs — parsley and sweet basil are notable examples — does not survive the drying process. Freezing is preferable for parsley. Put clean bunches into small plastic bags and store in a freezer. It will defrost into something limp but usable in soups, stews and dressings, and its strength will be comparable to fresh parsley. In the case of sweet basil, one suggestion is to fill a jar with clean chopped fresh basil leaves and then cover with olive oil and store in the freezer. It's even more tempting to turn the whole crops of basil into pesto (see page 193) and store that in the freezer. In this form, its flavour does survive surprisingly well.

There is such a profusion of appealing and useful herbs that it is difficult to make a short list, but these are most of the commonly used species that are easy to grow:

Chives *(Allium schoenoprasum)*: A hardy perennial that you can probably get from a friend, for chives increase and the clumps of tiny bulbs are easily divided and subdivided. The great pleasure in chives is their early appearance in the spring. Milder than onions, they have the same animating effect. They are best before blooming, and if you mean to continue using them past June, the handsome purple flower heads should be cut off. This will not affect the survival of the bulbs, and it will also save you from a completely unnecessary profusion of seedlings the following spring. Some can be potted and brought inside for the winter, but the winter sunlight is too meagre to encourage growth. Perhaps chives are best enjoyed in the spring, not dried, frozen or brought in the house for the winter. There are, after all, other members of the onion family.

Dill *(Anethum graveolens)*: An annual that germinates readily but does not transplant easily. It is best to plant seeds where you want them to grow. Dill is a tall plant with light feathery foliage, and all parts — leaves, flowers and seeds — are useful. Most commonly associated with cucumbers in dill pickles, dill may be used to good effect fresh in summer salads. Just chop the fine leaves and add to the dressing. It is also particularly good with yogurt or cottage cheese. Traditionally, dill was thought to help the digestion.

Since it is an annual difficult to transplant, dill is not a suitable candidate for moving indoors in the fall. It is best enjoyed during its season, though if you have extra seed heads, gather and dry them and use them for flavouring.

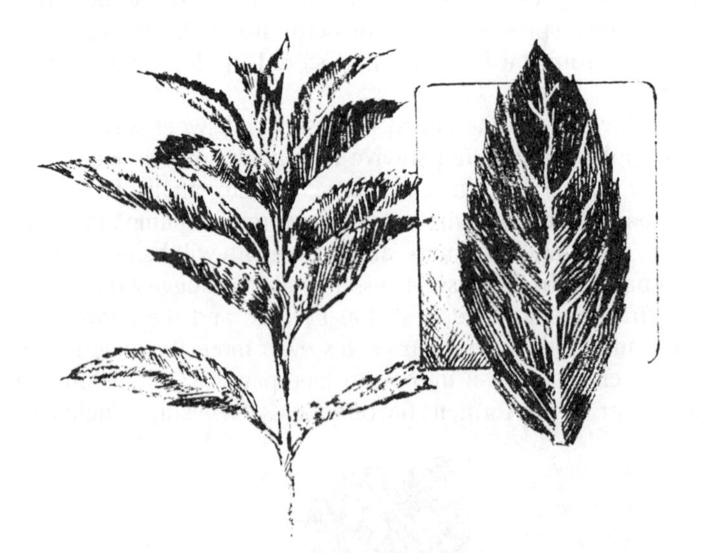

Mint: A perennial, of which there are many varieties. The traditional mint for mint sauce and jelly is spearmint (*Mentha spicata*). Because mint is so energetic, not to say invasive, it has been suggested that planting it in a plastic bucket, from which the bottom has been removed, will keep it in bounds. The alternative is to give it lots of room, harvesting it often, not merely to accompany lamb, but to dry for use as a herbal tea. Sprigs of mint are also agreeable in fruit salads, vegetables (especially peas), salads, and quite a large crop can be absorbed on hot summer evenings in mint juleps (see page 217). Fond of damp places, adapting well to light shade, mint has been used by the ancient Hebrews, the Romans, and all medieval Europe: it is no chance newcomer to the culinary scene. If space can be found for a second mint, then peppermint (*Mentha piperita*) should be the choice. Not so tall as spearmint, with leaves that are more round and dark, peppermint has a neater growing appearance, but still has a strong tendency to expand. Its leaves make a wonderful herbal tea. Oil of peppermint has long been used for flavouring and in pills for digestive problems.

Parsley: A sturdy biennial, the most common of the parsleys is the moss curled (*Petroselinum crispum*). It has had a good press from the ancient Greeks (Hercules is reputed to have worn parsley garlands, as did the victors at the Ismian Games) down to Helen Scott Nearing, complaining in 1980 that too often parsley is merely used as a garnish, when it should be incorporated in significant quantities in soups and salads. As she points out, it is as rich in vitamin A as cod liver oil and three times as rich in vitamin C as oranges. But parsley has had its detractors, too, from the terse "Parsley is garsley" to the complaint: "Parsley, parsley everywhere!/Damn. I like my victuals bare!"

Parsley seed is slow to germinate, and the tiny plants are slow to get moving. It is easier to buy a small box of plants already started. The plants really come into their own in the fall, enjoying as they do the cool, wet weather. It is useful to bring in a plant or so for the winter, using a fairly deep pot. Soak the plant thoroughly before transplanting, to minimize root damage; if it wilts, put it out of direct sunlight until it adjusts to its new setting. The beginning of September is the best time to do this, but leave the plant outside until the frosts become really severe. It will not grow so exuberantly in the house during the winter, partly because of the shortage of light, and partly because the atmosphere is apt to be too warm and too dry. Parsley, if it is left to winter in the garden, will bloom the second year and is self-seeding.

Sage: There are many varieties of sage, but garden sage (*Salvia officinalis*) is the one to aim for. It is another of those ancient herbs that have wended their way down through the centuries, from the Greeks to the Romans, who carried it throughout Europe (in place of Coca Cola, the Romans seem to have brought plants) to us, whose pioneer ancestors introduced it to North America. An old country saying goes, "Eat Sage in May and you'll live for aye," and it is endorsed by John Wesley, the founder of Methodism, who wrote in 1775: "The use of sage has fully answered my expectations: my hand is as steady as it was at fifteen."

Sage is an undemanding perennial with soft grey-green leaves and handsome blue flowers that appear at the beginning of July or even earlier. It may be started from seed and will take a little longer than an annual to germinate, but once under way it will last for years. In old age, the woody stems tend to become more evident and the leaves less numerous in proportion to the size of the plant. Either plant new seed or start new plants by layering some of the woody stems. Cover some of the long stems with earth, so that just the growing tip of the sage is above the soil. Soon new roots will form on the covered stems; after a month or so, the little plant may be cut free from the mother plant.

Traditionally, sage and onion dressing has been used as a stuffing for poultry and pork. There is also an excellent sage cheese, and it may be used sparingly (for it is very strong) in omelettes and cheese dishes. Early settlers drank sage tea, partly because they had no Chinese tea, but partly because of its high medicinal reputation: they thought it soothing to the nerves. Sage may be used fresh all spring and summer, then gathered and dried. Some may be potted for use indoors in winter.

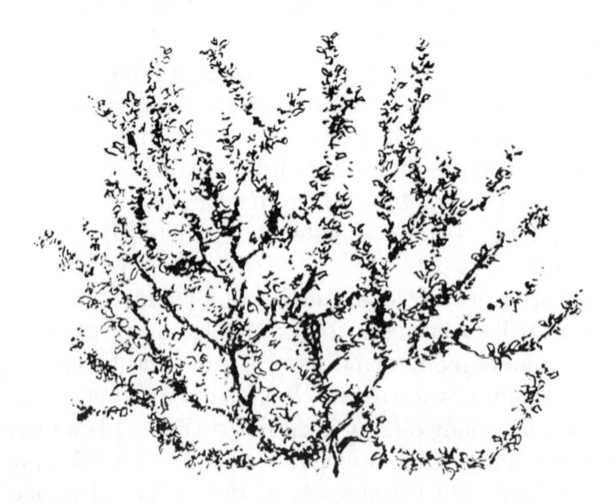

Sweet Basil (*Oeimum basilicum*): It has a mixed reputation among the authorities. It is "the herb which all authors are together by the ears about, and rail at one another, like lawyers." A sobering thought. Then there is the disturbing tradition that if a sprig of basil is left under a pot, it will eventually turn into a scorpion.

A native of India, sacred to Krishna, basil is associated with the devil in Crete. Whether it is a benign or a sinister herb, there can be no doubt about its culinary virtues, particularly when it is allied with tomatoes.

Basil is an annual and very easy to grow, but should not be started outside until the ground is warm — late May or early June is early enough. It should be treated a little like the tomato. (There is some advantage in starting the seeds indoors.) With the summer, it comes on fast, and the white flowers should be picked off to encourage the production of more leaves and no seeds. A pot of sweet basil may be brought in the house for the winter, but it will not last indefinitely, for it is an annual and will languish as the sun diminishes. Still, its season may be prolonged, and sweet basil lovers will find that worthwhile.

French Tarragon *(Artemisia dracunculus sativa)*: Tarragon is an enticing herb, but difficult in a number of ways. You cannot grow it from seed, but must buy the plant. When you do buy the plant, you must be careful not to be fobbed off with Russian tarragon (*Artemisia Redowski*), similar in appearance though lacking flavour. Give your prospective purchase a little pinch to make sure it has some smell. Though the leaves of French tarragon are far less aromatic in the spring than in late summer, in any season they outclass their Russian cousin. Finally, there is the wintering problem. Tarragon may or may not survive outdoors. Protecting it by surrounding it with a mulch of peat or compost should help. Bringing a pot in the house is equally problematic, for it by no means takes to indoor living.

Thyme *(Thymus vulgaris)*: Bees love thyme for its scent and abundant nectar. In Mediterranean countries thyme honey has been especially prized for thousands of years. The herb has long been used for a variety of medical and household purposes, and can be combined with lavender to make sachets for drawers and linen cupboards. Mostly we grow it in the garden for culinary purposes, using it in stuffings, soups and stews. In Arab countries, dried thyme is combined with roasted sesame and coriander seeds and salt and spread on bread.

As with other herbs, there are many varieties of thyme, but the common garden sort is a fairly hardy perennial, though subject to winter-kill in our more severe climates. The seeds are, like other perennials, relatively slow to germinate; they produce a small, woody, shrub-like plant with dark-green leaves and charming pink flowers. It makes a useful border and prefers a lot of sunlight. As it ages, the plant resembles sage, with many woody stems in relation to the quantity of leaves; this indicates that the plant should be divided or layered.

Thyme can be potted and brought indoors for the winter; being a sun-lover, it will not be especially active during the dark winter months, but a few leaves may be nibbled from time to time. Thyme dries well, keeping its aromatic scent for years; harvest the leaves just as the plant comes into bloom.

Hanging Flower Baskets

On my return toward Quebec, I proceeded more leisurely than I had done in coming down, and now found time to admire the beautiful plants, or rather vines, which were occasionally to be seen hanging from the lintel of an open window; the windows being hung with weights, to rise and fall as with us. These vines, it seems, are called fils d'araigner, *or spider's threads, from the singular delicacy of their tendrils; they are suspended in small pots, which the earliest leaves soon cover, so as completely to conceal the vessel which contains them; the plant then pushes forth its pendent strings of sprigs and flowers, green, red, and blue, the clusters of which seem to be growing in the air: frequently single pots of pinks, marigolds, and other flowers, occupied the sills of the windows in the meanest cottages, and gave them, more than any thing within, an appearance of domestic enjoyment.*

Joseph Sansom
Travels in Lower Canada, 1820

On an unofficial tour of a college, we once saw the most dramatic of hanging flower baskets — a long row of them interspersed among the weathered columns of a hidden cloister. Scarlet flowers blazed above vines that trailed six feet down to a velvet lawn.

You must have a knowledgeable gardener for that effect — as well as English rain and the ancient grey stones of Cambridge. But it *is* possible to create your own hanging baskets. It will be considerably less expensive than buying them at a nursery or market, and you will be less restricted in your choice of plants.

Although plastic hanging baskets abound, persevere until you find the old-fashioned moss basket, which is made of wire. Layer the wire with sphagnum moss (it helps retain moisture), pack with potting soil and plant. If you use one of the new water-retaining artificial soils, you will not have the annoyance of clambering on a chair, watering can awkwardly in hand, pouring the water and then watching it cascade through, doing little good to the thirsty plants and hastening the rotting of the porch. Apart from praying for rain, an alternative, equally awkward, is to lift the basket off the hook and submerge it in water in the sink. Apparently, the answer is ice cubes, which will melt slowly, releasing their moisture. Of course, if you have not been good at basketball, your porch may be awash in ice cubes instead. You should check your basket every 3 or 4 days for moisture, and water it at least once a week — more frequently if there is a succession of sunny days.

Do not be confined to porches. We have seen baskets hanging from old birdhouses and abandoned swingsets.

If there is plenty of light where you hang the basket, use sun-loving plants: ivy geraniums, petunias, nasturtiums or trailing verbena. For shady porches, select those that prefer the shade, such as fuchsias, begonias and impatiens. All kinds of ferns and ivies will flourish in the air, as will the lipstick plant, flame violet (*Episcia*) and trailing lantana. And don't forget the spectacular new plant on the block, the New Guinea impatiens with its large blossoms and dramatic striped leaves.

Vines

Vine-wreathed porches bring to mind languorous summer evenings in the old South, with the creaking of the swing, the chirp of the tree-frogs and the slow neighbourhood gossip about murder, madness and incest.

Vines, like gossip, can cover a multitude of sins. We know of a small inner-city backyard — all sunbaked cement, with a bleak cement garage to match. But the ingenious owners were given a root of a particularly aggressive Boston ivy, and within three years the glossy green leaves had masked the walls of the garage, which now also sports yellow-painted woodwork. With the large umbrella, white chairs, tubs of flowers, and rabbits and cats hopping about, this former eyesore now qualifies as a retreat.

Any good nursery should be able to supply you with a root and growing instructions. It will take time for your vine to become established, and you should consider the implications. With vague Whitmanesque memories, we once stuck a rather dead-looking Persian lilac twig in by the front door. Twenty years later, it is nearly 20 feet high, and shows no sign of stopping. Thank heavens we put it on the side that has no windows. Try to imagine what your vine will look like in winter, too. The luxuriant bower of scarlet roses encircling your white pillars in summer will be grey, scraggly branches in winter.

Consider honeysuckle, with its near-overwhelming scent, intoxicating to hummingbirds and humans alike. The old-fashioned trumpet vine with its drooping orange flowers is memorable on a white picket fence. The different varieties of wisteria with its clustered blossoms — white, purple, pink or blue — are also worthwhile. One magnificent specimen used to cause a traffic jam on Duplex Avenue in Toronto, as the cars paused to admire the purple curtain swathing a three-storey brick house. There's the clematis, too, with its gigantic star-like flowers of purple or white, red or blue.

Nor should the scarlet runner bean be forgotten, with its vivid flowers and edible crop — a great favourite with Alberta farmers.

Scented Gardens

Fragrance is an essential element in the pleasure that gardens give us, though it seems likely that plant breeders in recent decades have neglected it, concentrating on appearance and hardiness. Allergy sufferers aside, there is not one of us who does not stoop to smell a rose. In such a case, the visual treat is not enough, though very often it is all we get. A good deal of patient effort is needed to find roses and other flowers with real fragrance. The problem is complicated by the fact that growers seem to feel that plant buyers are indifferent to scent, and often fail to mention it even when it exists. Katharine White, in *Onward and Upward in the Garden*, writes about discovering for herself that Sutter's gold, a modern yellow rose, had a delightful perfume; that asset went unmentioned in several catalogues that listed it.

The spring garden presents no major problems, if fragrance is an object. Hyacinths and jonquils (a cousin to daffodils) in particular are richly scented. English violets are heavily perfumed in their own memorable way, and are reasonably hardy perennials. Still more hardy is the delicately scented lily-of-the-valley, and shortly after lily-of-the-valley bloom the lilacs, hardy shrubs whose flowers and fragrance are only a little less haunting than roses. It seems likely that the common lilac has the strongest scent, and space should be found for at least one of these, however many flashy French hybrids one is tempted to plant.

The summer garden offers a broad range of possibilities. Among bulbs, freesias have the sweetest scent imaginable, and certain of the day lilies, such as the regal lily, are very strongly scented. (Such lilies, brought indoors in too great a quantity, are apt to be overpowering; they will remind you, before you fall asleep, that you can get too much of a good thing.) There are scented peonies — the Chinese, not the European kind. Iris once had scent (perhaps if you are lucky you can find varieties in which it still exists), and the old-fashioned phlox still possesses it.

Among annuals, there is the much-neglected mignonette, which is very easy to grow. Its flowers are insignificant, but the fragrance is strong and immensely sweet. In Provence they are used to stuff pillows to induce sweet sleep. For night scents, there are a number of possibilities, including night-scented stock (*Matthiola bicornis*), the tall white nicotiana, whose fragrance is far superior to the coloured varieties, and the snowcap petunia. A clump of any of these will not only provide delightful fragrance for you but, if you are lucky, will attract handsome hawkmoths to sip and pollinate.

Saving Winter Plants

The azalea, the amaryllis and the cyclamen are engaging plants, all too often cast aside when they have finished blooming. This is a pity, for with a small amount of effort they can be carried on for years, increasing in size and beauty.

Azalea: This little cousin of the rhododendron is a charming shrub with evergreen leaves and masses of pink, red or white flowers. James Crockett remarks that if he had to sum up their care in one sentence, he would say, "keep them cool, keep them moist, and keep them after they flower." He goes on to describe a 150-year-old azalea that had been growing in the same pot for fifty years. Inspired by this thought, snip off the dead flowers and seed pods once the plant has finished blossoming, trim off any straggling branches that mar the shape, then repot. In the summer, once there is no danger of frost, move it outside to a shady spot and place the pot in a bed of peat moss or sand. Keep it moist all summer. In the fall, before the frost comes, set the azalea in a cool bright window sill. It should bloom again in the spring.

Cyclamen: Once considered helpful against baldness and snake bites, their blossoms seem like butterflies hovering in a winter window. After your cyclamen has stopped flowering, gradually cut back on watering it until the leaves fade. (When it is flowering, the cyclamen likes constant moisture.) In about a month, repot the corm in fresh potting soil (no deeper than it was before) and set it outside in a shady spot. Don't water it much during the summer and don't be alarmed when the old leaves fall off. New ones will appear. Bring it in in the fall and start again by giving it plenty of sunlight, water and feeding it every other week. It, too, prefers to be kept cool.

People frequently harbour the Christmas poinsettia (we do it ourselves), which can go on for months. One is blooming feebly on the back porch even as this is written — in mid-July. Such being the ungratefulness of human nature, one tires of it and wishes it would stop.

The poinsettia can be brought into bloom again the following year, but do you really want to spend six weeks (September 21 or so to the end of October) moving it back and forth from window sill to the darkest depths of the linen cupboard? The poinsettia demands 9 or 10 hours of bright light and 14 or 15 hours of total darkness daily, or it refuses to co-operate. Better to keep it as a handsome foliage plant and buy yourself a new one at Christmas.

The Kitchen

Strawberries

I now jogged on, without any farther adventures, to the inhospitable inn at Montmorency, where, however, the children now brought me plates of wild strawberries, for which I paid them to their heart's content. These Canadian strawberries are so very small, that I did not always think it necessary to pull off the stems, but ate them sometimes by handfuls, stems and all. Here they had been picked clean, and were served up to me like a delicacy, which they really are.

Joseph Sansom
Travels in Lower Canada, 1820

There is no greater culinary pleasure than eating wild strawberries, and it is not quite equalled by the misery of picking them. At least three generations of one Muskoka family will testify to that. Pick them they did, by roadsides and in neglected fields where the hay was thin, and always in the blazing sun. The berries are very small, best hulled while picking, and gathered in clean areas so they need not be washed. At whatever cost to personal comfort, they should be searched out and picked at least once in one's lifetime. Only a very little sugar need be sprinkled over them to bring out the juices, and perhaps a little cream added at serving time.

In the unlikely event of a great supply, the result of child labour, then the surplus can be made into the best of jams. Measure the crushed berries and cook them in a very little water until soft. Add 3/4 cup (175 mL) granulated sugar for each cup of berries and boil until thick. Just before it is ready to bottle, add the juice of half a lemon for each quart of berries. Skim, then bottle in hot sterilized jars.

Tame strawberries are not nearly as good, but as long as we are in no position to make comparisons, we enjoy the tame ones very much. And local berries, after the deceptive imported ones that have the appearance of strawberries but not the flavour, are very good. If you want a large supply — some for eating fresh, some for freezing and some for jam — go to the nearest farm that allows you to pick your own. Failing that, a local market is likely to have them in June at a good price.

Cultivated strawberries, unlike the wild ones, which are propped up by the other inhabitants of the meadow, are apt to get quite dirty, particularly after a heavy rainstorm. They need to be washed with care. One trendy soul recently claimed that strawberries should be gently rinsed with a little leftover white wine, lest they become soggy. This seems excessive.

Strawberries and Cream

Wash, drain and hull strawberries and cut the very largest berries in half. Place in a bowl and sprinkle with fruit sugar. Stir gently so the sugar is distributed. Cover and let sit for 30 to 60 minutes so they will be juicy. Serve with light cream.

Strawberry Shortcake

This is no doubt the most popular strawberry dessert, long a favourite at strawberry socials. Apart from using strawberries of good flavour, its excellence depends upon using a shortcake recipe with little, if any, sugar in it. Too much sugar in the cake will quell the flavour of the berries.

If you are too busy picking strawberries and making jam to produce strawberry shortcake in season, freeze some of the berries whole, on cookie trays, then bag them. You can pamper your family in January with a totally out-of-season treat. Strawberries freshly picked and frozen remain excellent indeed, but do not thaw them too long before serving time, for they tend to wilt a little.

6 cups (1.5 L)	fresh strawberries
	Granulated sugar to taste
2 cups (500 mL)	all-purpose flour
2 tbsp (25 mL)	granulated sugar
4 tsp (20 mL)	baking powder
1 tsp (5 mL)	salt
1/3 cup (75 mL)	shortening
1	egg
2/3 cup (150 mL)	milk, approx.
1/4 cup (50 mL)	butter
1 cup (250 mL)	whipping cream

In a large bowl, combine the berries with sugar to taste. Set aside.

Sift the flour, 2 tbsp (25 mL) sugar, baking powder and salt into a mixing bowl. Add the shortening and blend in with a pastry cutter until the mixture is rather mealy and the shortening is thoroughly distributed.

In a separate bowl, beat the egg, then beat in the milk. Add the liquid mixture to the dry ingredients and combine well (add more milk if necessary to make the dough very soft, but still stiff enough to handle).

Put the dough on a floured board and knead very gently a few times; then roll out so that it will fit a greased 8-inch (2-L) round cake pan. Place the dough in the pan, prick the surface with a fork and bake at 425°F (220°C) for 12 to 15 minutes, or until the biscuit sounds hollow when tapped.

To serve, cut the biscuit into serving pieces while still slightly warm. Slice each piece in half horizontally and spread with butter. Crush the berries slightly, reserving several whole berries for garnish. Spread the crushed berries on the bottom half of each biscuit.

Whip the cream (with a little sugar and vanilla, if desired), and dab a little on top of the crushed berries. Place the top half of the biscuit on top and garnish with more whipped cream and a few whole berries. Serves 10.

Pavlova

This delectable English and Australian sweet made its way here in the recipe boxes of twentieth-century settlers.

3	egg whites
1 cup (250 mL)	granulated sugar
1 tsp (5 mL)	white vinegar
1 cup (250 mL)	whipping cream
2 cups (500 mL)	sliced strawberries or other fresh fruit

If you can avoid it, don't try to make a meringue on a rainy or humid day.

Beat the egg whites until they are very stiff. (Test by placing a knife in the mixture to see if it comes out clean.) Add the sugar and vinegar and beat for 1 minute. Spoon the meringue into a 9-inch (23-cm) pie plate lined with waxed paper.

Preheat the oven to 400°F (200°C) and then turn it off. Bake the meringue for 10 minutes, then turn the oven to 200°F (90°C) and bake for a further 30 minutes, or until it is lightly brown on top.

Remove the meringue from the oven and cool. Whip the cream. Top the meringue with the cream and sliced fruit. Blueberries and bananas make an agreeable mixture, but you must have strawberries to be authentic. Serves 6.

Fresh Strawberry Pie

1 quart (1 L)	strawberries
3/4 cup (175 mL)	water
3 tbsp (45 mL)	cornstarch
1 cup (250 mL)	granulated sugar
1 tsp (5 mL)	fresh lemon juice
1	baked 9-inch (23-cm) pie shell
1/2 cup (125 mL)	whipping cream
1/4 tsp (1 mL)	vanilla

Add one cup of the berries to the water and bring to a boil; simmer for about 4 minutes. Combine the cornstarch and sugar and add to the berry mixture. Bring to a boil and continue to cook and stir until the syrup becomes thick and clear. Add the lemon juice and cool slightly.

Arrange the remaining berries evenly over the pie shell. Pour the syrup over the berries and chill for about 4 hours.

Before serving, whip the cream and add the vanilla. Spread over the top of the pie.

Strawberry Rhubarb Jam

Strawberries make delicious jam, but they have one grave defect: they lack pectin and so do not gel easily. The old-fashioned system is to measure the crushed berries, then cook them with a little water until they are soft, add 3/4 cup (175 mL) granulated sugar for each cup of berries used, then boil vigorously and at length until the jam is sufficiently thick. A little lemon may be added in the later stages of cooking. This produces a dark, rich jam of high quality, but small quantity in relation to the number of berries used.

The price of strawberries being what it is, the temptation is strong to increase the yield. One means of doing this is by combining strawberry with rhubarb, a very pleasing combination in desserts or jams.

Wash, drain and hull 3 quarts (3 L) strawberries. Crush, then measure them. There should be about 6 cups (1.5 L). Put the strawberries and 4 cups (1 L) chopped rhubarb in a large pan. Bring to a boil, stirring constantly. Cook gently, uncovered, for about 20 minutes, or until the fruit is thoroughly soft. Then add 7 cups (1.75 L) granulated sugar, bring to a boil and boil vigorously until thick. Stir throughout this process.

It is tempting to go on and on with strawberries. One sinful but sociable way of serving them is to place them in a bowl, washed but unhulled, beside a bowl of sour cream and another smaller bowl of Demerara sugar. Dip the individual strawberries first in the sour cream and then in the sugar. Not to be done every night, but delicious occasionally. Try strawberries sprinkled with chopped mint, combined with honey and lime juice, or with a dash of pepper as they do in New Brunswick. Or make a nutritious milkshake by combining 4 strawberries, 1 banana, 1 cup (250 mL) yogurt and a little honey in a blender.

Among the earliest berry to ripen is the strawberry.... These welcome events are celebrated by longhouse ceremonies in which thanks are given, while quantities of the fruit are eaten in the feasts which follow.

F.W. Waugh
Iroquois foods and food preparation, 1916

Lettuce

Lettuce has long had its admirers. The Emperor Diocletian, a passionate gardener, abdicated in 305 A.D. When his co-emperor, Maximian, urged him to reconsider, Diocletian declined. "If you saw what beautiful lettuces I am raising, you would not urge me to take up that burden again." Sensible man. John Evelyn thought highly of lettuce, too, writing that it "ever was and still continues the principal foundation of the universal Tribe of Salads; which is to cool and refresh."

There are many varieties to be explored, apart from the common iceberg (maligned by food critics but, in our experience, preferred by children) — the soft and delicate butterheads (Boston and bibb), Belgian, curly endive (chicory), escarole, the long-leaved Romaine, and the Chinese. Nor should the loose-leaf "cut and come again", known in France as *"laitue à couper"*, be overlooked. Arugula puzzled us, until we discovered that it was the ancient roquette, a variety that arouses mixed emotions among salad-lovers: "coarse-leaved, fuzzy, aggressive in flavour," says one noted authority. "Its wonderful nutty, peppery leaves add excitement," enthuses another.

Lettuce has many uses, apart from its soporific effects so apparent in *The Flopsy Bunnies*. Where would salads and sandwiches be without it? (Ordinary lettuce on brown bread with mayonnaise, salt and pepper is very good in its own right.) The loose leaves make tasty beds for cold meat platters; the stalks of the lettuce can be chopped, steamed and served with a cream sauce. But too often, when faced with a flourishing crop in summer, we scratch our heads and wish, as *The Joy of Cooking* so frankly puts it, that we "had rabbits instead of children."

Braised Lettuce

1 tbsp (15 mL)	butter
2 tbsp (25 mL)	vegetable oil
1/2	head lettuce, coarsely chopped
1	clove garlic, minced
1 tsp (5 mL)	anchovy paste

Heat the butter and oil in a medium frying pan. Add the lettuce, cover and cook over fairly high heat until steam escapes. Add the garlic and turn down the heat. Simmer for 5 minutes. Add the anchovy paste, blend in and serve. Serves 4.

Peas with Lettuce

1/4 cup (50 mL)	butter
5	green onions, cut in 2-inch (5-cm) pieces
8 oz (250 g)	shelled green peas or young green beans, topped and tailed
	Salt and pepper
1/4	head lettuce, halved
1 tbsp (15 mL)	chopped fresh parsley
1/2 tsp (2 mL)	chervil

In a large frying pan, melt the butter and add the green onions. Cook for 2 minutes. Add the peas or beans and cook gently for 20 minutes, or until tender. Season with salt and pepper. Add the lettuce, parsley and chervil and cook for an additional 5 minutes. Serve immediately. Serves 4.

To liven up frozen peas, put a generous helping of butter in a saucepan with a minimal amount of water or stock. Add the peas, a few sprigs of chopped mint and cover with a large lettuce leaf or two. Cook gently until the peas are tender. Remove the lettuce leaf, slice it and mix into the peas.

When Monsieur d'Egmont and his young friend entered the house after a short walk round the grounds, Andre placed on the table a dish of fine trout, and another of broiled wild pigeons, covered with raw chervil.

"It is not a very luxurious supper," said Monsieur d'Egmont. "I caught the trout myself before the door an hour ago, and Andre shot the pigeons at sunrise, in that dead tree at half a gun-shot's distance from here. You see, without being a seigneur, I have a fish pond and dove-cot on my domain. A salad of lettuce dressed with cream, a bowl of raspberries, and a bowl of wine will complete your supper, my friend Jules."

Aubert de Gaspé
Les anciens Canadiens, 1863

Swiss Chard

Swiss chard is the zucchini of the lettuce family, endlessly productive, bowling ahead through fair weather or foul. A row in the garden is apt to outstrip the appetite of a small family for salad. Because it cooks down so much, like spinach, serve it hot on occasion.

Creamed Chard

1 lb (500 g)	Swiss chard
2 tbsp (25 mL)	butter
4	green onions, finely chopped
1/2 tsp (2 mL)	lemon juice
1/2 cup (125 mL)	unflavoured yogurt

Wash the chard and drain. Cut off the white stems (increasingly prominent as the season progresses) and chop finely. Chop the leaves coarsely.

In a large frying pan, heat the butter. Add the stems and green onions and cook until soft. Add the chard leaves, cover and cook for a few minutes until soft and wilted. Season with lemon juice. Turn off the heat and add the yogurt. Combine well and serve at once. Serves 4.

Chard with Rice and Cheese

This agreeable recipe absorbs quite a lot of garden chard, assures that the stems are tender by cooking them longer than the leaves, and triumphantly solves the whole cooked vegetable problem for a family dinner.

1 lb (500 g)	Swiss chard
2 tbsp (25 mL)	butter
2	onions, chopped
1	clove garlic, finely chopped
1 1/2 cups (375 mL)	cooked long-grain rice
1/2 cup (125 mL)	grated Cheddar cheese
1/2 tsp (2 mL)	Worcestershire sauce

Wash and drain the chard. Cut off the white stems and chop them finely; chop the leaves coarsely. In a large frying pan, heat the butter and cook the stems, onions and garlic until transparent. Add the cooked rice and mix together, then place the chard leaves on top. Cover and cook for a few minutes, until the chard is soft and wilted. Stir in the grated cheese and Worcestershire sauce until the cheese begins to melt and the ingredients are thoroughly combined. Serve at once. Serves 4.

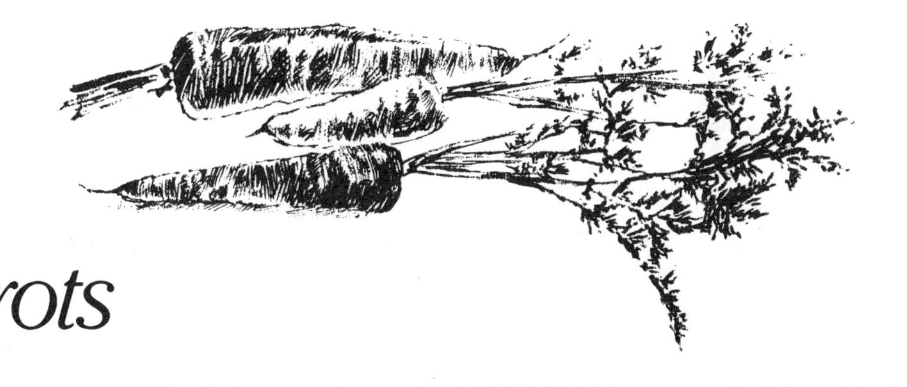

Carrots

A farmer in our neighbourhood, who was partial to their growth for the sake of his horses and cattle, beat us...in the quantity raised on a given space having actually gathered at the rate of thirteen hundred bushels per acre of carrots. We had a carrot show some years after in the neighbouring township, at which this fact was stated and its accuracy fairly established by the fact of others having gathered at the rate of as many as eleven hundred bushels per acre. I remember the meeting chiefly from the assertion of an Irishman present, who would not allow that any thing in Canada could surpass its counterpart in his native island, and maintained that these carrots were certainly very good, but that they were nothing to one which was grown near Cork, which was no less than eight feet nine inches in length!

John Geikie
Adventures in Canada, 1864

Carrot Salad

This useful salad will serve a crowd or keep for up to two weeks in the refrigerator.

2 lb (1 kg)	carrots, sliced diagonally — about 6 cups (1.5 L)
1	large onion, thinly sliced
1	green pepper, thinly sliced
1/2 cup (125 mL)	vegetable oil
1 tsp (5 mL)	dry mustard
1	10-oz (284-mL) can tomato soup
3/4 cup (175 mL)	white vinegar
1 cup (250 mL)	granulated sugar
1 tsp (5 mL)	Worcestershire sauce
1 tsp (5 mL)	chopped fresh basil or tarragon

Combine the carrots, onion and green pepper in a large bowl. In a separate bowl, combine the remaining ingredients to make a marinade. Pour over the vegetables. Refrigerate, covered, for at least 24 hours. Serve chilled or at room temperature. Serves 6 to 8.

Carrot Soufflé

2 cups (500 mL)	cooked mashed carrots, hot
1/3 cup (75 mL)	butter
1/4 cup (50 mL)	finely minced onion
4	sprigs parsley, finely chopped
3	eggs
1 tbsp (15 mL)	all-purpose flour
1 tbsp (15 mL)	granulated sugar
1 tsp (5 mL)	baking powder
1/2 tsp (2 mL)	salt
1 cup (250 mL)	milk

In a blender or food processor, combine the cooked carrots, butter, onion and parsley. Add the eggs and beat together briefly.

Mix the dry ingredients together and add to the carrot mixture. Add the milk and blend in. Pour into a greased 2-quart (2-L) casserole dish and bake at 350°F (180°C) for 45 minutes. Serves 4 to 6.

Herbed Carrots

2 tbsp (25 mL)	butter
5	medium carrots, coarsely grated — about 3 cups (750 mL)
2	green onions, finely chopped
2	sprigs parsley, finely chopped
1	sprig rosemary, finely chopped
	Salt and pepper

Melt the butter in a large frying pan. Add the carrots and cook over fairly high heat for 3 minutes, stirring constantly. Add the remaining ingredients and cook 1 minute. Season with salt and pepper and serve at once. Serves 2 to 3.

Herbs

Summer is the best time for herbal cooking — just when we are too busy. However, we include a few recipes.

Rosemary Cookies

1/2 cup (125 mL)	butter
1/4 cup (50 mL)	granulated sugar
3/4 cup (175 mL)	all-purpose flour
2 tbsp (25 mL)	chopped fresh rosemary

Cream the butter and sugar well. Add the flour and rosemary and combine. Roll out about 1/4 inch (5 mm) thick and cut into shapes with a cookie-cutter. Bake on cookie sheet at 450°F (230°C) for 12 minutes, or until golden-brown. Makes about 3 dozen.

Herbed Roast Pork

4 tsp (20 mL)	dried sage, marjoram or thyme
1/2 tsp (2 mL)	salt
1/4 tsp (1 mL)	pepper
3/4 tsp (4 mL)	ground ginger
1	6-lb (3-kg) pork roast
	Vegetable oil

To make an herbal crust for meat pies, add a little chopped parsley, thyme, etc., to the pastry.

Mix the herbs and seasonings together in a small bowl. Spread on the roast and brush with oil. Roast, fat side up, at 350°F (180°C) for 3 hours, or until the meat is tender. Serves 8.

...and her mother in the kitchen making the last of the mincemeat into pies, which sent out a real baking odor of cinnamon and cloves; a roast of pork that had been "doing too fast", was now sitting on the top of the high oven, its angry, sparking, sizzling trailing off into a throaty guttering.

Nellie L. McClung
Purple Springs, 1926

Herbal Vinegar

Tarragon is the most commonly made, but other herbs such as mint, sweet basil, thyme or rosemary may also be used. Fill a clean glass jar with tarragon leaves, cover with white wine vinegar and let stand for two weeks to infuse. Then strain and pour into bottles. A fresh sprig of the herb added to each bottle is attractive and further strengthens the flavour. Use in salad dressings as you wish — mint vinegar when you are serving lamb, basil with tomato dishes, rosemary with spinach, dill with salmon.

Mint Jelly

During the summer, make fresh mint sauce for the roast lamb. Finely chop a handful of clean mint leaves, adding 2 tbsp (25 mL) white vinegar and the same quantity of water. Season to taste with granulated sugar, salt and pepper. Let sit in a cup or small serving dish, covered, in a warm place (such as the top of the stove when the roast is cooking), so the flavour of the mint diffuses through the liquids.

In the winter, however, it is time for something different, and that is when mint jelly proves so useful. Gather the fresh mint for jelly-making just before the plant comes into bloom, sometime in July.

Other kinds of herbal jelly may be made using rosemary or basil (particularly good with cold meats; try it with fish or desserts, too). Thyme jelly accompanies cold meats sympathetically, as well as poultry.

1 1/2 cups (375 mL)	firmly packed mint leaves and stems
3 1/4 cups (800 mL)	water
1	package dry commercial pectin
4 cups (1 L)	granulated sugar
	Green food colouring, optional

In a saucepan, crush the mint and add the water. Bring to a boil and remove from the heat. Cover and let stand for 10 minutes. Strain — there should be about 3 cups (750 mL) mint infusion.

Combine the pectin and mint infusion in a large pot and bring to a strong boil. Stir in the sugar, then return to a full boil, stirring constantly. Boil hard for 1 minute. Remove from the heat and add the colouring. Pour into hot sterilized jars. Cover with a thin layer of wax. Makes about four 6-oz (175-mL) jars.

Dilled Green Beans

4 quarts (4 L)	string beans
3 cups (750 mL)	water
2 cups (500 mL)	white vinegar
2 tbsp (25 mL)	coarse salt
3/4 cup (175 mL)	granulated sugar
10	sprigs dill

Wash and drain the beans. If large, cut them in 1-inch (2.5-cm) pieces. Combine in a saucepan with 1 cup (250 mL) water and boil for 10 minutes.

In a separate pot, bring the vinegar, remaining water, salt and sugar to a boil. Add any remaining liquid from the green beans.

Put 1 sprig dill in each hot sterilized pint jar. Add the beans. Place a second sprig of dill on the top. Cover to 1/4 inch (5 mm) of the top of the jar with boiling liquid. Seal. Makes about 10 cups (2.5 L).

Parsley Capon

This method of stuffing fowl (try it with chicken or turkey, too) is simple, healthy and refreshing; it gives the capon a delicious flavour.

1 tsp (5 mL)	salt
1/4 cup (50 mL)	lemon juice
1	6-lb (3-kg) capon
1 cup (250 mL)	coarsely chopped parsley
1/2 cup (125 mL)	melted butter
1 cup (250 mL)	chicken stock
1 cup (250 mL)	dry white wine

Mix the salt and lemon juice together and rub into the capon cavity. Stuff the cavity with the parsley and pour in the melted butter.

Place the bird in a roasting pan and pour over the stock and wine. Roast for 2 to 2 1/2 hours at 350°F (180°C), until the capon is tender, basting from time to time. Serve with the basting juices, oven-baked potatoes and green salad. Serves 6.

Pesto

A wonderfully basil-flavoured sauce that is meant to be stirred into hot pasta, but can also be used as a spread for open-faced sandwiches, topped with sliced tomato; or a couple of spoonfuls can be added to minestrone for seasoning. No need to regard this as strictly a summer pleasure, for it can be frozen for winter use.

20	large basil leaves
2	sprigs parsley
1/3 cup (75 mL)	freshly grated Parmesan cheese
1/3 cup (75 mL)	pine nuts or walnuts
5	cloves garlic
1/2 tsp (2 mL)	salt
1/2 cup (125 mL)	olive oil

You can use a mortar and pestle, but a blender is faster. Blend the basil, parsley, cheese, nuts, garlic and salt until they form a smooth paste. Gradually add the oil, blending it in steadily until absorbed. Makes about 1 cup (250 mL).

The Edible Bouquet

Lucy Boston, the redoubtable children's author who lives in a Norman house (restored to its original period) and claims to have a Roman rose in her garden, liked to serve wine to her hapless guests, using roses as goblets. Flower cooks can overdo it — marigolds stuffed with chicken salad, and violet omelettes do not appeal mightily — but the fresh peppery flavour of a nasturtium or the unique taste of candied rose petals are not to be overlooked. (Nibble a sprig of elderflower, and you will find that it tastes slightly like a cream soda.) And how agreeable is the thought that it's possible to have a light snack as one wanders down the primrose path.

Nasturtiums

Nasturtium, with all its colours
from old moon to cut vein,
flower of deprivation,
does best in poor soil,
can be eaten, adds
blood to the salads.

Margaret Atwood

Their colours are glorious — red, yellow, rose and above all, that glowing orange and burnished gold. In the language of flowers, nasturtium stands for patriotism.

This admirable plant prefers poor soil, but it does need plenty of sun. There are climbing types, too, for hanging baskets and fences. It is one of the best of all plants for small children's gardens, because it grows easily from seed and flowers profusely if it is constantly picked. Use a few young leaves (and their stems) in consommé or in a green salad, or to surround a dish of marinated cucumbers. The seeds can be pickled and used in place of capers.

Nasturtium Mayonnaise

The agreeably pungent taste of nasturtiums explains their old name of Indian cress. The blossoms, too, are peppery, although milder. One authority says that there is always a little drop of honey in them.

12	nasturtium blossoms
1/2 cup (125 mL)	mayonnaise
2 tbsp (25 mL)	whipping cream

Remove the stamens and pistils from the blossoms and discard. Put all the ingredients in blender and run at top speed for 1 minute. Use with a lettuce-tomato-cucumber salad. Makes about 1/2 cup (125 mL).

Nasturtium Sandwiches
Are a novelty, and have a picquant flavor. The flowers shredded with the addition of a few of the tender seeds, placed between slices of buttered bread, make a dainty sandwich.

Margaret Taylor and Frances McNaught
The Early Canadian Galt Cook Book, 1898

Marigolds

Pot marigolds (*Calendula officinalis*), sometimes known as "the sun's bride" or "Mary's Gold", also have unexpected uses. Early writers tell us that they are handy for trapping burglars (lay them under your head at night and you "shall see the thief and all his conditions"). Steep them in vinegar and rub well for "a sovereign remedie for the assuaging of the grevious paine of the Teeth." Marigold oil is reputed to be good for tired feet, and some vain medieval maidens "use to make their hair yellow with the flower of this herbe not being content wyth the natural colour which God hath gyven them."

You can add marigold petals to plain muffins, cakes, cookies, crabmeat sandwiches or to custards as a flavouring. Blend them into butter or cream cheese, devilled eggs or salads. They will also add an extra zing to mint tea.

Marigold Rice

The yellow and gold leaves, dried, can be used in any recipe that calls for saffron. There is a pleasant claim that in pioneer times, grocers kept barrels of the spicy dried petals for use in soups and stews.

2 tbsp (25 mL)	butter
1	small onion, chopped
1 cup (250 mL)	long-grain rice
2 cups (500 mL)	chicken stock
1/2 tsp (2 mL)	salt
2 tbsp (25 mL)	chopped marigold petals
1/2 tsp (2 mL)	dried rosemary

Heat the butter in a frying pan. Add the onion and cook until tender and transparent. Add the rice and cook until golden. Add the stock, salt, marigold petals and rosemary, bring to a boil and simmer, covered, for about 20 minutes, or until tender. Uncover and toss with a fork. Serves 5 to 6.

Roses

And so we come to roses, beloved by poets, significant in wars and legend. (The tears Venus shed for the loss of Adonis fell on the white rose and turned it red.) They were strewn on the floor and decorated tables at the feasts of the emperors — at one Roman banquet, so many petals showered from the ceiling that several of the guests were suffocated.

Old-fashioned roses have the best flavour for cooking (and scent), so take your petals from a rugosa, cabbage, moss or damask, and be sure that the bush has not been sprayed. Use the petals to flavour vinegar, sugar or butter; or scatter them over a cherry pie before covering with pastry and baking.

Rose Petal Salad

Make a green lettuce salad with parsley, watercress, sliced green onions and a rose-vinegar vinaigrette. Add two large spoonfuls of rose petals and toss gently.

Candied Rose Petals

It's best to be nimble-fingered if you attempt these.

With a small brush, paint rose petals with slightly beaten egg white on one side. Sprinkle with fruit sugar, turn over and repeat the process. Dry in the sun on a cake rack, or in a 150°F (65°C) oven for 15 minutes. Do not let the petals brown. When the petals are entirely dry, store in an airtight jar between layers of waxed paper. They are delicious by themselves, or as decorations for cakes and ice cream, and they will keep for up to a year. The same technique can be used with mint leaves and borage flowers.

Put 2 cups (500 mL) granulated sugar in an airtight container, with about a dozen rose petals at the bottom. Let stand, covered, for 2 weeks and then use with stewed fruit or icings, or sprinkled on top of cookies. You can sift out the petals or use them crumbled in the sugar.

I can assert that on the fifteenth of June there were wild roses here [Hudson Bay], as beautiful and fragrant as those at Quebec. The season seemed to me farther advanced, the aire extremely mild and agreeable.

Charles Albanel
Jesuit Relations, 1671-72

Raspberries

Raspberries are another fruit that makes living in the summertime not merely easy but luxuriant. The wild ones have been enjoyed for a long time. The flavour of the wild ones is superior to the tame, but if you can't find any wild ones, the tame ones taste very good. You can cultivate wild raspberries in your garden, but it would have to be a very large one, for the yield is not heavy. Even tame ones take up a good deal of space, so for most people the best source will be a pick-your-own commercial garden.

Raspberry Omelette

As always, we are happy to eat the early berries very plainly, with a little sugar and cream at most. Later in the season, this sweet omelette will be welcomed.

This recipe will not work for a dinner-party, unless it is an intimate gathering of two. We tried it once for four, and there was omelette all over the place. It still tasted good, though.

1 cup (250 mL)	raspberries
2 tbsp (25 mL)	fruit sugar
2 tbsp (25 mL)	Grand Marnier
2	egg whites
pinch	salt
4	egg yolks
2 tbsp (25 mL)	granulated sugar
2 tbsp (25 mL)	butter
	Sifted icing sugar

Mash and crush the berries (not too violently) and mix with the fruit sugar and Grand Marnier.

Beat the egg whites with a pinch of salt until stiff. Without washing the beater, in a separate bowl beat the yolks and granulated sugar until foamy. Fold the whites into the yolks gently.

In an ovenproof omelette pan, melt the butter over high heat until it turns white, then lower the temperature to medium and pour in the egg mixture. Cook for 5 minutes, or until it is solid rather than liquid and doesn't return to the side of the pan when pushed aside. Put the omelette under a preheated broiler for 1 minute, or until lightly browned and puffy. Slide it onto a warm plate, spread half of it with the raspberry mixture, fold over and sift sparingly with icing sugar. Eat at once. Serves 2.

Meringues with Raspberry Puree

2	egg whites
3/4 cup (175 mL)	granulated sugar
1/2 tsp (2 mL)	vanilla
3 cups (750 mL)	raspberries, fresh or frozen and defrosted
2 cups (500 mL)	vanilla ice cream

Beat the egg whites until they are stiff and dry. Add 1/2 cup (125 mL) sugar, a little at a time, beating after each addition, until all the sugar is added and the mixture is stiff enough to hold its shape. Add the vanilla and give a final beat.

Line a cookie sheet with waxed paper. Arrange the meringue mixture by spoonfuls on the sheet, making eight meringues. Shape slightly to form "nests". Bake at 250°F (120°C) for 50 minutes.

Put the raspberries in a blender or food processor and puree. Add the remaining sugar and combine.

Arrange the meringues in serving dishes. Place a scoop of vanilla ice cream in each and top with the raspberry puree. Serves 8.

Raspberry Syllabub

Gourmet stores will have rose water. It is easier to buy it there than make your own.

4 cups (1 L)	raspberries
1/4 cup (50 mL)	granulated sugar
2 tbsp (25 mL)	rose water or 3 tbsp (45 mL) lemon juice or kirsch
1 cup (250 mL)	whipping cream
1 cup (250 mL)	sweet white wine (Sauterne)

Puree the berries, saving any juice. Blend the raspberry puree with the sugar and rose water (or the lemon juice or kirsch). Beat the cream until stiff, then add the wine and any raspberry juice, beating well. Gently fold in the puree, put in individual glass dishes and chill for several hours. Garnish with extra berries. Serves 6.

Why fool around? Raspberries laced with Grand Marnier will never be rejected.

Our common raspberries *are so plentiful here [at Quebec] on the hills near grain fields, rivers and brooks, that the branches look quite red on account of the number of berries on them. They are ripe about this time and eaten as a dessert after dinner. They are served either with or without fresh milk and powdered sugar. Sometimes they are kept through the winter in glass jars with syrup.*

Peter Kalm
Travels into North America, 1753-61

Red Currants, Gooseberries and Black Currants

Used by native peoples, explorers and pioneers, and cultivated by farmers and sold in markets and stores for generations, members of the *ribes* tribe — red currants, black currants and gooseberries — have fallen strangely out of fashion. They are hard to find in stores (and are very expensive when found), and recipes using them are absent from most modern cookbooks. The only obvious explanation is that they are hosts to the white pine blister rust, and in many areas their cultivation has been discouraged, even prohibited. Now that varieties of pine trees resistant to rust have been developed, it is likely that the currants and gooseberries will once again be cultivated.

Currants and gooseberries make excellent jams, jellies, pies, juices and wines. Being full of pectin, they gel easily. And they freeze well, so a supply can be reserved for winter use. The black currant, in particular, is rich in vitamin C and has been used time out of mind in northern Europe as well as North America, as a soothing syrup for colds, coughs and sore throats.

The wild varieties are all very well, but most of us will not be able to find them in usable quantities. Nor is there the dramatic difference in flavour between, for example, wild gooseberries and tame ones, that there is between wild and tame strawberries.

Red Currants

There are white currants, too, but the red ones are cheerier. Whatever the colour, currants are apt to be too tart to be eaten fresh. About half a cup, scattered in a fresh fruit salad for four, will have an inspiring effect. They combine well with most summer fruits — raspberries, peaches, melons and cherries.

Red Currant Jelly

Red currants are usually made into jelly, their seeds being a bit too large for jams. Pick the whole stem with the currants attached. They should be predominantly red, but a few unripe ones will provide an even higher quantity of pectin.

Wash the currants, but do not stem. Place in a kettle with about half a cup of water to each quart of fruit. Crush the fruit with a potato masher. Cover the container, heat and simmer gently for 15 minutes, or until the berries are thoroughly softened. Sieve. Reserve the sieved fruit for a second pressing.

Measure the juice. For each cup of juice, add a cup of sugar. Bring the juice and sugar rapidly to a boil, stir and boil vigorously until the gel point is reached. This can take anywhere from 5 to 20 minutes. Bottle in hot sterilized jars.

Currant jelly is delicious with roast chicken; it is not unlike cranberry, but a shade more civilized. It suits roast veal, too, and there are some who prefer it to mint jelly with roast lamb.

The Second Pressing

After all the possible juice has been extracted, put the sieved fruit in a saucepan and cover with water. Heat and simmer for 10 to 15 minutes. Sieve again. The resulting juice will be surprisingly strong. Add sugar to taste. Combine with orange juice for a fine summer drink, or add a little to herbal teas, instead of lemon.

Raspberry and Red Currant Jam

Raspberries and red currants have a special affinity. One old cookbook advises mixing fresh raspberries and red currants, adding sugar and serving with plain cream. It "makes a very nice dish." More conventionally, raspberries and red currants are combined in jam or jelly.

2 cups (500 mL)	red currant juice (from first pressing)
5 cups (1.25 L)	raspberries, crushed and firmly packed
5 3/4 cups (1.425 mL)	granulated sugar

Combine the red currant juice and raspberries in a large pot. Bring to a boil and simmer, covered, until the raspberries are thoroughly soft. Add the sugar and bring rapidly to a boil. Boil and stir vigorously until the gel point is reached. Bottle in hot sterilized jars. Makes about 4 cups (1 L).

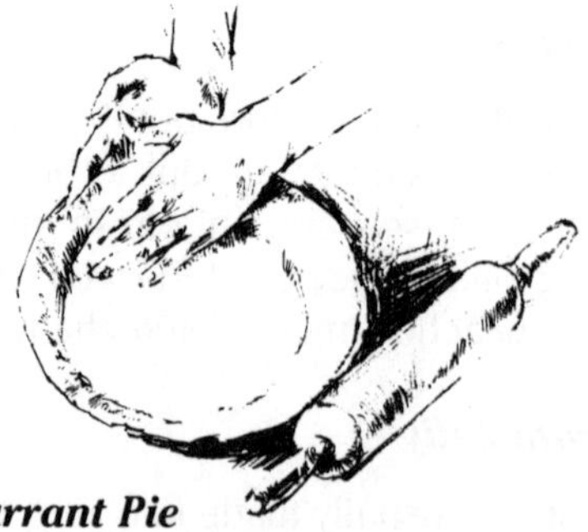

Raspberry and Red Currant Pie

2 cups (500 mL)	raspberries, firmly packed
1 cup (250 mL)	red currants, stems removed
3/4 cup (175 mL)	granulated sugar
2 tbsp (25 mL)	all-purpose flour
	Pastry for 9-inch (23-cm) pie and lattice top

Combine the fruits. Add the sugar mixed with flour, and combine well. Spread evenly over the pie crust and cover with a lattice top. Bake at 450°F (230°C) for 10 minutes; reduce the heat to 350°F (180°C) and bake for 30 minutes.

Our men worked well until dinner-time, when, after washing in the lake, they all sat down to the rude board which I had prepared for them, loaded with the best fare that could be procured in the bush. Pea-soup, legs of pork, venison, eel, and raspberry pie, garnished with plenty of potatoes and whiskey to wash them down, beside a large iron kettle of tea.

Susanna Moodie
Roughing It in the Bush, 1852

Black Cherry and Red Currant Jam

Black Bing cherries are delicious fresh, but a dead loss in cooking. However, if the black cherries are combined with tart red currant juice, a grand jam is produced. It will gel, too, although it must be boiled longer than straight red currant jelly because the black cherries lack pectin.

3 cups (750 mL)	red currant juice (from first pressing)
5 cups (1.25 L)	pitted black cherries
6 3/4 cups (1.675 mL)	granulated sugar
1/4 tsp (1 mL)	salt
1/2 tsp (2 mL)	almond extract

Combine the red currant juice and cherries in a large pot. Bring to a boil and simmer, uncovered, until the cherries are soft. Add the sugar and boil vigorously, stirring constantly, until the gel point is reached after about 30 minutes. Add salt and almond flavouring and bottle in hot sterilized jars. Makes 8 cups (2 L).

To preserve plums and cherries, six months or a year, retaining all that bloom and agreeable flavour, during the whole of that period, of which they are possessed when taken from the tree.

Take any quantity of plums or cherries a little before they are fully ripe with the stems on; take them directly from the tree, when perfectly dry, and with the greatest care, so that they are not in the least bruised—put them with great care into a large stone jug, which must be dry, fill it full, and immediately make it proof against air and water, then sink it in the bottom of a living spring of water, there let it remain for a year if you like, and when opened they will exhibit every beauty and charm, both as to the appearance and taste, as when taken from the tree.

The Cook Not Mad, 1831

Red Currant Pie

This recipe comes from an old edition of Fannie Farmer. The fresh red currants give the pie a fine, bright flavour; frozen currants are only slightly inferior.

1 1/3 cups (325 mL)	granulated sugar
1/4 cup (50 mL)	all-purpose flour
2	eggs, separated
2 tbsp (25 mL)	water
1 cup (250 mL)	red currants, washed and stemmed
1	unbaked 9-inch (23-cm) pie shell

Mix together 1 cup (250 mL) sugar and the flour. Combine the egg yolks and water and add to the dry ingredients along with the currants. Spread evenly over the pie crust. Bake at 450°F (230°C) for 10 minutes, then at 350°F (180°C) for 20 minutes, or until the custard is set. Remove from the oven and cool.

To make the meringue, beat the egg whites until they are very stiff. Add the remaining 1/3 cup (75 mL) sugar gradually and continue beating for 1 minute. Spoon over the pie and bake at 325°F (160°C) for 15 minutes.

Gooseberries

Southby and Anthony went into the woods to get some gooseberry plants, of which they find there is a species remarkably good to be used green. They grow in marshes and with them a species of strawberries very much like our scarlet. These two plants are therefore to occupy jointly a bed in the lowest part of the garden.

Mary O'Brien
Journals, 1828-38

An English catalogue of 1872 lists 122 varieties of red, green, yellow and white gooseberries; in 1951, an English gardener mourned that the numbers were down to thirty or forty varieties. Canadians must make do with far fewer. There are about six wild varieties in all, some of them with marked regional preferences. As to the tame ones, a popular garden catalogue lists just two; and an Ontario Ministry of Agriculture bulletin suggests three.

Tame gooseberries have their good points: the berries are larger and have no prickles, and are therefore much easier to pick. (The bushes have prickles, though.) It's nice to have a bush or so in the garden, because even in mid-summer, gooseberries can only be found in stores and markets for a price. They are very nearly worth it, for they make an excellent jam and jelly, and a wide variety of desserts. It's also easy to freeze them, topped and tailed, and postpone making some of the desserts until winter.

Gooseberry Jam

This is a particular favourite of many north Europeans and is best made from gooseberries that are unripened, but not so immature as to lack flavour.

2 quarts (2 L)	green gooseberries
2 cups (500 mL)	water
5 cups (1.25 mL)	granulated sugar
	Juice of 1 orange

Wash, top and tail the gooseberries. Put the gooseberries and water into a large pot and simmer for 15 minutes, until the berries are thoroughly soft. Add the sugar and orange juice. Boil vigorously and stir constantly until the gel point is reached. This may take no more than 5 minutes if the gooseberries are green, for they are rich in pectin. Put in hot sterilized jars and seal. Makes about 6 cups (1.5 L).

Note: If a jelly is preferred, simply cook gooseberries and water as already described; then put them through a sieve. Measure the juice and allow one cup of sugar for each cup of juice. Boil and stir the juice and sugar until the gel point is reached. Bottle in hot sterilized jars. Use instead of red currant jelly with lamb.

Thursday, 23 August, 1838
In the Evening we went upon Lake George, the water of which is so Clear *& beautiful that it was formerly sent by the Jesuits to France for sacred purposes & called St. Sacrament. Shot a* little rapid *for the 1st time — rather frightened. Landed on an Island, made a sketch. Eat wild gooseberries —* red *— very good, but almost impossible to eat being covered with* formidable prickles *— almost thorns — which hurt one's mouth uncommonly.*

Jane Ellice
Diary, 1838

A contemporary of Jane Ellice, coping with life in the woods, had a way of dealing with these prickles. "To avail yourself of the fruit," wrote Catharine Parr Traill, "you must pour boiling water on them: let them lie in it a minute; then rub them in a coarse clean dry cloth on the table: this will remove, or soften the spines so that their roughness will be taken away." We must confess to not having tried this, but have found that the spines cook down in jam — to a certain extent.

Better, perhaps, to use domesticated gooseberries for this most summery of recipes.

Gooseberry Fool

3 cups (750 mL)	green gooseberries
1/4 cup (50 mL)	water
1 cup (250 mL)	granulated sugar
1 cup (250 mL)	whipping cream

Simmer the gooseberries in the water and 1/4 cup (50 mL) sugar until soft. Put the berries through a sieve, and to the resulting pulp add the remaining sugar. Chill.

Beat the cream until light and thick. Fold gently into the chilled gooseberries. They should "combine as a soft green cloud." Chill until ready to serve. Serves 6 to 8.

Gooseberry Sauce

This fine astringent sauce offsets the richness of roast goose (see page 97).

1 cup (250 mL)	gooseberries, topped and tailed
1/3 cup (75 mL)	water
1/3 cup (75 mL)	granulated sugar

Boil all the ingredients together until the gooseberries pop their skins; then simmer gently for 5 to 10 minutes until soft. Makes about 1 cup (250 mL).

Spiced Gooseberries

This unusual relish, sparked with fresh ginger, is a great enlivener of cold meats.

2 quarts (2 L)	green gooseberries, topped and tailed
3 cups (750 mL)	brown sugar
1 cup (250 mL)	cider vinegar
1 tsp (5 mL)	cinnamon
2 tsp (10 mL)	grated fresh ginger root

Put all the ingredients in a large pot, bring to boil and cook at a medium heat until thick, stirring frequently. This will take approximately 30 minutes. Makes about 4 1/2 cups (1.125 L).

Gooseberry Pie

For an extra-zesty pie, mix a heaping tablespoon of finely chopped fresh mint with the sugar and flour.

2 1/2 cups (625 mL)	gooseberries, topped and tailed
	Pastry for double-crust 9-inch (23-cm) pie
1 cup (250 mL)	granulated sugar
2 tbsp (25 mL)	all-purpose flour

Distribute the berries evenly over the pie crust. Mix the sugar and flour together, then spread on top of the fruit. Cover with pastry and prick. Bake at 450°F (230°C) for 10 minutes, then reduce the heat to 350°F (180°C) and bake for 30 minutes.

Black Currants

The Pillager Ojibwe eat these berries fresh, in jams and preserves and dry them for winter. In the winter, a favourite dish is wild currants cooked with sweet corn. The Flambeau Indians use them in a like manner. . . .

H. Smith
Ojibwe, 1921

The concentration of vitamin C in black currants is nearly three times as great as in oranges, so this is a useful fruit as well as a flavourful one. Black currants have a very strong flavour and need to be diluted when used in desserts. They can be used to make cordial, wine or juice, and they make a deservedly popular jam or jelly.

To make black currant puree, cook the currants in a little water, sieve them to get rid of the seeds and add sugar to taste. The puree is delicious on top of yogurt or ice cream. For black currant fool, whip 2 cups (500 mL) whipping cream and fold in 3/4 cups (175 mL) puree. Serves 6 to 8.

Black Currant Jam

6 cups (1.5 L)	black currants, washed and stemmed
3 cups (750 mL)	water
9 cups (2.25 L)	granulated sugar

Simmer the black currants in the water in a large pot for about 15 minutes, until they are thoroughly cooked. Add the sugar and boil vigorously, stirring, until the gel point is reached. Bottle in hot sterilized jars. Makes about 9 cups (2.25 L).

Note: Although black currant seeds are not nearly as large as those of red currants, some people like to minimize their exposure to any size of seed, and so will prefer jelly. To make it, simmer the currants and water as above and then sieve. For each cup of juice add one cup of sugar (or more to taste). Boil together until the gel point is reached, then bottle in hot sterilized jars.

This useful fruit may be dried whole, or boiled down and spread on tin plates and dried, with or without sugar; made into jam or jelly, or merely stewed with a little sugar, sufficient to sweeten, not preserve them. The convenience of this method is very apparent. In Canada, preserves are always placed on table at the evening meal, and often in the form of tarts. This method enables any one who has ripe fruit to prepare an agreeable dish at a small expense, and very little trouble, if a party of friends arrive unexpectedly to tea.

Catharine Parr Traill
The Canadian Settler's Guide, 1854

Black Currant and Apple Pie

It's useful to freeze a few cups of stemmed black currants so that you can produce this pie during the fall and winter months.

4	cooking apples, preferably Northern Spies
	Pastry for double-crust 9-inch (23-cm) pie
1 cup (250 mL)	black currants
3/4 cup (175 mL)	granulated sugar
1/4 tsp (1 mL)	salt

Peel and core the apples, then slice them into the unbaked pie shell. Mix the black currants, sugar and salt together and spread over the apples. Cover with pie crust, making slits in it to allow the steam to escape. Bake at 450°F (230°C) for 10 minutes. Reduce the heat to 325°F (160°C) and bake for 30 minutes longer, or until the apples are thoroughly cooked.

In the course of the summer I planted an orchard, consisting of various kinds of fruit trees — the best apple, with plum and cherry — and furthermore inserted, in the rich shallow surface of soil which covered a large flat sloping rock much exposed to the rays of the sun, slips of grape vine which I was informed produced the most delicious fruit. On the same description of ground I moreover planted water-melons which, nourished by the sun's heat also, promised fruit of a superior quality. Nor were my grounds wanting in other productions, the seeds of which had been planted there by the hand of nature alone. The wild strawberry, the gooseberry, the raspberry, and the huckleberry, grew in abundance on those parts of the grounds which had never been broken by the plough.

Major Richardson
Eight Years in Canada, 1847

Picnics

The picnic day was the loveliest sort of a day — bright and warm, yet cooled by a gentle wind, and the prairie on July the first with its sweet brier roses in massed bloom was a sight to remember....

Down by the river the tables were set, and benches from the boarding-house brought down for seats. There were raisin-buns and cinnamon rolls curled like snail shells, doughnuts and cookies (ginger and molasses), railroad cake; lettuce cut up in sour cream, mustard, and sugar; cold sliced ham, home cured; and Mother had made half a dozen vinegar pies, using her own recipe. The filling of a pie is rather a delicate matter when you have no fresh fruit or eggs, but she made her filling of molasses and butter thickened with bread crumbs and sharpened and flavoured with vinegar and cinnamon. Her one regret was that she had not the white of an egg to make a frosting, but we had no hens that year.

Nellie L. McClung
Clearing in the West, 1935

And a very good picnic it would be nowadays, too, although modern tastes might prefer fewer sweet things.

There are all sorts of picnics: Stratford elegant, where one takes large hampers, tablecloths and white wine, but must fend off the swans; and the more homespun kind, where one goes on foot with the children and a small brown paper bag of squashed peanut butter and jam sandwiches and a leaky chunk of watermelon.

We offer a few suggestions for the picnic hamper, some quick and easy, some to be prepared ahead so that you won't be too tired to do anything but sleep under the trees while the others play Frisbee. (Perhaps not a bad idea, at that.)

Pack foods that travel well: hard-boiled or devilled eggs (they'll survive if you put them in egg cartons), vegetable sticks, cold chicken, potato salad, a Thermos of cold soup, pickled herring or marinated artichoke hearts.

Cold Soups for Hot Weather

These soups, of course, are equally good consumed on the porch. Vichyssoise — leeks, potatoes and chicken broth, cooked together and seasoned in various ways — is the classic cold soup. For the less energetic, there is jellied consommé straight from the tin and the refrigerator. To add a note of distinction, combine chopped fresh dill with yogurt and use as a topping instead of a slice of lemon — if you're on the porch, that is.

Cold Borscht

2 cups (500 mL)	diced raw beets
1	green onion, chopped
2 cups (500 mL)	sour cream or unflavoured yogurt
	Chopped fresh dill
	Salt

For this it is best to use young beets, washing the roots and cutting off rootlets and stem ends, but not peeling. Chop the beets in fairly small pieces, add the onion and yogurt, and mix together. Blend half the mixture in the blender; then add the second half and blend again. Season to taste with fresh dill and salt and serve well chilled. (It is the Doukhobors who use dill in this way, and surely they are right; it has a wonderfully cooling effect, both on beets and on summer heat.) Serves 4.

Summer Salad

This recipe from a friend in Thunder Bay is perfect for picnics because you do all the work the night before. You take whatever amounts please you of all sorts of vegetables: raw broccoli, cauliflower, celery, carrots, beans, mushrooms, tiny zucchini — anything that can be eaten in a normal salad. Cut in bite-sized pieces and marinate overnight in Italian dressing. Before the picnic, stir and drain.

Make-Ahead Green Salad

This curiously constructed salad seems to do most of the work itself, emerging delicious after twenty-four hours in the refrigerator. Excellent for a summer buffet supper.

1	small head lettuce
1/2 cup (125 mL)	chopped celery
1/3 cup (75 mL)	chopped green pepper
1	10-oz (284-mL) can water chestnuts, drained and sliced
1/4 cup (50 mL)	chopped red onion
1	10-oz (300-g) package frozen peas
2 cups (500 mL)	mayonnaise
2 tsp (10 mL)	granulated sugar
1/2 cup (125 mL)	grated Romano cheese

In the order given put the vegetables in a shallow 12-cup (3-L) serving bowl or casserole. Cover with mayonnaise and sprinkle with sugar. Top with cheese, cover and store in the refrigerator for 24 hours. Serve as is; this salad is not for tossing. Serves 8 to 10.

Old-fashioned Potato Salad

The peculiar excellence of this salad probably lies in the dressing, and the secret there is likely the combination of dry mustard and cider vinegar. The exuberant language of the original recipe is a little hard to translate. Is it fair to turn "tons of salt when refrigerating potatoes, then more before serving" into "1 tablespoon salt"?

10	medium potatoes
1 tbsp (15 mL)	salt
1/2 cup (125 mL)	granulated sugar
1 1/2 tsp (7 mL)	all-purpose flour
1 tsp (5 mL)	dry mustard
1	egg
1/3 cup (75 mL)	cider vinegar
3 tbsp (45 mL)	water
	Salt and pepper
2 tbsp (25 mL)	butter
1	onion, finely chopped
8	radishes, thinly sliced
2	stalks celery, finely chopped
1/4	green pepper, finely chopped
1/4 cup (50 mL)	olives, pitted and chopped, optional
3	hard-boiled eggs
	Few sprigs fresh parsley

Boil the potatoes, then peel them while warm. Chop them into 1/2-inch (2-cm) cubes. Sprinkle with the salt, then cool in the refrigerator.

While the potatoes are cooling, combine the sugar, flour and mustard in the top part of a double boiler. In a small bowl, beat the egg slightly and add the vinegar and water. Add the liquid mixture very slowly to the dry ingredients and stir until well blended. Add salt and pepper to taste. Heat until the mixture thickens, then remove from the heat and stir in the butter. Refrigerate instantly.

When the potatoes are cool, add the onion, radishes, celery, green pepper, olives and 2 of the hard-boiled eggs sliced very thin. Gently stir in the cool salad dressing, then refrigerate for a few more hours. (The potatoes and eggs, if they live together for a little while, improve each other enormously.) Just before serving, taste to see whether more salt is needed, then garnish with a few sprigs of fresh parsley and a thinly sliced hard-boiled egg. Serves about 12.

Devilled Eggs

These are sloppier than usual, so well suited to outdoor eating. What does it matter if you spill? If you remove a minute slice from the bottom of the small end of the egg (add it to the yolks) the eggs will stand more easily. Or slice them in half lengthwise.

Boil however many eggs you require. When they are done, drain and then let sit covered in cold water until you are ready to peel them. For once, it's best not to use "country-fresh" eggs, because they will be difficult to peel and you will wind up with a batch of what will look like devilled plover eggs.

After they are peeled, slice the eggs in half and gently scoop the yolks into a bowl. Add a generous amount of mayonnaise, Dijon mustard, salt and pepper, chopped parsley or chives, a sprinkling of oregano and mix well. Add a splash of vinaigrette or herbal vinegar (see page 192). Fill the egg whites with the mixture and sprinkle with paprika. Refrigerate until ready to serve.

Shishkabob

Many picnic spots now provide barbecues or hibachis. Or you can take along your own for this seemingly elaborate, but actually very simple, dinner.

1	medium rib-eye steak — about 2 lb (1 kg)
2/3 cup (150 mL)	vegetable oil
1/3 cup (75 mL)	white vinegar
1 tsp (5 mL)	dry mustard
1/2 tsp (2 mL)	salt
1/4 tsp (1 mL)	pepper
8	mushrooms
8	cherry tomatoes
1	green pepper, cut in 1-inch (2.5-cm) pieces
1/4 cup (50 mL)	ketchup
1/4 cup (50 mL)	barbecue sauce
1/4 cup (50 mL)	chili sauce

Cut the steak in 1-inch (2.5-cm) cubes. Make a vinaigrette dressing by combining the oil, vinegar, mustard, salt and pepper. Pour over the steak and vegetables and marinate for 12 to 24 hours in the refrigerator, spooning the marinade over from time to time.

Put the ketchup, barbecue sauce and chili sauce in a small jar with a tight lid, shake well and store in the refrigerator until you are ready to leave for the picnic. Just before leaving, thread the meat and vegetables on skewers and wrap them in foil.

To serve, unwrap the skewers, spread the sauce over them and grill for 5 minutes on each side, or until as well cooked as you like them. Serve at once with rolls or pita bread. (If you're serving this at home, put your shishkabobs on a bed of rice.) Serves 4.

Herbed Cottage Cheese with Tomatoes

2	sprigs parsley, finely chopped
3	green onions, finely chopped
8	large leaves basil, finely chopped
5	cherry tomatoes, quartered
2/3 cup (150 mL)	cottage cheese

Toss all ingredients together and serve. Serves 1 or 2.

Quick Chicken

Chicken prepared this way is also delicious served at home, and hot. Cook some extra to take along as the main feature of the next day's picnic with a jar of peach chutney (see page 27).

6	single chicken breasts
1/4 cup (50 mL)	melted butter
2 tbsp (25 mL)	lemon juice
	Salt and pepper
2 tbsp (25 mL)	sesame seeds or 1 tbsp (15 mL) celery seeds

Put the chicken in a roasting pan, skin side up. Pour over the butter and lemon juice and sprinkle with salt, pepper and sesame or celery seeds. (You can also sprinkle the chicken with soy sauce instead of lemon juice for a different flavour.) Bake, uncovered, at 400°F (200°C) for 20 to 30 minutes, or until the chicken is cooked and skin is crisp. Serves 4 to 6.

Vinegar Pie

The flavour of this pie is subtle, and not at all vinegary.

2 tbsp (25 mL)	melted butter
1/2 cup (125 mL)	granulated sugar
3 tbsp (45 mL)	all-purpose flour
1 tsp (5 mL)	cinnamon
1/4 tsp (1 mL)	ground cloves
1/4 tsp (1 mL)	ground allspice
1/4 tsp (1 mL)	salt
1	egg, beaten
1 cup (250 mL)	water
2 tbsp (25 mL)	white vinegar
1	baked 9-inch (23-cm) pie shell

Combine all the ingredients (except the pie shell) in the top of a double boiler. Cook until thick. Pour into the baked pie shell and cool. Serve topped with whipped cream. Serves 6 to 8.

Pound Cake

This plain yet satisfying loaf is easily transportable.

2/3 cup (150 mL)	shortening
1 1/3 cups (325 mL)	granulated sugar
2/3 cup (150 mL)	milk
1 tsp (5 mL)	vanilla
1 tsp (5 mL)	lemon extract
2 cups (500 mL)	cake and pastry flour
1/2 tsp (2 mL)	baking powder
1 tsp (5 mL)	salt
1 tsp (5 mL)	ground mace
3	eggs

Cream the shortening with the sugar in a large bowl. Add the milk, vanilla and lemon extract. Sift the dry ingredients slowly into the mixture and stir well. Beat in the eggs one at a time. Pour the batter into a grated 9 × 5-inch (2-L) loaf pan and bake at 350°F (180°C) for 1 hour, or until a fork inserted comes out clean.

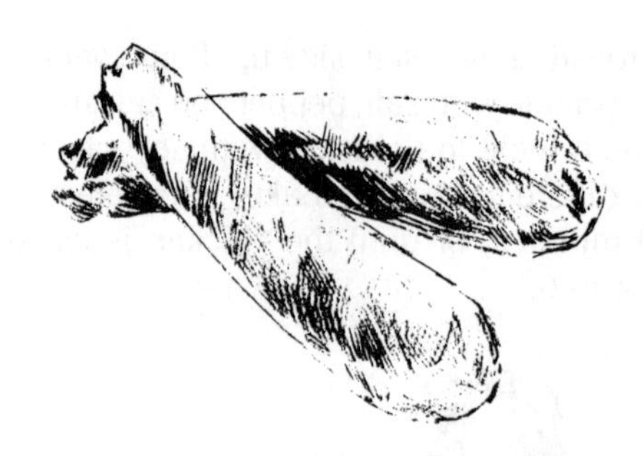

Zucchini

The esteem I have given you of late years for the squash of the Iroquois has given you an appetite for them. I am sending you some seed, which the Hurons brought us from the Iroquois country, but I do not know whether your soil will change the taste. They are prepared in divers manners — as a soup with milk, or fried. They are also cooked in the oven like apples or under the embers like pears, and it is true that, thus prepared, they have the taste of cooked reinette apples.

Marie de l'Incarnation
Letters, 1668

Squash and cucumbers begin to appear in increasing numbers and sizes in late summer, their desperate owners eager to offer them to all and sundry. We once saw a pile heaped on a front lawn with a sign, "Free, to a good home," propped behind them. And very good they were, too.

The best way to eat zucchini (like most vegetables) is when they are very small, simply sliced (no need even to peel them). Sprinkle generously with salt, pepper and oregano and cook gently for a few minutes in butter until golden.

Zucchini Quiche

Not a true quiche, but wonderfully easy to prepare. If you are very well organized, you will have your own baking powder biscuit mix (minus liquid) stored in the freezer; otherwise, reach for the packaged mix.

3 cups (750 mL)	thinly sliced zucchini
1	small onion, chopped
1 cup (250 mL)	biscuit mix
4	large eggs
1/2 cup (125 mL)	vegetable oil
1/2 cup (125 mL)	grated Parmesan cheese
1/2 cup (125 mL)	grated Gruyère cheese
1/2 tsp (2 mL)	dried marjoram
2	sprigs parsley, chopped
1/4 tsp (1 mL)	salt
pinch	pepper

Mix all the ingredients together in a large bowl. Place in a greased 12 × 8-inch (3-L) casserole dish. Bake at 350°F (180°C) for 30 minutes, or until golden. Serves 8.

Zucchini Quince Marmalade

Although the now-rare quince is reputed to resemble a large, misshapen golden apple, the only ones we have ever managed to locate (in a secret spot confided to us by a friend) were small and green and wrinkled. Quinces were highly regarded by our ancestors and are still a great favourite in Australia. *The Cook Not Mad* gives recipes for quince pudding, sweetmeats, pies, marmalade and preserves. Somewhere there must be an orchard. Or plant the ornamental Japanese quince in your garden.

1/2 cup (125 mL)	chopped quince (seeds, skins and all)
5 cups (1.25 mL)	coarsely grated zucchini
5 cups (1.25 mL)	granulated sugar
2	oranges, unpeeled and thinly sliced
1	lemon, unpeeled and thinly sliced
2 cups (500 mL)	lemonade

In a saucepan, combine the chopped quince with enough water to keep it from boiling dry in the pot. Simmer until soft. Sieve through a coarse sieve or colander. Return the quince to the pot with the zucchini, sugar, oranges, lemon and lemonade. Boil and stir until the mixture is thick or registers 220°F (112°C) on a candy thermometer. This will take at least 30 minutes. Bottle in hot sterilized jars.

Blueberries

It was probably due to the profusion of berries (Vaccineae) that the original name of Newfoundland, given by its early Norwegian visitors — Winland — was due, a country frequently alluded to in Norwegian and Icelandic historical records. The huckle-berries, especially are so large and juicy that they might naturally have passed for the wild grapes for which the island was said to be famous, and which, it is almost needless to state, do not therein exist.

Campbell Hardy
Forest Life in Acadie, 1869

People seem to feel strongly about various kinds of summer fruit, fiercely arguing the merits of raspberries versus strawberries, peaches as opposed to plums. Perhaps, when all is said and done, wild blueberries are the most satisfying of all. Fresh blueberries and cream make a superb dessert. The berries freeze easily, too. They won't be as good as those picked from a bush along the Saguenay or beside the Atlantic in Nova Scotia, but will be better than the bloated, tasteless fruit from New Jersey or Michigan that masquerades as a blueberry in most supermarkets.

Apart from turning voles' teeth blue, blueberries stain clothes, fingers, kitchen countertops and anything else they come in contact with.

An idyllic nineteenth-century description shows the long-standing popularity of this splendid berry:

This [Swamp Blueberry — Vaccinium corymbosum] is a large handsome shrub, from five to eight feet high, found in many varieties growing in swamps. The corolla is larger than either of the above and of a purer white. The leaves are ovate and entire, and slightly pubescent. The rich berries begin to ripen in August, and are the latest of the season.

These pretty shrubs, laden with their luscious berries, may be found on all dry open places. The poor Indian squaw fills her bark baskets with the fruit and brings them to the villages to trade for flour, tea, and calico, while social parties of the settlers used to go forth annually to gather the fruit for preserving, or for the pleasure of spending a long summer's day among the romantic hills and valleys, roaming in unrestrained freedom among the wild flowers scattered in such rich profusion over those open tracts of land where these useful berries grow. These rural parties would sometimes muster to the extent of fifty or even an hundred individuals, furnished with provisions and all the appliances for an extended picnic.

Catharine Parr Traill
Studies of Plant Life in Canada, 1885

In *Food*, Waverley Root says that Alaskan red-backed voles like blueberries, too, being "so partial to this fruit that most of them have blue teeth during the berry season."

Blueberries were much esteemed by the native people, who used them in endless ways, including dried (as food for winter and hunting trips), baked in cornbread loaves, and as wine and dye. The root was used for medicinal teas, and (has this been investigated recently?) as "the great medicine that squaws use at the birth of their children."

Visitors to Quebec should hunt down Dubluet, which resembles a kind of purple Dubonnet. At first it tastes medicinal, but then it grows on you....

Blueberry Rhubarb Jam

Rhubarb sharpens the flavour of blueberry more effectively than lemon does, and gives the jam a livelier flavour than is achieved by using straight blueberries.

2 quarts (2 L)	blueberries
4 cups (1 L)	diced rhubarb
1 cup (250 mL)	water
4 cups (1 L)	granulated sugar

Combine the blueberries, rhubarb and water in a large pot and bring to a full boil. Cook, uncovered, for 10 minutes. Add the sugar, return the mixture to a boil and boil vigorously for 10 to 30 minutes, stirring constantly, until the jam is thick. Bottle in hot sterilized jars. Makes about 8 cups (2 L).

Blueberry Lemon Soufflé

One of life's most memorable meals, exquisite in its simplicity, consisted of fresh lobster followed by fresh blueberries smothered in cream. But if one is sitting in eastern Ontario, instead of by the Bay of Fundy watching the tide go out, one can still enjoy this elegant variation.

5	eggs, separated
1/2 cup (125 mL)	granulated sugar
1/4 cup (50 mL)	lemon juice
1 cup (250 mL)	fresh blueberries

Beat the egg whites until they are stiff but not dry. In a separate bowl, beat the egg yolks until they are foamy and light. Gradually beat in the sugar and then the lemon juice. Fold the egg whites into the yolks, then gently stir in the blueberries. Pour into a 1 1/2-quart (1.5-L) soufflé dish set in a pan of hot (not boiling) water and bake at 325°F (160°C) for 40 minutes, or until the soufflé is firm. Serve immediately with maple syrup or cream. Serves 6.

You can incorporate blueberries into your favourite muffin mix, use them as the fruit for a syllabub (see page 55), make a pie out of them or that longtime Maritime favourite, Blueberry Grunt, which consists of stewed blueberries with dumplings on top.

Wild Blueberry Sauce

In Norway House in northern Manitoba, they serve this with wild rice pancakes (see page 44) and wild rice pudding, but it is good over ice cream, steamed pudding or ordinary pancakes and rice pudding, too.

2 cups (500 mL)	blueberries
1/2 cup (125 mL)	granulated sugar

Crush half the berries in a saucepan. Add the sugar and the remaining whole berries. Bring to a boil, then reduce the heat and simmer for 5 minutes, stirring occasionally. Serves 4.

Blueberry Blintzes with Sour Cream

We first encountered this sublime dish, not in a remote auberge in the Gaspé, but at a restaurant called Weinstein's in Squirrel Hill, in the heart of Pittsburgh.

	Blintzes:
3	eggs
1 cup (250 mL)	milk
1/2 tsp (2 mL)	salt
3 tbsp (45 mL)	vegetable oil
3/4 cup (175 mL)	all-purpose flour
	Filling:
1 cup (250 mL)	cottage cheese, well drained
1	large egg yolk, beaten
1 tbsp (15 mL)	melted butter
3 tbsp (45 mL)	fruit sugar
1 1/2 cups (375 mL)	blueberries
1 tsp (5 mL)	lemon juice

Beat the eggs, milk, salt and oil together in a bowl. Gradually add the flour until the batter resembles thick cream. Let it rest for at least 30 minutes.

Meanwhile, in a separate bowl, stir together the cottage cheese, beaten egg yolk, melted butter, fruit sugar, blueberries and lemon juice.

Heat a little butter in a 6-inch (15-cm) crêpe or omelette pan. Pour about 3 tbsp (45 mL) batter into the pan and tip until it covers the bottom. Cook for about 1 minute, or until golden-brown, then place, brown side up, on a warmed dish. Put about 2 tbsp (25 mL) filling on the blintz, fold over the ends and roll up like a small jelly roll. (Once you get the rhythm, you can cook one blintz while you fill another.) Fry the filled blintzes in melted butter (probably the best way, but you need to be neat-fingered). The clumsy can bake them in an ovenproof dish at 425°F (220°C) for about 10 minutes, or until they are brown on top. Sprinkle with grated nutmeg and serve with sour cream. Makes 12 to 18 blintzes. (Most people are willing to eat several.)

The Cellar

Many of the gentlemen present...asserted that the following method had been successfully employed to keep wine, beer, or water cool during the summer. The wine or other liquor is bottled; the bottles are well corked, hung up in the air and wrapped in wet cloth. This cools the wine in the bottles notwithstanding it was quite warm before. After a little while the cloths are again made wet, with the coldest water that is to be had and this continued. The wine or other liquor, in the bottles is then always colder than the water with which the cloths are made wet. And though the bottles should be hung up in the sunshine, the above way of proceeding will always have the same effect.

Peter Kalm
Travels into North America, 1753-61

Strawberry Bowl (Erdbeerbowle)

Put about 1 tbsp (15 mL) fruit sugar over 2 cups (500 mL) ripe strawberries (cut the big berries in half). Pour in inexpensive white wine to cover. Cover and leave overnight in the refrigerator. Just before serving, pour 2 bottles chilled (and still inexpensive) white wine over the berries. At the last minute add a bottle of Champagne or mineral water. Serve in small glasses with a spoon. Do not add ice cubes.

Our source (from Stuttgart) thought that the litre cartons of semi-dry white domestic wine were perfect for this favourite German drink. She said that as a rule of thumb, "the less sugar you use, the less likelihood there is of a headache. It's so sweet and pleasant," she added in heartfelt tones. "People don't realize. They can get an awful headache."

Mint Julep

I guess, said Mr. Slick, the heat today is like a glass of Mint Julip with a lump of ice in it, it tastes cool and feels warm — its real good, I tell you....

T. Haliburton
The Clockmaker, 1839

The main ingredient, apart from the bourbon, which you must use to be authentic, seems to be shaved ice. Tall thin glasses should be as well chilled as possible. You then place a sprig of mint, a teaspoon of sugar and a teaspoon of bourbon at the bottom of each glass and mash them together. Fill the glasses to the brim with ice, add enough bourbon to cover (about 2 oz) and stir until the glass is frosted. Garnish with sprigs of fresh mint.

Charles Dickens, who visited the South in the 1840s, commented that "the mounds of ices, and the bowls of mint-julep and sherry cobbler they make in these latitudes, are refreshments never to be thought of afterwards, in summer, by those who would preserve contented minds."

Black Currant Liqueur

You can make damson liqueur in the same fashion in the fall. It's hard to tell which is the most delicious.

1 lb (500 g)	black currants
2 cups (500 mL)	granulated sugar
	Vodka or clear alcohol

Put the currants and sugar in layers in a sterilized 3-quart (3-L) bottle with a screw top. Cover with vodka or alcohol and put away. Once every two weeks, turn the bottle upside down to help dissolve the sugar. At the end of 3 to 6 months, strain off the liquid. Makes 3 quarts (3 L).

Black Currant Juice

Wash whatever quantity of currants you plan to use and remove the stems. Place in a large saucepan, cover with water and simmer until the berries are thoroughly soft. Crush with a potato masher and press through a sieve. Sweeten the juice to taste with sugar, bring briefly to a boil to sterilize and bottle in hot sterilized jars. This will provide a very strong drink, which should be diluted with water or ginger ale before serving.

For immediate use, do a second pressing. Put the sieved berries back in the saucepan, cover with water, simmer for 10 minutes and sieve again. Sweeten to taste. This, too, will provide a strong drink that can be diluted with water or mixed with other juices.

Bergamot Tea

Scarlet bergamot (bee balm, Oswego tea, Indian paintbrush, *Monarda didyma*), a favourite perennial in many gardens, means "your whims are quite unbearable" in the language of flowers. A member of the mint family, the bergamot has striking scarlet blooms. Mrs. Simcoe commented that "the roots...infused in brandy make a wholesome cordial. It is called Oswego bitter" (*Diary*, 1792-96).

Bergamot tea is reputed to be good for sore throats, colds and chest troubles. To make it, use 1 tsp (5 mL) dried leaves for each cup of boiling water (double the quantity when using fresh leaves). Pour boiling water over the leaves and let steep for 5 minutes. Sweeten to taste with honey. If the plant is in blossom, add a few flower heads, but be careful to inspect them first. Otherwise, as Geoffrey Grigson warns, you may find yourself drinking earwig tea instead.

Further Reading

Obviously, for a book such as this, we have consulted dozens (at times it seemed like thousands) of cooking and gardening books, poetry books and accounts by early writers. It would be impossible to name them all. However, we would like to mention a few that have provided us with particular pleasure.

Food and Cooking:
Everyone who cooks in North America owes a debt of gratitude to *Fannie Farmer* and *The Joy of Cooking*. Many of us also swear by Julia Child, Craig Claiborne and James Beard. In Canada, Mme Benoit, Helen Gougeon and Margo Oliver are sources of inspiration and good recipes, with the added advantage that they are in tune with our seasons, holidays and supplies.

Other fine Canadian books include *A French-Canadian Cookbook* by Donald E. Asselin (Edmonton: M.G. Hurtig, 1971), an amiable and down-to-earth guide to this substantial cuisine, and two books by Blanche Pownall Garrett, *Canadian Country Preserves & Wines* (Toronto: James Lewis & Samuel, 1974) and *A Taste of the Wild* (Toronto: James Lorimer, 1975). Published well before the current craze for wild food, these two handsomely designed volumes still more than hold their own.

Dorothy Hartley's *Food in England* (London: Macdonald, 1954) and *Food and Drink in Britain* by Anne C. Wilson (London: Penguin, 1984) both offer much wisdom on the history of British food through the ages. And anyone spending a longish time in Britain should look for the splendid little books issued by Sainsbury's, which are attractive and inexpensive, perfect for souvenirs, small gifts and everyday cooking. The Penguin list is a constant source of authoritative books on both cooking and gardening, and includes standard works by Elizabeth David, Jane Grigson and Bea Nilson.

Newspapers have supplied some of our favourite recipes, as have the sides of lard packages. Company cookbooks can often be worthwhile, too. Many of us cherish our Five Roses cookbooks of whatever vintage, and Colman's Mustard has issued books, admirable for the restraint in the use of their product.

Leaves from Our Tuscan Kitchen by Janet Ross and Michael Waterfield (London: Penguin, 1977) has vegetable recipes to please the most carnivorous. In *The Spice Cookbook* by Avanelle Day and Lillie Stuckie (New York: Grosset and Dunlap, 1964) you will find many unusual recipes and entertaining oddments of information. Finally, we recommend *Food* by Waverley Root (New York: Simon and Schuster, 1986), a book that entered our lives in the nick of time—a fascinating history and dictionary of the foods of the world, with detailed information, legends and funny stories.

Gardening and Related Subjects:

Amateur gardeners seem to begin youthfully with instructions from family and gardening friends, and progress to literacy by a close reading of instructions on seed packages. Later they will read anything they can get, with somewhat mixed results. Useful articles can be found in periodicals such as *Harrowsmith*, *Organic Gardening* and *Nature Canada*.

There is a great tradition of writing among English gardeners, from John Gerard's *The Herball* (1597) through to Victoria Sackville-West. Two American books of comparable quality are Katharine S. White's *Onward and Upward in the Garden* (New York: Farrar, Straus & Giroux, 1979) and Eleanor Perenyi's *Green Thoughts: A Writer in the Garden* (New York: Random House, 1981).

For Canadian gardeners, the Canadian Department of Agriculture and the National Museum of Natural Sciences are sources of much potentially useful information, ranging from simple pamphlets and booklets on growing house plants, making jams and jellies and collecting mushrooms through to quite elaborate books such as Nancy J. Turner's and Adam F. Szczawinski's *Edible Wild Fruits and Nuts of Canada* (Ottawa: National Museum of Natural Sciences, 1979) and J. Walton Groves' *Edible and Poisonous Mushrooms of Canada* (Ottawa: Queen's Printer, 1962). Nor should the publications of provincial departments of agriculture be overlooked.

On more specific subjects, the following are recommended: James Underwood Crockett, *Crockett's Indoor Garden* (Boston/Toronto: Little Brown, 1978); Eustella Langdon, *Pioneer Gardens* (Toronto: Holt, Rinehart and Winston, 1972); Jacqueline Heriteau, *Potpourris and Other Fragrant Delights* (New York: Simon and Schuster, 1973); Lee Peterson, *A Field Guide to Edible Wild Plants of Eastern and Central North America* (Boston: Houghton Mifflin, 1977); Roger Tory Peterson and Margaret McKenny, *A Field Guide to Wildflowers of Northeastern and North-central North America* (Boston: Houghton Mifflin, 1968); The Audubon Society, *Field Guide to North American Wildflowers Eastern Region* (New York: Alfred A. Knopf, 1979).

Index